Hart Town Environs

A Chronicle of People, Places & Events
Carroll County, Georgia
1825–1900

John B. Bailey

and

Elaine Bolden Bailey

 Lillium Press

Books by Elaine Bolden Bailey:

Pompadour and Pearls: a Patchwork of Poetry

Buttermilk Clouds

Tracks

Explosion in Villa Rica

Co-authored with Patricia Lamar Mullinax

Draketown Tragedy

Collaboration with John Bailey on his book:

The History of Dark Corner Campbell County, Georgia

Books by John B. Bailey

The History of Dark Corner Campbell County, Georgia

Hart Town Environs

A Chronicle of People, Places & Events

Carroll County, Georgia

1825–1900

Hart Town Environs A Chronicle of People, Places & Events
Carroll County, Georgia 1825–1900

Copyright © 2020 by John B. Bailey & Elaine Bolden Bailey

Hart Town Environs may be used freely by individuals for research, teaching and personal use and for genealogy as long as credit is given to the name of the book, author and publisher.

This book is a Lillium Press Historical Book.

Website: lilliumpress.net

Cover design: Fred Finch Graphics
www.fredricfinch.com

Editor: Richard Argo

ISBN: 978-0-9628023-5-5

Front Cover Photo: John Bailey
Back Cover Photo: Elaine Bailey

 Lillium Press

This book is dedicated to

The Villa Rica Area Historical Society

And To All Lovers of History

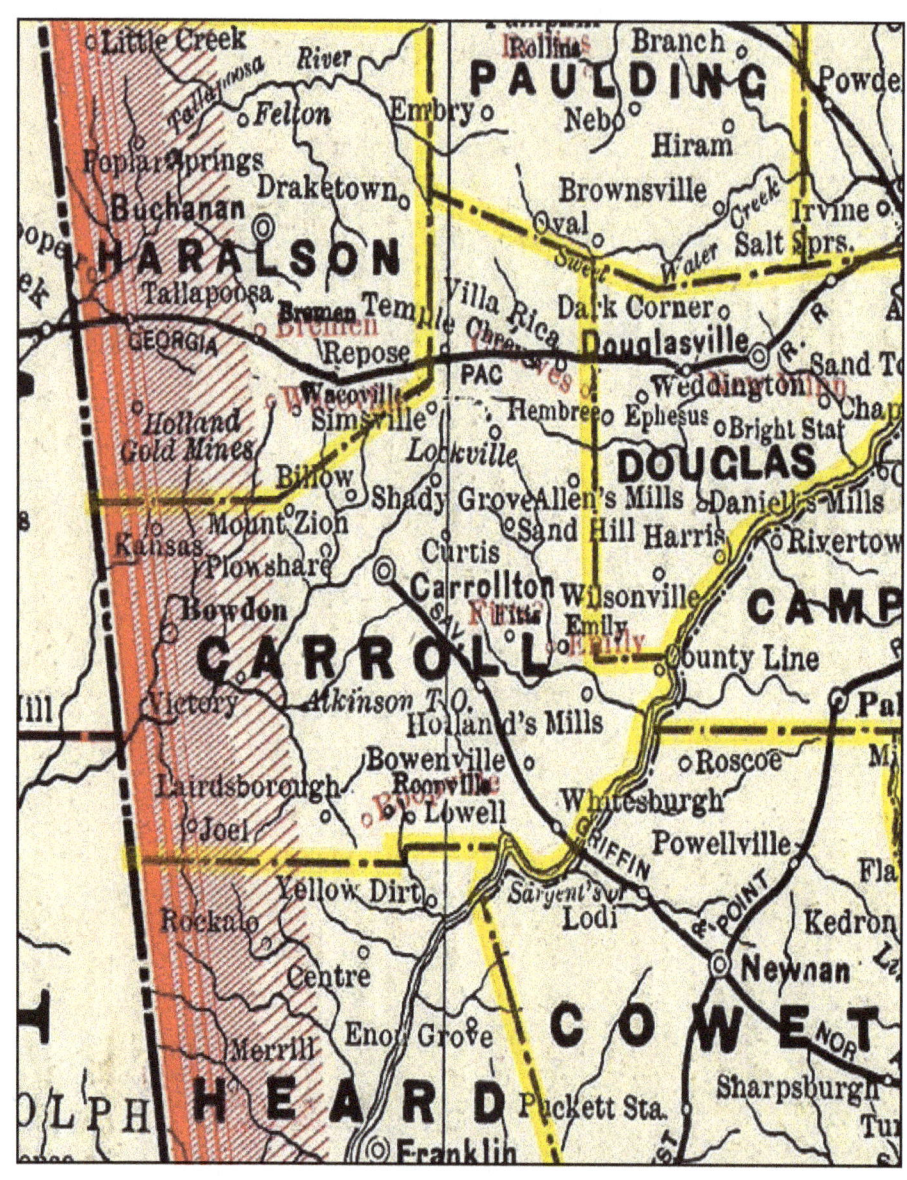

An 1883 map of west Georgia. Note
the towns which no longer exist: Hixtown
Cheeves, Simsville and Joel, among others.

Contents

Acknowledgements p. 8

Prologue p. 9

1: Native Americans, Early Pioneers & Early Roads p. 11

2: Waystation, Stores, Churches, Schools, Post Offices, Masons p. 23

3: Gold Deposits & Climatic Anomalies p. 41

4: Intruders, Pony Boys and Slicks p. 55

5: Early Settlers of Hart Town & Pleasant Grove p. 65

6: Early Settlers of Hickory Level p. 83

7: The Civil War Affects Families: Candlers, Chambers, Haynes p. 97

8: Early Settlers of Old Town—Hixtown & Chevestown p. 115

9: Early Settlers of the Wesley Chapel Community p. 135

10: Early Settlers of Hill's Crossing & Simsville p. 147

11: Families of the Hart Plantation p. 167

Appendix A: Photos of artifacts p. 184

Appendix B Muster Roll of Villa Rica "Gold Diggers" p. 186

Appendix C: 1864 Census for Reorganizing Georgia Militia p. 197

Appendix D: Abstracts Carroll County, GA 1827–1854 p. 201

Bibliography p. 208

Index p. 224

Acknowledgments

History fades as time travels into the future. Hart Town was one of those places that has faded into the past.

This project has been a two-year labor of love. This is the only Lillium Press Historical Book that will have both my husband's name and my name on the cover as the authors. That fact alone has spurred us forward. The support of family and friends encouraged us. Many times there were stop and then start again times.

An important acknowledgement is to the authors of past history books: Mary Talley Anderson for, *The History of Villa Rica* (1976); James C. Bonner for *Georgia's Last Frontier* (1971); and Joe Cobb for his most valuable book, *Carroll County and Her People* (1906). In developing a biographical sketch, I always review what has been written previously about our research. I was in constantly amazed at the technology we had available to find photos, maps, and details. Data that I had at my fingertips, made this an amazing undertaking.

Being a charter member and historian of the Villa Rica Area Historical Society has proven invaluable. I am especially grateful to Sarah Pitts for her encouragement, help, knowledge, and ability to find things when I had given up. We talked almost daily. Carl Lewis' research brought many unknown facts to light. His knowledge of Villa Rica Gold Mining and Old Town has added an extra dimension to this endeavor. Thanks for your willingness to share your years of historical research.

How great to have friends who have written history books and given us permission to use an excerpt and to paraphrase from these books. Thanks to Ruth Holder for permission to share from *The History of Temple, Georgia - A West Georgia Town of Carroll County* (2013), and thanks to Ray Henderson for information from his *The History of the Pony Club* (2011).

How very willing were those whom we called for an interview or just to answer a question or to verify for the second time a certain fact from the past, or to share a family photo! Thanks again to: Alisa Doyal, Frank Duke, Jack Hart, Larry Hart, Nancy Stolz-Jeffares, Don Levans, Milton Leathers, Greg & Donna Lisenby, John McFall, Barbara Wynn Mitchell, Rebekah Willoughby Morgan, Trish Mullinax, Jerry & Pat Saxon Morris, Mary Phillips, Jimmy Pitts, Pauline Roberts, Roger Smith, Monroe Spake, Jerry Vogler, Myra Wade, and Catherine Yates West..

We would also like to thank the Villa Rica Masonic Lodge #72 Members for sharing information and photos.

The Villa Rica Area Historical Society's Electronic Archaeology Team, led by Larry Arnold, with historian Carl Lewis, were invaluable in going on site and helping with the GPS coordinates.

Prologue

The faintest ink is better than the strongest memory.

The idea for this book began with the relocation of the Hart historical home in August of 2016. Our historical society was privileged with the task of raising money for the foundation, clearing of land and stabilizing the front porch. We were also given permission to metal-detect the site. Photos of the artifact which were found are included in Appendix A of this book.

As we began to research the Hart family, we inadvertently found information on the gold mines in Villa Rica. We began to research who owned the gold mines.

We saw how much of Villa Rica history was in danger of being lost forever. We wanted to have a memory of the Hart House preserved, so we made this old plantation house the focus of the book. We also wanted to add to the history of the immediate area surrounding that plantation. Thus, we planned to develop the history within a three-mile radius with the Hart House as the center. Our mission seemed reasonable. Look three miles south, east, north, then west. These were the parameters for researching the people, places and events.

The input of this book was dictated by the research we found, not our original plan. So what do we do when we find something wonderful just *four* miles south? Include it. So what do we do when the early pioneers traveled a little over three miles to attend a church and that church history was available? Included it. So our original parameters were altered a bit.

Then there was the matter of photographs. Many were collected. All were edited. Some were colorized. So what happened when we found a very old photograph, but one face is not distinguishable? Include it. I believe it is better to have a not-so-perfect picture than no photo.

What about a timeline? 1825 was chosen as the beginning because we wanted to show that marauders—intruders and settlers who came to Georgia and Carroll County before they were allowed to—arrived even before the Land Lottery of 1827.

Ending our timeline was certainly more difficult. 1900 should include the railroad that came through Villa Rica and the new Villa Rica which was incorporated on October 5, 1883. But this is not the history of Villa Rica—that has already been written. This is a history of the outlying areas around Hart Town. We did focus one chapter on Old Town.

So what do we do when we have access to a wonderful family history which includes color pictures taken after the 1900? You guessed it. They're included.

We hope the history, the stories and the photographs will stir those who love history as we do.

John & Elaine Bailey

1

Native Americans, Early Pioneers and Early Roads

*A Native American Creek Indian trail passed along the
Tennessee Road/Middle Alabama Road
intersection and through the grounds of the Hart plantation.*

Before Georgia had roads, it was laced with Indian trails and paths. These trails served the needs of Georgia's native populations by connecting their villages and allowing them to travel great distances in quest of game, fish and shellfish mineral resources as salt, flint, pipestone, steatite, hematite, and ochre. Many groups followed an annual economic cycle that saw them undertake seasonal migrations in pursuit of the plants and animals they needed to survive.

They used these trails and paths to travel for war making; these trails lead to the homelands of hostile groups. Abundant evidence indicates that some of the trails used by the early Indians of Georgia were already formed by large grazing animals, particularly the Eastern buffalo which were smaller than the western buffalo.

Most trails became major routes beginning in the early 1800s. They were widened for wagon use, sometimes marked with a double-dash line on old maps.

Indian paths were secondary routes, short cuts, connecting the larger pathways.

The southern part of Carroll County, Georgia possibly has the best known Indian trails, McIntosh and Five Notch, but there were important pathways elsewhere in the area.

The largest most widely used trail on the north side was the Sandtown Trail. This east/west route started at a village on the Chattahoochee River at the Douglas County—Fulton County line. This village was formally known as Buzzard's Roost.

Some of the Oktahasasi families settled on the Chattahoochee at Buzzard's Roost and the village became known by the white man's interpretation of Oktahasasi:

Sandtown.

The Sandtown Trail ran west across Sweetwater Creek and followed parts of present day U. S. Highway 78 into Lithia Springs, then to Douglasville, and then toward Villa Rica and Temple. After reaching Villa Rica, the trail veered northwest to pass a mile and a half above Temple, then on west to Tallapoosa. The path passed into Alabama and followed the Tallapoosa River south.

A short cut route from the Sandtown Trail to the old Alabama villages was established by cutting southwest at Villa Rica and following the Little Tallapoosa River. The modern day Blackstock Road was part of the original "Alley's Trace." A trace was a path made by animals, like buffalo and deer, large enough to leave the grasses and undergrowth beaten down: leaving their trace. It was easier to follow the trace than to cut new ones. A cutoff toward Carrollton, called "Alley's Trail," split off about where Land Lot #131, District 6 is located. The trail ran north of the present day Hickory Level Road to the river and turned south.

One short cut branched off "Alley's Trail" at Carrollton and ran south to McIntosh Trail and on to the west. There were many other trails connecting the major routes. Trails ran from village sites on Turkey Creek, Indian Creek, Buck Creek, Buffalo Creek, and many others forming a transportation network for the Creeks in Carroll county and the surrounding areas.

Another important ancient American Indian route was the Five Notch Trail that ran along the Chattahoochee River through Carroll County into Cherokee territory. When travelers took these trails through the wilderness, they needed to know which trail to take at a fork or split in the path. Notches were cut into the side of the largest or most prominent tree at the fork to indicate the direction.

The McIntosh Trail and the Five Notch Trail joined near Acorn Creek. This trail in Carroll County was one of the most important crossroads in Georgia, directly connecting Georgia with Florida, South Carolina, Alabama, Mississippi, Tennessee and North Carolina. Trade goods from all the major southeastern Indian tribes were transported through this area for hundreds of years.

The road north of this crossroads was the Four Notch Trail that ran north through Crossplains and Sand Hill into the Cherokee territory north of Villa Rica. Four Notch Road split at Ephesus Church, with the left (or northwest) fork called Old Stagecoach Road. This stage route ran from Carrollton through McIntosh Reserve to Newnan and other points.

Another important historic site lies just a few hundred yards to the east of the Five Notch and McIntosh crossroads, the William Wagnon home where county residents first met to elect county officials in May, 1827. They elected the first sheriff, tax collector, tax receiver, coroner, surveyor, county clerk and justices of the inferior court. It was also the site of the first post office in the county.

One of the main trails that split off the Five Notch Trail was a path that ran along Snake Creek from the major village sites on the Chattahoochee to the village complex near Carrollton on the Little Tallapoosa River. Many other small trails split off the main "interstate" routes that never had names or have been forgotten.

A dividing line ran between the Creek and Cherokee Nations from Buzzard's Roost along the Tallapoosa Ridge to Alabama. Twenty-five miles on each side of that line, these two tribes hunted together peacefully—a fifty mile neutral zone later changed to five miles.

The Sandtown Trail, was later known as the The Middle Alabama Road and even later, the Atlanta-Jacksonville Highway and now, today, Highway 78. Sandtown Trail was one of the first roads going east to west through Georgia. What is today known as North Van Wert Road was once The Tennessee Road, one of the earliest roads running north to south through Georgia.

An 1830 6th district map shows that an early Native American Creek Indian trail passed along the Tennessee Road/Middle Alabama Road intersection and through the grounds of the Hart plantation.

From *The Temple Enterprise 1883—Centennial Edition—1983*, dated September 24, 1983:

> The First Settlers in Carroll County were Creek Indians. Before the white man settled this section of northwestern Georgia, it was inhabited by the Creek Indians. The vast forest land which they owned was called the Creek Nation. The name "Creek" was given by the English because of the many small streams beside which the Indians lived.
>
> For many years prior to the establishment of Carroll County, white men lived among the Indians. Through the years the Creeks began to live more and more like the white man, and some of the Indian women became their wives. The Chief of the Cowetas, a leading subtribal group was William McIntosh, the son of a Creek Indian mother and a Scotch father.
>
> By the 1820's the Creeks had adopted, somewhat, the manner and dress of their white neighbors. Many were speaking broken English, and a few of their children had been taught to read and write the language. They cultivated vegetables and fruits; they raised cattle, hogs, and poultry. Small patches of cotton were also grown. The Creeks hunted the abundant wild game, fished the sparkling clear streams, and gathered fruits and nuts produced by the forest.
>
> In the early 1800's the white man began more and more to want possession of the land of the Creeks. Consequently, after a period of persistent persuasion, treaties with the Indians ceded land to the U. S. Government. White families moved in from older parts of Georgia, cleared small plots of land and established farms.
>
> In 1825 at Indian Springs, Georgia, Chief McIntosh signed a treaty which ceded the land that included what is now Carroll County. McIntosh lived at his home at Acorn Bluff, near Whitesburg.

All the Creek Indians did not approve of the treaty which provided an exchange of their land for equal acreage in the West. They were also to be paid for the improvements they had made on the ceded land.

Early Pioneers

The early pioneers who came to the Hart Town, Simsville, Pleasant Grove, and Hickory Level area were Absolom Adams, Alcimus Allen, James Baskin, David Brock, James Bryce, Willis Bagwell, Thomas Chandler, Henry & William Coleman, Isaac & William Cobb, James Coltharps, John Conner, Will Driscoll, Abel Embry, Frances Fielders, Alex & Mercer Green, the Jonathan & Henry Haynes, William Hixon, Samuel Hart, Abel Harrison, Benjamin Long, the James, William and Wright Majors families, J. G. W. Lassiter, James Reeves, John Riggs, Parker Rice, Luke Skinner, J. O. Stone, Thomas Frank Sykes, and William West. These were the first postmasters, school teachers, merchants and ministers. They owned the first mercantile stores, manned the first stagecoach waystations, opened the first blacksmith shops, joinery shops, and gold mines.

Before 1825

From *The History of Villa Rica*:

Contrary to the opinion held by most people today, the area we know as Creek Indian Lands or Western Georgia had a few white dwellers or settlers before the territory was acquired by the State in 1825.

Benjamin Hawkins, Indian agent, describes some of these places in his "Sketch of the Creek Country", 1798. From the U. S. Dept. of Agriculture's "Soil Survey of Carroll County, Georgia of 1924", page 132, appears this statement. "The second treaty with the Creek Indians in 1825 marked the beginning of agriculture in the county, however, there were a few whites in this section prior to that date." One of the well known "Federal Roads" passed through what is now the upper part of Carroll County. It began at Augusta and proceeded through the older settled section of Georgia to what was known as Standing Peachtree, then turned westward through Cherokee and Creek lands. It crossed the Chattahoochee at Buzzard's Roost, on to Lick Skillet, Deer Lick (Lithia Springs), Vansant Place, Skinned Chestnut (Douglasville), Hix Town (Villa Rica), Hart Town, Buckhorn, Wolf Pen (Bremen), Possum Snout (Tallapoosa) and on to Jacksonville, Alabama, and on through Chickasaw Country to the Mississippi River.

Gold was discovered around what was later to become Villa Rica in 1824, and several whites moved into the section.

1825 Settlers at The Little Tallapoosa River Area

The Progeny of John Long, page 31:

Hart Town Environs

James Y(oung) Long (son of John and Jane Long) was born January 7, 1781 (in Monroe Co. Tenn). He married Jane Walker on March 3, 1803. James emigrated in 1826 to the Little Talaposa [sic] river in Carroll County, Georgia, where he was killed in 1828. He left four children, one of whom was Nancy Davis Long b. March 12, 1806 in Tennessee. She married her cousin John Long III (son of Robert & Isabell Leeper Long) and had children: Benjamin McFarland Long, John Long, Isabella Long, Louise S. Long, William Leeper Long and Carrie Long Shields.

The Progeny of John Long states:

John Long III, (1798-1870), son of Robert Long and Isabelle Leeper Long, lived on the Little Tallapoosa in 1825. This was an area which was opened circa 1825, formerly the property of the Creek Indians. John Long was amonst [sic] the first white settlers to the area.

Migration took the route from northeast South Carolina to Georgia or southwest North Carolina to Georgia. There was also an influx of travelers from Tennessee to Georgia. Several members of a community would travel together as those did from Haywood, North Carolina to Carroll County: the families of John Columbus Hicks, Joseph and John Chambers, Henry and Jonathan Haynes and the Alexander Green family. Interest in coming to Georgia had something to do with the fact that the gold fever had hit Villa Rica . . . , and people were coming in from all parts to work in the mines and "get rich."

Early Carroll County

Carroll County was created by acts of June 19, 1825 and December 11, 1826, from Creek Indian Cessions. The new county was named for Charles Carroll of Maryland, a signer of the Declaration of Independence.

When Carroll County was first laid out in 1827, it included a vast area much larger than Carroll County is today. In later years parts of the original county were cut away and became parts of Heard, Douglas, Troup, Campbell, and Haralson Counties.

Within the original boundaries of Carroll County there were 1,600 square miles. This land was distributed by the lottery system at Milledgeville in 1826. At that time Milledgeville was the capital of Georgia. Among others, a bachelor who had reached his 18th birthday, was a United States citizen and had lived in the state at least three years was entitled to one lottery ticket. Others meeting certain qualifications were given two tickets. Veterans of the Revolution, widows and orphans of veterans killed in war, and certain other groups received special consideration.

The land lots were composed of 202 1/2 acres. Those who drew lots paid a fee of $18 per lot. All fractional lots were withheld from lottery and sold later at public auction.

Only a few of the richest spots were selected for farming. The other land, which was used for grazing and timber, was very cheap with some selling for less than ten cents per acre. Holders of successful lottery tickets generally sold their lots very cheaply. A bed quilt, gun, dog, or cow was sometimes swapped for an entire lot of 202 1/2 acres. An inn keeper refused an offer of a land lot in exchange for a night's lodging. It was not unusual for men to stake whole lots in small wagers, or to give two hundred acres to "boot" in a horse trade.

Many of the drawees of Carroll County lots never moved to the county.

The law provided that the freeholders living in the new county could meet on the first Monday in May of 1827 to elect county officials. This meeting was held at the McIntosh Reserve near Whitesburg. Five justices of the Inferior Court, a county clerk, sheriff, tax collector, tax receiver, coroner, and a surveyor were selected.

The first Carroll County Inferior Court met May 31, 1827. In June the justices of the court who had charge of roads, bridges, and all public property, met again and authorized one of their number to buy a lot in the Fifth District for a county seat. A lot was bought from land lot 115 from Thomas Bolton near where Sand Hill is today. This place was later known as Old Carrollton.

On November 14, 1829, the county seat was moved to its present site in the Tenth District, land lot number 128. The new site was first named Troupsville, in honor of Governor George M. Troup. On December 22 the state legislature incorporated the new county seat under the name of Carrollton rather than Troupsville.

Carroll County Rangers:

Carroll County was formed from Creek Cession of January 24, 1826. The County Seat was (and is) at Carrollton, Georgia. Land in Carroll County was distributed through the Lottery of 1827.

> A List of a company of Voliteers [sic] Cold (called), the Carroll Rangers or Spies. We the undersigners Do tender our services to His Excellency William Schly, the Commander in Chiefs as Mounted men for the term of three months for the purpose of Garding [sic] the Lines of Carroll against the Hostilities of Indians.
>
> Wm. O. Wagnon, Capt.; Lee Bird, 1st Lt; Valentine Burnett, 2nd Lt; Mathew Read, Ensign; John Duke, 1st Sgt; George W. Ward, 2nd Sgt; Auther Beal, 3rd Sgt; Henry T. Read, 4th Sgt; George S. Sharp, 1st Cpl; James S. McDowell, 2nd Cpl; George Hiden, 2nd Cpl; Leonard Fullbright, 4th Sgt; Slomon Wynn; Thomas Bryce; Amos Helton; David W. White; John Bante; Andrew McMullan; Mansell Tidwell; Thomas W. Guierer; Joseph N. Spencer; Jackson Hewit; William Majors; Anderson Green, Amos Dyer;
>
> S. C. Parker; Abel H. Harrison; Edward Dyer; James Stripling; Y. C. Camon; Jonathan Haynes; Michael Aderholt; Absolom Adams; David Liles; James Liles; Joseph Phillips; Mathew Knight; John L. Hambleton; Jeremiah Walls; George Read; James Herrin; Tyre Watson; Moses Morris; James Michael; L. L. Turner; Daniel Harlin; Elisha Barber; James

Hart Town Environs

Brown; James Harcrow; Keneth Murkinson; Rora Mirkinson; Eli Miller.

Thomas Johnson; Henry T. Chance; John Bayley; Jeremiah Cole; Richard Shackleford; Absolm Howard; Jesse Mayfield; Joseph Thompson; Levi Bohanon; Jobe Adams; Harkin Phillips; Gilles J. Adams; Young J. Long; John Long; Jesse Brown; William White; Thomas Newton; Samuel B. Landrum; David Smith; William D. Stephens; Ezekel Hall; Samuel Knight.

Return 11 June 1836. Corp. Thomas. Return of Property belonging to Carroll Rangers.

July 11, 1836—Army evaluated their property.

In 1836, during the Creek War, the Carroll County Rangers camped at Camp Thomas on July 11th, 1836. The Army occasionally evaluated their property which included horses, saddles, and guns. On this date, the property of the Carroll Rangers was evaluated by John Long, 1st Lt., Valentine Burnett, 2nd Lt. and Mathew Reid, Ensign. Their signatures were John Long, Valentine Burnett, and Mathew Reid. Beside each name of a Carroll Ranger was listed first the kind of horse he had, the age of the horse, the price of the horse (as evaluated by the above men), the price of the saddle, and the price of the gun. All these men were some of Carroll County's earliest settlers and many of these names are found in Carroll County today.

William O. Wagner, Captain, Spotted M, age 7, $100, $20, $20; John Long 1st Lt, Sorrell M, age 4, $100, $20, $15; Valentine Burnett, 2nd Lt., Claybank M, age 5, $100, $15, $30; Mathew Reid, Ensign, Roan M, age 8, $80, $15, $30; John Duke, 1st Sgt., Sorrell M, age 6, $100, $25, $20; George W. Ware, 2nd Sgt., Bay M, age 7, $60, $20, $10; Arthur Bell, 3rd Sgt., Bay M, age 8, $50, $20, $10; Henry L. Reid, 4th Sgt., Sorrell H, age 9, $80, $30, $20; George S. Sharp, 1st Corp., Bay H, age 5, $100, $20, $25; James B. McDowell, 2nd Corp., Sorrell H, age 10, $115, $25, $18; George Hiden, 3rd Corp., Bay H, age 6, $100, $15, $12; Leonard Fullbright, 4th Corp., Bay H, age 3, $70, $15, $12; Privates: Absolom Adams, Gray M, age 5, $150, $10, $18. *(Just the inventory of the officers and one private listed here.)*

Early Roads

Miscellaneous Carroll County Georgia Inferior Court Minutes as abstracted from the first book of the Inferior Court records:

Monday January 3rd 1831

The Honorable the Superior court met this day pursuant to adjournment present their Honors A. M. McWhorter, Eldred M. Hibbler and Daniel N. Parr Esquires. The following persons were drawn to serve as jurors at July . . . for the Superior Court. . .

James Cardwell 1; David Hendon 2; Josaah Becker 3; Abner Sherdon 4; Nathan Gan 5; Jacob Awtery 6; Riley McWalker 7; John Easterwood 8; Hiram Mehaffy

9; Ezekiah Felton 10; Ephriam B. Hiccombeffon; John Aimes 12; David Cannes 13; William Worsham 14; John Cline 15; James Michael 16; John Merridith 17; Alexander Goggen 18; Enoch Parker 19; Caswell Bark 20; Reubin Read 21; Elisha Barber 22; Lemuel Perddy 23.

It is hereby ordered by the court that James Majors . . . and he is hereby appointed a road commissioner of the sixth district to fill the vacancy . . . if [sic] Wright Majors deceased (see Wright Majors, Chapter 6).

We do hereby certify that we have reviewed and marked out the road running from Carrollton to Campellton to have as the county line the names and best route to the best of our knowledge and information in compliance with an order of the Inferior Court for that purpose. This day of January 1832. Sworn to and Subscribed before me the day and date above mentioned. Wallas Wapner, William Philips and A. M. McWhorter.

An 1831 Road

Punkintown Road from Fulton County into Villa Rica was impassable when its ford was flooded by the Chattahoochee River. In 1831 the inferior Court of Carroll County commissioned Aaron Jones and Hiram Sharp to build (mark out) a road from Villa Rica to the Alabama Road, near Sally Hughes Ferry on the Etowah River, over which gold miners could haul their equipment by wagon from Atlanta and elsewhere to Villa Rica—in all kinds of weather. The official survey plat of the 3rd District, 3rd Section of Paulding County, Georgia, made by M. G. Anderson on December 10, 1832, shows the course of the road built (marked out) by Jones and Sharp and contains two names for it: Sally Hughes Road and Carroll County Gold Mine Road. This road is now known as Georgia Highway 61 and extends from Villa Rica to Cartersville, Georgia.

1834

Also ordered by the Court that Puckett Wood, Robert S. Bailey and William L. Parr be appointed to review & mark a road from Carrollton to Phillips Ferry by the most convenient rout [sic] . . . Ordered by the Court that the Tax Collector for the year 1834 add fifty per cent on the State Tax for county purposes and twelve & a half per cent on the State Tax for the Poor.

March 1834

James Baskin J. P. It is ordered by the court that the treasurer pay to John Ward the within amount this 4 March 1834.

Agreeable to an order of the Inferior Court of the county aforesaid we have laid out and marked a road commencing at the line of the sixth District near Sandy Creek and not far from the Youngs Ferry road and thence on the sixth district passing the homes of James Brantley and B. Huckabee and thence the most practicable way passing the gold mines and intersecting the Sally Hughes road near Jonathan Walker

& C . . . ordered to be open. (Signed) Daniel McDowell, Frances Richards, Jonathan Walker."

April 7, 1834

William L. Parr is sworn in as Trustee of the Poor School. Inferior Court of Carroll County Dr. (directed?) [sic] to John Ward Jr. April for three days serving jurors at the September Court—$3.00. October two days serving—$2.00 (totaled) $5.00.

(Signed John Ward). Sworn to & Subscribed before me this 3rd Febry [sic].

July 18, 1835

To Samuel Leathers, Benjamin Chapman & James L. Adair. You are hereby appointed commissioners to review and lay out a road to begin at or near the house of Benjamin Chapmans in the 642nd district to the line of the County at or near the house of Samuel Leathers in said district so as to intersect a road about to be opened by the County of Paulding to come to said place and report the same at our next Inferior Court . . . " Carroll Inferior Court February Term 1837.

Ordered by the court that the Road Commissioners in the 649th and 642nd Districts of said county have this Road (my note: road was described in earlier minutes as "a road of public utility to follow from this place the old road about one mile then turn to the right thence the new blazes a north course until it intersects the old road then the old road to the Paulding County line) in their districts opened out and agreeable to the within report. .

The following persons is appointed Road Commissioners for the Year 1838. 642nd Dist: John Hilderbrand J. P., J. F. Johnson, McKleroy & Johnson Haynes. 649th Dist: Henry J. Chance J. P. , Peterson Black (the names of Sloman Wynn and Alexander Haynes struck through) and William Burns.

September 15, 1835

Villa Rica. To the honorable the Inferior Court of Carroll County your petitioners respectfully showeth to your honors the present road running through Villa Rica as laid out by the reviewers if ever any such reviewers is ilconvenient [sic] to the citizens of said Village and your petitioners prays an order from your honorable body to remove and establish said road as it now runs through said Village laying aside the former roads. Your petitioners further sheweth to your honors and wish your body to remove the present road running through Qualls lain formerly McLains or Poes lain and establish and pass an order to alter said road so fare as viz. Commencing at the corner of Henry Hulsey farm.

February 1837

Ordered by the court that the Road Commissioners in the 649th and 642nd Districts of said county have this Road (my note: road was described in earlier minutes as 'a road of public utility') to follow from this Place the old road about one mile then turn to the right thence the new blazes a north course until it intersects the old road then the old road to the Paulding County line.

August 9, 1837

Ordered by the Court that Samuel C. Candler, Abel H. Harrison, and James L. Adair review a rout [sic] for a road from Villa Rica to the County line in the direction of Paulding Court house so as to intersect a road now leading from said Court house in the direction to Villa Rica by way of Swains Mills and report as soon as practicable.

Ordered by the Court that the district commissioners of the 649th district G. M. cause [sic] to be opened and kept in good repair a road leading from a little spring on the Phillips Ferry road near the store of James Coltharp to Jones Mill road on the Paulding County line.

It is ordered by the Court that Clayton Williams, Phillip Chambers & Thomas Raburn review a road commencing on the road near Coltharps and McSpading's Store in the 649th Georgia Military District leading to Phillips' Ferry on the Chattahoochee river the rout to be reviewed and marked out the nearest and best way from said point to intersect the road leading from Cedar Town Paulding, County Georgia at or near Elisha Brookes.

We James Coltharp and John McElreath being appointed by the honorable Inferior Court of said County to review and mark out a road through a part of the 649th district G. M. beginning at a spring near Coltharp's Store and thence running by the way of the home of Lewis Davis and striking the Paulding line on Jones Mill road and after viewing and examining the rout as fare as we think practable [sic] we believe the road will be of great utility . . . Sworn to before Charles Hulsey, a Justice of the peace, July 21, 1837.

Ordered by the Court that the Clerk notify the road Commissioners of the 813th district G. M. to appear before said Court on the first Monday in next month to show cause if any they have why the road leading from Corolton [sic] to Robinsons through the district is not kept in good repair.

It is ordered by the Court that James H. Holland road commissioner of the 682nd District Georgia Military pay a fine of Ten dollars for contempt of Court for failing to appear before said Court when notified to appear and answer to charges prefered [sic] against him as Commissioner as aforesaid . . .

James F. Garrison, William Rooks and William B. Gilley, Commissioners, swore before A. M. McWhorter, J. P., the following:

We . . . have reviewed and marked the way for a road to run from where the five notch road comes in to the McIntosh road or near that place from thence to the place where J. McKleroy lives in the sixth district said county . . .

1838

The following persons is appointed Road Commissioners for the year 1838:

642nd District, John Hilderbrand J. P.; J. F. Johnson; McKleroy & Johnson Haynes.
649th Henry J. Chance J. P.; Peterson Black (the names of Sloman Wynn and Alexander Haynes struck through) & William Burnes.

Inferior Court, Carroll County, Georgia.

February 3, 1840
The following Road Commissioners were appointed for the year 1840:
642 Dist—John Hilderbrand, J. P.; Abel H. Harrison, John T. Chambers. . . .
649 Dist—Henry S. Chance, J. P.; Peter E. Junkin; Nathaniel Adams. . . .
Edward W. Holland, Samuel C. Candler and Abel H. Harrison are appointed Commissioners to lay off and straighten the present stage road from Villa Rica to the Paulding line near the house of John Cole and to make the present road and the past straightened the publick [sic] highway.
The Commissioners of the 642nd District G. M. are ordered to open the road ordered from Villa Rica on the direction to McCoys ferry as fare as the Carroll line.
H. P. Mabry, David Smith, Peter Warren, Jesse L. Hix, Anderson Boggs & Willoby Knight to lay off a road the nearest and best way from Carrollton to the home of H. P. Mabry.
The following men were appointed commissioners for the Common School for the ensuing year: James Reaves, Charles Sheets, John McCorcle, James F. Garrison & Appleton Mandeville.

August 3, 1840, Monday
It is ordered by the Court that Needham Jarnagin, Jacob Awtry and Jonathan Sanders be appointed Reviewers to review and mark out the road from Villa Rica to Youngs Ferry Road near Jacob Awtrys residence in that part when it has been turned between Villa Rica and the Tallapoosa Bridge road . . .

February 2, 1841
District Road Commissioners for the year 1841:
649 Dist—Wilson Cartright J. P., Abel H. Harrison, James Coltharp.
64(3)(2?) Dist — R. V. C. Ruffin J. P., Samuel C. Candler, Charles Sheets.

October 13, 1841
It is ordered by the Court that Robert S. Bailey, Jesse Boon, Mason Daughtery, James Lasseter & B. S. Camp be appointed as Reviewers to review and report upon the utility of a Road from the house of Thomas Hughey to the home of Christopher Bowen—Ferry on the Chattahoochy [sic] . . .

November 13, 1841:
E. S. Candler is sworn in as Deputy Sheriff of Carroll County.

January 17, 1842:
>Road Commissioners appointed for 1842:
>649 Dist—Thomas Raburn, J. P., James Baskin, Nathaniel Adams.
>642 Dist—R. V. C. Ruffin, J. P., Leonard C. Huff, James Coltharp.

2

Waystation, Stores, Churches, Schools, Post Offices, Masons

After 1832, Majors & Coltharp Store moved 1/2 mile east of the Little Tallapoosa River to Hart Town.

Some waystations became stagecoach stops, relay points for post riders, inns, and taverns. They were situated about sixteen miles apart, considered the average day's travel for foot traffic. Those who ran these stations sometimes charged exorbitant prices for poor meals and insect-riddled beds as the weary traveler was at their mercy. In the earliest times, creek crossings were often run by an Indian with a white partner. Some Indians learned they could charge (extort) high ferry and guide fees.

Buckhorn Tavern
William West built a large, double-log cabin in 1833 in northwest Carroll County about three miles west of Hart Town on what was later Old Temple-Villa Rica Road. The cabin and land were later purchased by Isaac E. Cobb. On March 8, 1842, William West sold it to Isaac E. Cobb for the sum of $400.00: Land Lot #169, Land Lot #170 in the 6th district of Carroll County, except nine acres owned by David Hiden. Also Land Lot #184, and Land Lot #151 lot containing 15 acres all in the 6th district of Carroll. Isaac Cobb and his family lived on this land, which was an almost unbroken forest for miles around the house.

Cobb was industrious and busy, but found time to hunt. All kinds of game were abundant. He killed some wolves and bears and a great many deer. He nailed the horns of the bucks under the eaves of the house and on the trees in the grove in front and made hitching racks of them. When antlers were nailed along the entryway, travelers used these as hangers for their hats, coats and saddle bags. The place took the name Buckhorn.

The country was sparsely settled. It became necessary to have a place where a traveler could repose for the night. The cabin was built on the crest of a red hill and

Buckhorn Tavern
Courtesy Hart Cobb and Ray Rial

became a famous hostelry on the stagecoach route between Marthasville and Jacksonville, Alabama. Isaac E. Cobb set apart certain rooms known as Traveler's Rooms and he "took them in," furnishing refreshments and food. The house was a big double-log house with a dogtrot down the center. In later years, this dogtrot was enclosed to create more rooms for the growing family. Isaac and his wife, Francis Carter Chandler Cobb, raised a large family of nine children.

This waystation for travelers became known as Buckhorn Tavern (33°44'13.41"N 85°00'16.97"W). It was noted for hospitality and fare prices. Stagecoaches that stopped at the tavern were drawn by four or six horses. The seating capacity of the coaches was six, with room on top for a man or two where the baggage was usually piled high.

When a stage was about a mile from the tavern, the driver would sound a blast on a hunting horn for each passenger he carried. By the time it arrived, the table was set for the exact number of guests. When the guest spent the night, they slept in two large rooms—ladies on the ground floor and men in the attic.

Isaac E. Cobb was appointed postmaster at Buckhorn in February 1849, establishing the post office at Buckhorn Tavern and becoming Buck Horn, Georgia. His son, William W. Cobb, became postmaster on October 16, 1852; then, Joseph L. Hart became postmaster on September 16, 1856. The post office was discontinued after 1857.

During the Civil War, Confederate soldiers camped around the tavern and were extended hospitality by the innkeepers.

After Isaac E. Cobb was a member of the Legislature three times in succession and was Sheriff of the county, he moved to northwest Carroll County.

A Frontier Store

A frontier store carried a variety of merchandise that was necessary on the frontier. The size of carts, wagons and pack animals determined what could be loaded and what the early settlers could carry home or to their camp. Until houses were built, they lived in tents or in wagons—sometimes under the wagon. After unloading the wagon, the bed would be removed from the frame and turned over for sleeping or the storage of goods.

Merchandise sold in a frontier trading station were fabrics such as wool, cotton and silk. They carried needles, thread, thimbles and buttons, all for the making and mending of clothes.

They sold clothing such as shawls, socks (long & short), hats, and hat covers made of oil cloth to protect the wool and flannel hats from rain. They sold shoes and moccasins for $ .25; calico shirts were $1.25. In the store were woolen blankets —$4 each, horse saddles, saddle bags, reins and leather straps.

Guns ($12.50) and ammo (powder, lead balls and flint), large knives and pocket knives were also sold. Belt knives were $1.00. They also stocked tomahawks, cooking utensils, pots, kettles, pans and eating utensils. There were hand tools, hammers and nails. Saws were $1.25. You could buy grind stones, wire or a window glass (an 8 x 10 being the largest). There were traps of all sizes, plus iron bars of various thicknesses, wax and wax candles, smoking pipes, tobacco (smoking and chewing), paper, quills and ink. Mercantile stores offered spices of all kind, sugar made from maple syrup, tallow, beads, combs, mirrors, spectacles, scissors and fish hooks.

Early Churches, Schools & Stores

New Hope Primitive Baptist Church of Christ

This famous church (33°43'50.13"N 84°54'17.22 W) was founded by Mrs. Mary Carnes and thirteen others in 1828 which possibly makes it the oldest church structure in Carroll County. It was the first Baptist church established in Northwest Georgia west of the Chattahoochee River.

June 27, 1829 Brother Majors preached and after worship, he inquired for the fellowship of the Church and proceeded to open a door for the reception of members. None came forward. Nominations were made: John Brookes, Jonathan Walker, James Dickson, George Harass, Jessee Blackwell, John Carnes and John Long were chosen to find a place to build a meeting house on Sunday, June 28. The Church, being in order, to opened a door for the reception of members and received Polly Carnes.

Several members of the Hart Town community traveled the three and a half miles east from Hart Town to attend the New Hope Primitive Baptist Church at the intersection of the now Conners Road, Old Punpkintown Road and Highway 78. Families included the Majors and Coltharp families, Anderson Green, John and Elizabeth Brooks, John Long, Hester P. Beall, Justin Beall, David Hiden, Mary Hyden, Joseph

W. Chambers, Washington Chambers, John and Sarah Chambers, Catherine, Jesse and Lucindy Chambers, H. Chambers and wife Katherine, Merrel C. Awtry, Albinia Awtry, Elizabeth A. Awtry and Nancy Awtry, James Leathers & wife Arminda, Mary Leathers, Meria (Maria) Leathers and John A. Jones, are shown on the church minutes, dated from 1829 to 1867.

The Haynes' brothers, Henry, Jonathan, Edward and William (originally from Haywood County, North Carolina) came from Providence Church in Habersham County, Georgia along with others to Carroll County. On September 24, 1830 they appointed a committee to purchase land for a meeting house. Henry Haynes became the long-term minister. Jonathan Haynes was elected as a trustee to assist in laying the new church's foundation on November 27, 1830. On February 1, 1834 church services were still held at Jonathan's home.

From New Hope Primitive Baptist Church of Christ Minutes:

> This the 27th of November 1830. We the Church at New Hope setting in order opened a door for the Reception of members Received Elizabeth Dudley and Elizabeth Harris by Letter and Dismist [sic] William Adams and his wife Sarah Adams and Rebekah Lott by Letter and then as Alexander M. Creis has given his Bond to make Rites to two acres of Land in the north East Corner of lot number 145 in the Second District the Church then proceeded to appoint Trustees Jonathan Haynes and William Majors and James Dickson to assist in Laying of the plan and to receive the rights for the Same for the life of the Church Dismist in order.

The attitude and customs of the times is that church members could be brought before the church on charges ranging from drinking excessively, to fighting to "getting in a violent passion" (probably meaning excessive anger), to attempted murder, to hiding a bastard child from the church, to working on Sunday. Members often took their letters with them when they moved or left a particular church. Sometimes members were added after a conversion experience.

Members were dismissed by letter, meaning that they were transferring to another church of like order, or sometimes they were excluded from unresolved charges. Even non-attendance for three meetings in a row was cause for a committee to visit members and admonish them to return to fellowship or face church discipline which could mean exclusion if unresolved. Pastors were subject to an annual call or re-election of their position which had to be unanimous.

Slaves were members of the church from its earliest days and are mentioned in the church minutes, along with the owners' name. They are probably buried in the cemetery in unmarked graves as many people in those days could not afford tombstones and engraving them.

Hart Town Environs

In the early 1800s, Villa Rica was, for practical purposes, frontier territory, attractive to prospectors once gold was found there. The minutes from New Hope Church reveal a feisty population at the time. Villa Rica was a rough mining town in the 1830s. From minutes of December 24, 1833: The church preferred a charge against Brother David Hyden for getting into an affray with William Burns at the house of William Green and wanting or proposing to fight; also for drawing his knife and making many cuts at said Burns with an intent to wound him."

Records also indicate that the church served as a court. On June 25, 1836, members met to decide charges made by William Majors against Thomas Rabun "for falsely packing" two bales of cotton by which means Brother Majors claims to be injured in the sale of said cotton $23 when sold in market. On Oct. 22 the church decided the charge was groundless, "not being established by gospel testimony."

On November 26, Brother Majors apologized to Brother Rabun, "convinced that he had been misled by his waggoner."

In March 1828, Majors and Rabun were in trouble again, as both came forward on March 23 to make satisfaction: for the "difficulty (Majors) got into" and for "the fight (Rabun) had."

These Primitive Baptist believed that foot washing, as done by Christ for his disciples in the upper room, was an ordinance of the church, just as much as baptism and communion. They also did not hold with the idea of missions as a duty of the church, and they were staunch in their belief of the doctrine of election.

Minutes of the church were kept with initials beside the names of the members: RBL = Received by Letter; DBL = Dismissed by Letter; EXCOM = Excommunicated; EXCLU = Excluded; RES = Restored to Fellowship.

On February 23, 1833, a rule was passed that each male member of the church was to pay 12 & 1/2 cents each quarter for the expenses of the church.

On July 23, 1837, the church committee reported that the church house was to be built near the campmeeting ground, near to Charles Sheets'. Trustees were set up to be in charge of this undertaking.

On March 24, 1838, new rules of decorum called for all male members to be present at each church conference and delinquents would be called to answer to the church. Additional rules for handling disputes within the church fellowship was also added.

On October 27, 1838, the church "received a petition" from a part of the members of this church for dismission from the church to become a constituted body themselves. Twelve men applied for letters of dismissal and sixteen women applied for dismissal. All were DBL—Dismissed by Letter.

September 25, 1841, the members took up the issue of building a church, and the majority voted to build it in "the same old place." They also voted to send delegates to the New Liberty Church in Carroll County where their association was meeting.

On April 5, 1845, John T. Chambers was **excommunicated** for "communing with the Missionary Baptist."

May 22, 1858, William Keeton "Service by Brother Williams" is now the new pastor and moderator in the place of Henry Haynes."

April 3, 1859, the church "took up the Articles of Faith and Rules of Decorum," and appointed delegates to the Tallapoosa Association.

October 22, 1860, "Whitten Hambric is now preaching and serving as moderator."

While major battles were being fought in the Atlanta Campaign in 1864, and during the war years the church often did not meet or else conducted little business.

"June 1864, in consequence of the Yankee army being in the settlement there was no conference held," Allison Cheves, Church Clerk.

August 1864—conference held. Brother J. M. Muse is the new pastor.

April 1, 1865, a subscription was taken up for the purpose of repairing the roof of the church.

Pleasant Grove Baptist Church

About one-half mile down Middle Van Wert Road in Hart Town is Pleasant Grove Church, (33°43'47.35"N 84°57'56.64"W) formed in July 1849. The early members were: Samuel Hart, Dobbs, Alexander Porter Green, Sneelgroves, Haynes, Muse, Davis, Astins, Dobsons, Willis Bagwell, Shinn, Tom Turners, Conners, Hogues, Burtons, Yates, William Hixon, Leathers, Frank Sykes, Velvin, Cheves, Lassetter, Beall, Florence, Newborn, and Marion Fielder. The first pastors were: Parker M. Rice, James Reeves and Leroy McWhorter. Other members were William Hixon, F. M. Fielder, Willis Bagwell and W. W. Cobb. Jane Cobb, widow of William Washington Cobb, was the oldest living member for many years; she died March 2, 1909. The church has one of the most beautiful and well-kept cemeteries to be found anywhere.

From a pamphlet, 1943, *History of Pleasant Grove Baptist Church:*

Francis Marion Fielder was among the best men who ever lived. He was one of the founders and pillar at Pleasant Grove Church, of which he was chorister for fifty years. Mr. James C. Hixon (also) served for so long as chorister here at Pleasant Grove, and was famous throughout the county for his teaching of "Singing Schools."

Billy Hixon was also an early settler. Like the above mentioned gentlemen, he was noted for his devoutness and honesty.

The first building was constructed of logs and the congregation is presently worshiping in the fourth building.

Pastors who have served the church from the time it was constituted: James Reeves, Thornton Burt, James Rainwater, 1850-1860; John M. Muse, 1960-1869; John M. Key, 1869-1874; W. A. Lane, 1875-1880; John M. Muse, 1880-1884; J. R. T. Brown, 1884-1890; J. M. B. Stallings, 1890-1891; W. W. Roop, 1891-1902; R. C. Rhodes, 1902-1907; F. J. Amis, 1907-1909; H. H. Connell 1909-1911; A. J. Morgan, 1911-1914; J. G. Hunt, 1914-1921; A. J. Morgan, 1921-1924; W. M. Suttles, 1924-: J. J. Hagood, L. P. Lambert, J. A. Bonner, J. W. Holland, Glenn Waldrop and L. P. Lambert, the present pastor (1943).

Pleasant Grove Baptist Church
Courtesy Sarah Pitts & Villa Rica Archives

On March 13th, 1913 the church house, a frame building at that time, was completely demolished by a cyclone. The roof and all walls were swept away entirely by the terrific wind. The floor, however, remained intact except for being set over several inches on the pillars, but all pews and everything were blown away and the floor swept clear of everything with the exception of a small table, which stood just in front of the pulpit, on which table was a Bible, a water pitcher and drinking glass which remained undisturbed as by a miracle. The noble and consecrated band of Christians of Pleasant Grove Church lost no time in making plans to rebuild following the destruction of the church building.

. . .The church was replaced with a beautiful brick structure, which is the present building. (1943).

Some descendants of these early church members still live in the area and have attended one or both: Pleasant Grove Baptist Church and the present-day Villa Rica First Baptist Church. Descendants of the early members of the Pleasant Grove Baptist Church who also lived in the Hart House were the Hixons, Brooks, Leathers, Wynns and Mitchells.

From Abstract of Deeds, Book F, Page 229 Carroll County, 13 Oct 1851. THOMAS W. BURTON to JAMES C. ECHOLS, Telfair County. $800.00. Part of land lot #166, 6th district except 39 acres where Pleasant Grove meeting house stands. 1/2 gold reserved to THOMAS RABUN. Attest: Gilbert Cole, Leonard Fullbright, Joseph L. Hart, O. A. Henson, J.P. 5 May 1853.

Pleasant Grove School

Jane Hart Cobb taught at Pleasant Grove School after her husband was killed in 1864 in the Civil War. She and her three boys, Ossie, John and E. H. "Bud" walked three miles every school day from their home on the Old Jacksonville Atlanta Road (also known as the Old Villa Rica -Temple Road).

The school, located on Land Lot 155, (33°43'21.00"N 84°58'00.60"W) sat back from the road, and faced Pleasant Grove Church Road near where Flat Rock (Missionary) Baptist Church is today and only about a half mile from Pleasant Grove Baptist Church. This school continued into the 1940's but at that time the front of the school faced today's Rocky Branch Road.

Pleasant Grove Baptist School
Courtesy Sarah Pitts

From the 1918, *Education Survey of Georgia*:

On lot No. 155; two miles to (New) Brooklyn school. Grounds: Area and titles uncertain; lot neglected; no school garden; small playground; no toilet. Building: value $600.00; one room; no cloak room; improperly lighted; ceiled; unpainted; in fair condition. Equipment: Rough home-made desks; no teacher's desk; poor blackboards; no maps; no charts; no globe; no pictures; no library; no dictionary; a covered water cooler. Organization: one teacher; seven grades; six months school year; average attendance for last three years, 48 pupils. Maintenance: From County Board $330.00.

Villa Rica Male and Female Institute

From the *Carroll County Press*, March 11, 1851:

This institution is situated in the retired, beautiful and healthy village of Villa Rica, Carroll County, and is now under the direction of Mr. Asa Griggs, who found it just twelve months since. Situated in a healthy region of country, and under the supervision of its presentable and efficient Principal, this institution is destined to occupy a high rank among the schools in our country. It has already reached a commanding eminence and on the road to a still higher destiny when it was founded, one year since, it numbered just thirteen pupils, but before the close of the scholastic year that number had swollen to one hundred.

Girls or boys may here find adequate facilities for acquiring a thorough and extensive English and classical education. Send us your children and we will endeavor to make good scholars and good citizens. The next term will commence on the first Monday in February. By order of the villagers.

Concord Methodist Church at Hickory Level

The Concord Methodist Church (33°40'39.23"N 85.00'02.71"W) was organized in 1828. It is located at Hickory Level, a community at the intersection of Hickory Level Road and the Sandhill-Hickory Level Road. This community is four miles south of Hart Town.

The first settler, Reverend James Baskin, arrived in February 1828. He bought the property which was timberland, cleared much of it, and built a home. The land was almost level and the timber was largely hickory, thus the name given by the first settler to that community. Reverend Baskin also donated a plot of land for a church and school, together with considerable other lands.

The Methodist Church, known as Concord (meaning, "living in love and harmony") was organized in the summer of 1828. The first building was constructed of logs and was eighteen feet square. It was lighted by candles placed at intervals on the wall. The church began with thirteen members. Charter members included Rev. James Baskin, Dave Stripling, Wright Majors, James Upson, Larkin Allen, Baxter, James Bryce, Cash, Rev. Thomas G. Powell, Billy Taylor, Turner, Slomman Wynn and Ballard.

The second church building was constructed in 1836, also of logs, and was twenty-four feet square. The third church was a frame building and was built in 1854 for about $500. The fourth church was built in 1891. The present building was constructed in 1909 after a storm wrecked the former structure. The building, costing $4,000, was dedicated by Bishop Warren A. Candler. Through the years, the buildings have always been rebuilt on the same location. The cornerstone marking the original property line laid out by James Baskin in 1828 remains as he erected it.

In the early years, the church was served by circuit riders who came to preach every six to eight weeks. During the absence of the circuit riders, the spiritual life of the church was carried on by local preachers (unordained men who could "exhort" but not serve the sacraments) and by class leaders who organized groups to study the meaning of Christian living. They met in homes of members.

Sabbath School was begun in 1868. The Women's Missionary Society started in the mid-1890s with Mollie Wynn as the first president.

In the 1860's, twenty-four African-American members were listed on the roll. From this group emerged an outstanding minister, Rev. Larkin Walker, who preached at Concord to the African American congregation and to other congregations in surrounding areas. He was buried at Concord.

In 1865, during the worst of the Civil War, Concord had no pastor for the only time in its history. The records indicate that through local preachers and class leaders, the spiritual life of the church and community was maintained.

In the early years, following the "laying by" of crops, great revivals were held at Concord. This tradition is kept alive today, for the third week in August is still set aside for revivals. One of the high moments in the history of the church was in August of 1896 when fifty-four persons were received into the church on one day during the revival. Rev. W. T. Irvine served as pastor.

Pastors who have served Concord Methodist Church: 1828 James Baskin; 1829 Simeon L. Stephens; 1830 George W. Powell; 1831 Appleton Haygood; 1832 George Bishop; 1833 William Stegall; 1834 M. Gresham; 1835 James Jones; 1836 J. W. Yarbrough; 1837 Thomas W. Thomas; 1838 Alford Dorman; 1839 Phillips Groves; 1840-1841 Sidney M. Smith; 1842 Jesse M. Carroll; 1843 Thomas Fowler; 1844 B. E. Lucas; 1845 Robert R. Johnson; 1846-1847 William B. Moss; 1848 J. Blakley Smith; 1849 William E. Lucy; 1850-1851 Thomas H. Whitley and W. B. McHand Jr.; 1852 Alfred Dorman; 1853 Cleyburn Trussell; and J. G. Worley, Jr.;

1854 W. J. Wardlaw and M. W. Arnold, Jr.; 1855 Cleyburn Trussell; 1856-1857 Thomas Boring; 1858 Miles W. Arnold; 1859 Jackson W. Brady; 1860 Samuel Clark; 1861 James Lupo; 1862 David Stripling; 1863 John Murphy; 1864 No pastor (War); 1865 David Stripling; 1866-1867 W. C. Dunlap; 1868 Cleyburn Trussell; 1869 Robert R. Johnson; 1870-1872 J. N. Myers; 1873 Sanford Leek; 1875 Joseph Chambers; 1876-1877 F. F. Reynolds; 1878-1879 J. D. Weems; 1880-1881 Britton Sanders; 1882 O. C. Simons; 1883--1885 S. H. Braswell; 1886-1887 E. H. Wood; 1888-1889 Sanford Leeke; 1890 W. M. Sewell; 1891 W. J. Wood and 1892 S. W. Rodgers.

The first postmaster was Reverend James Baskin who also built the post office. Reverend Thomas G. Powell served as the first schoolmaster. The first settlers at Hickory Level were Larkin Allen, Alysmus Allen, the Baxter family, James Bryce, Jesse Gray, Ned Gresham, Billy McCain, John Smith, David Stripling, Rev. Billy Taylor and Slomman Wynn.

Methodist Episcopal Church, South

Listed in Carroll County Abstracts for Deed Book G, page 152: Deed on page 81, July 10, 1852. James Baskin sold to Slomman Wynn, James Bryce, William H. Taylor, David Stripling and James Stripling trustees in trust part of land lot #56, 6th district, Carroll County, two acres to build or cause to be built a house of worship for the Methodist Episcopal Church South. Attest: Larkin A. Allen, Henry S. Chance J. P. November 3, 1852.

Hickory Level Store & Hospital: (33°40'44.11"N 84°59'57.41"W)

From *At Home in Carrollton* page 76:

At one time there was a hospital called the 'Community Hospital' located on the second floor of the "Hickory Level Store. Dr. Franklin Seaborn Scales was the doctor. He came to Hickory Level about the turn of the century. His wife was his nurse. The front room was his medicine room including herbs. There was a waiting room and three beds. He per-

Hickory Level Store
The Heritage of Carroll County

formed surgery here as well as made house calls.

"Old" Bethel Primitive Baptist Church
From the *Temple Enterprise* newspaper dated September 24, 1883:

Old Bethel Primitive Baptist Church was originally made of logs and had no steeple. Though the church was most rustic in appearance, the farmers gathered, the old elder rode up, tied his horse to a sapling, and preached the gospel as he saw it. The singing of the old gospel sons could be heard afar as the melodious notes pealed through the quiet countryside.

From Abstract Deed Book F, Page 173 Carroll County, 22 Jun 1848. ROBERT A. GREENE to GILBERT COLE. $300.00. South half land lot #152. Attest: G. M. Hiden, H. S. Hulsey, M.A. McRae 6 Nov 1848.

Then from the Abstract Deed Book F, Page 353 Carroll County, 10 Mar 1849. GILBERT COLE to ELISHA BROOKS, WILLIAM NEELEY DAVIS and ISAAC E. COBB, trustees of the PRIMITIVE BAPTIST CHURCH at BETHEL MEETING HOUSE. $9.00. Part of land lot #152, 6th district Carroll County. 3 acres. Attest: Anderson Green, G. M. Hiden, Henry S. Chance, J.P. 25 Dec 1849.

William Neeley Davis' (above) father, John Davis, travelled preaching baptist faith. It's possible John with the help of Gilbert Cole, Elisha Brooks, Isaac E. Cobb and his son, William, helped organize the Bethel Primitive Baptist Church.

Book G, Page 547 Carroll County, 28 Nov 1853. GILBERT COLE to ALFRED WADDELL, Meriwether County. $950.00. South half land lot #152, 6th dist. Carroll County. Except 3 acres where BETHEL MEETING HOUSE now stands. Attest: L. C. McAlmon, John T. Meador, J.I.C. 11 Oct 1854.

The Villa Rica Presbyterian Church at Old Town Villa Rica.
The Villa Rica Presbyterian Church was organized in 1855 by Reverend Benjamin Dupree and has met for 163 years except for the years of the Civil War. It began with fourteen members who met in individual's homes. The first members were Miss Mary Hodgen and W. B. Candler, Sr; the first elders were James Davis, T. M. Hamilton and W. P. Hill. When Reverend Dupree died in 1863, the regular services were discontinued until 1867 when Reverend James Stacy became pastor and added four new members. The Presbyterian's history states that their services were, at one time, held in the old town Methodist Church alternating Sundays with the Methodists.

Also in 1867 several new members joined including more of the Candler Family who have played a crucial role in the church to this day. The original structure which served both the Methodist and the Presbyterian on alternate Sundays, sat where Punkintown Road intercepts into Highway 61. When this building was abandoned after new churches were built, the Haynes family used the old church building as a barn as it sat across the road (then dirt) from the Haynes Home. About 1940 it burned down. Later, Punkintown Road was extended through where the church/barn had set to the present day extension to intercept Highway 61.

In 1885, the Presbyterian membership built their first church building, a wooden structure, erected on Candler Street behind the present-day police

Villa Rica Presbyterian Church
Courtesy Greg & Donna Lisenby

station. This frame building was constructed through the efforts of W. B. Candler, Sr., J. T. Hamilton, John Mabel, Frank A. Pritchett and J. N. Wilson. The next pastor was Reverend William Desmuke who served from 1872 to 1889. Reverend R. L. King was the next pastor.

By 1925, the congregation had grown to sixty people. Sometime around 1930, the clapboard church was moved from Candler Street—about 1/4 mile away from its present location. The older structure was moved on poles pulled by a horse owned by Harlan Lane. Later, Harlan served as an elder of the church. His daughter, Mary Bell, was a member.

The present church on Main Street was the site of the former home of W. B. Candler, Sr and was given for the site of the church in memory of W. B. Candler (1847-1928) and his wife, Elizabeth Slaughter Candler (1854-1915) by their children. The home, being on the back of the property, served as an office space, fellowship center and Sunday School.

After its move, the church was bricked and a basement added. The bricks, delivered via train which stopped in front of the church, were unloaded by the men of the congregations. The current pulpit, mahogany pews and stained glass windows were purchased from the Old Wesley Memorial Church in Atlanta when it was demolished in the 1920s and were stored until the renovations were complete. This original structure was renovated, bricked and extended to become the beautiful sanctuary which is still in use today. (33°44'05.42"N 84°55'17.98"W)

Methodist Church at Willoughby Farm, then the Methodist Church at Old Town

The first Methodist Church was laid out in 1830, four years after gold was discovered in the Villa Rica area (named thus meaning City of Gold by the mother of Bishop Warren Candler, Martha Beall Candler. According to local information, the first Methodist church, a log building, was the first erected in the mining community and served all denominations. Later, this log cabin was moved closer to Highway 61, less than a mile to become the Macedonia Baptist Church.
(33°45'15.93"N 84°54'03.24"W)

About 1845, an attractive wooden church was built in Old Town across from the Haynes and Slaughter property where Punkintown Road today intercepts Highway 61. The Methodists shared their pulpit with the Baptist and Presbyterians, and a strong Union Sunday School was loyally attended by all denominations for years. Mr. W. P. Stone served as the Superintendent for many years. Records show that the church was established and supported by such godly men as Samuel C. Candler, the father of Bishop Warren Candler; Tom Perkerson; Dr. John Slaughter, grandfather of Dr. N. G. Slaughter of Athens, Georgia; Alfred Baggett; and others. Reverend Claiborn Trussell was one of the first ministers.

In 1883 a new town, Villa Rica, was laid out a mile south of the old town, to connect with the marvel of the age, the Georgia Pacific, now the Southern Railroad. In 1886 a new Methodist church was built in present day Villa Rica for $1200. For Methodists, there existed the church at Old Town, the new church, one in Temple, and one at Concord. Mr. F. A. Trussell was Sunday School Superintendent in 1891 during the ministry of Rev. M. S. Williams and filled the place for many years. However, it was customary for members to return to the Old Town church for Sunday School.

In 1890, the old church building was abandoned and sold in 1896. The money was used to repair the new church. Since this former church building was located across the road from the Haynes home, it became their barn. Many years later it burned down and later Punkintown Road was extended to its present location.

The trustees at the new Villa Rica Methodist were W. A. Floyd, A. B. Davis, B. F. Floyd, W. H. Malone, and W. A. Maxwell. The white frame church was used until 1905 when a committee composed of G. B. Malone, J. M. Moore, G. P. Braswell, B. C. Powell and A. J. Simmons was appointed to build a new church. The present-day brick church designed along Gothic lines and costing $3500 was completed in time for services in July 1906. Reverend T. M. Elliott was pastor.

Early records reveal a long line of noble pastors. The pioneer circuit riders who began the church to modern times were Rev. Claiborn Trussell, Rev. Henry Haynes, Rev. James Reeves, Rev. S. Freeman, Rev. Thornton Burke, and Rev.

Later pastors: 1867-1868 Rev. M. D. Norton; 1869 Rev. R. R. Johnson; 1871-72 Rev. J. N. Myers; 1873 Rev. Sandford Leake; 1875 Rev. James Chambers; 1876-77 Rev. F. F. Reynolds; 1878-79 Rev. D. J. Weems; 1880-81 Rev. B. Sanders; 1882 O. C. Simmons; 1883 Rev. G. W. Hardaway; 1884 Rev. G. W. Thomas; and 1885 Rev. C. S. Owens.

Book E page 147, Carroll County, 25 May 1842. EDMUND W. HOLLAND, agent for DAVID CLOPTON, EDWARD A. BROADDUS, EDMUND W. HOLLAND, BENJAMIN CHAPMAN, JOSEPH CHAMBERS, JESSE H. CHAMBERS, CLAYTON WILLIAMS to CHARLES B. HENTON, EZEKIEL S. CHANDLER, LEONARD C. HUFF, DENISON B. PALMER AND WILLIAM A. R. PATRICK trustees and their successors METHODIST EPISCOPAL CHURCH VILLA RICA. $1.00. 11/12 town lot in Villa Rica, land lot #193, 6th district Carroll County, Town lot #3. 70 feet in front, 250 feet back, 50 feet wide south end, 1/3 acres. To be used to erect Methodist Episcopal Church denominations, also to be used as a school house. Edmund W. Holland, agent for Villa Rica Town Company. Attest: John B. Wick, John Hilderbrand, J. P. 3 Sept 1844. (33°44'53.81"N 84°54'40.98"W)

Villa Rica First United Methodist Church

In 1883, when the railroad came through Villa Rica, merchants in Old Town wanted to build a new town close to the railroad. Those who attended the Methodist Church and the little Red Schoolhouse at Old Town continued to do so, but a church was needed close to the new town. First, a wooden structure was built. Then, in 1905-1906, a modern building was constructed and bricked on Land Lot 161. It was large enough for Sunday School rooms.

Villa Rica Methodist Church
Courtesy Mary Elizabeth Phillips

Pastors of the Villa Rica First United Methodist Church: 1886-87 Rev. E. H. Wood; 1888-89 Sanford Leake; 1889 S. R. Belk; 1890- 93 M. S. Williams; 1894- William Dunbar; 1896-98 Rev. F. Walton; 1899 Rev. C. M. Verdell, Sr; 1900-01 D. M. Edwards; 1902-04 Rev. M. S. Williams; 1905-06 Rev. Loy Warwick and 1907-08 T. M. Elliott." (33°44'02.71"N 84°55'11.97"W)

Villa Rica First Baptist Church

Organized in 1850, the first church was held in a log school house with Reverend J. R. T. Brown as pastor. In 1880 a two-story church was build with W. A. Land and Reverend A. J. Morgan as pastors. The Church meetings were held on the second floor and the first floor was used for a school. John A. "Jack" Jones donated land in 1885, for ninety-nine years, for a new Baptist Church to be built on what is now known as Main Street in Villa Rica. A Sunday School was organized and services were held once a month.

Pastors at Villa Rica Baptist Church were Reverend Morgan (1885-1889), Reverend J. B. Jenkins (1889) and Reverend J. R. T. Brown, who died as he was conducing services at Pleasant Grove. Then came Reverend J. I. Oxford, Reverend T. E. McClutcheon, Reverend Griffis, Reverend H. H. Connell, Reverend Parish, Reverend J. M. Spinks, Rev. J. T. Maltbie and Rev. J. M. Suttles. (33°44'09.49"N 84°55'22.83"W)

Wesley Chapel United Methodist Church

In 1854 W. J. Wardlaw and Miles Wesley Arnold served on the Carrollton Circuit. They held a brush arbor revival which was the beginning of the church they organized as Wesley Chapel Methodist Church (about three and a half miles north of Villa Rica). Soon after the church was organized a house [sic] (church) was built during the same year, which remained until 1890, when it was torn down and a new one begun.

Shortly before the church was organized, some of the Arnolds and Turners from middle Georgia moved into the community. They were among the first and most prominent members of the new church. They were Methodist before they left middle Georgia and as soon as they could, they built a church of that denomination near their new homes. Among those who came from middle Georgia to Carroll County were Asbury Coke Arnold and family, James R. Turner and family, and Thomas Turner and family. These all united with the new church.

The first trustees were Asbury Coke Arnold, James R. Turner, Larkin H. Davis, Thomas Turner and Josiah Tolbert. Asbury Coke Arnold was a son of Wllliam Arnold (Billy), of the Georgia Conference, and a brother to Miles Wesley Arnold of the North Georgia Conference.

James R. Turner was the father of Rev. William S. Turner, of the Georgia Conference. Larkin H. Davis was a brother to Cris C. Davis, a popular local preacher of Atlanta. Thomas Turner, brother of James R. Turner was a local preacher. He died before the church was completed. He was buried on July 4, 1854, at the graveyard near the church; his grave being the first ever dug there. Among those who sleep in the old graveyard is "Uncle" Claiborn Trussell, one of the purest and best men that ever lived in this section. He was a member of the Georgia Conference and of the North Georgia Conference for fifty-two years. "A grand old man was he."

Wesley Chapel has given two preachers to the itinerancy. William S. Turner joined the Georgia Conference in 1854, the year the church was organized. In 1867 he transferred to Alabama. He died at Fort Valley, Georgia on March 14, 1891. He was a good man, and a useful preacher.

The Turner family's role in the history of the church and the community covers one hundred fourteen years. The family moved to the community in 1840. Miss

Lizzie was daughter, grand-daughter, and niece of charter members. There was never a closer family, nor one who was closer in everything that was done in their church.

In the beginning of 1890, members were few. That year, Rev. S. R. Belk was in charge of the Villa Rica Circuit and Wesley Chapel belonged to the circuit. The preacher was full of faith and the Holy Ghost. He went to work with all his power consecrated to the service of the Lord. God blessed his efforts; a wonderful revival was the result. About sixty members joined the church. The old members took on new life and determined to build a new church.

Wesley Chapel Methodist Church
Villa Rica Archives Sarah Pitts

The money was subscribed and the work begun. The house was forty by sixty feet. On the third Sunday in September 1891, the new church was dedicated. An intense crowd was present; Rev. S. R. Belk dedicated the house [sic], church. Signed M. S. Williams MC.

This article was written by the pastor of Wesley Chapel and published in the Carroll County Paper, dated September 20, 1891.

When the Villa Rica Methodist Church was organized it took many members away from Wesley Chapel.

The annual All Day Singing at Wesley Chapel was held on the third Sunday in September. Singers came from over the southeastern part of the United States. All day singing had been held for more than forty years. The singers brought well filled baskets of food, and the people of the church brought enough for the regular congregation and the singers. The Homecoming, which was held the third Sunday in May and the All Day Singing always brought a full house, and usually enough money came in on these two special days to pay for the cleaning of the cemetery.

Wesley Chapel Pastors Presiding:
    1854 Pastor W. J. Wardlaw; 1854 Pastor Miles Wesley Arnold; 1855 Claiborn Trusell; 1855 Pastor Peter Groover; 1856 Pastor Thomas Boring; 1857 Pastor Thomas Boring;
    1858 Pastor Miles Wesley Arnold; 1859 Pastor John W. Brady; 1859 Pastor S. A. Clark; 1860 Pastor J. W. Brady; 1861 & 1862 Pastor J. L. Lupo; 1863 & 1864 Pastor John Murphy; 1865 Pastor David Stripling; 1866 Pastor W. C. Dunlap;
    1867 Pastor W. C. Dunlap; 1868 Pastor Claiborn Trussell; 1869 Pastor R. R. Johnson; 1870, 1871 & 1873 Pastor J. N. Myers;

1873 & 1874 Pastor Sanford Leak; 1875 Pastor J. Chambers; 1876 Pastor F. F. Reynolds; 1877 Pastor F. F. Reynold; 1878 & 1879 Pastor D. J. Weims;

1880 & 1881 Pastor Britton Sanders; 1882 Pastor O. C. Simmons; 1883, 1884 & 1885 Pastor S. H. Braswell;

1886 & 1887 Pastor F. R. Smith; 1888 & 1889 Pastor J. M. Sewell; 1890 Pastor S. R. Belk; 1891,1892 & 1893 Pastor M. S. Williams;

1894 Pastor J. L. Curtiss; 1895, 1896, 1897 & 1898 Pastor Fletcher Walton; 1899 Pastor C. M. Verdell; and 1900 Pastor D. M. Edwards. (33°46'28.94"N 84°57'42.67"W)

Lebanon Campground

Book A, Page 462, Carroll County, 13 Apr 1835. WILLIAM KENNON to ANDREW AGNEW, JEREMIAH HARRISON, FRANCIS WINN and JAMES BASKIN, Trustees of Lebanon Campground. Relinquish of rights because of past (land) deeds. 4 acres of land lot #131, 6th district Carroll County, including Lebanon Meeting House and Campground for use of the Methodist E. Church. Attest: Pennel Quales, A. M. McWhorter, J.P., 17 Jun 1835.

Post Office/Postmasters
Allen's Mill
Andrew J. Aderhold 8 April 1876; Discontinued 3 May 1886.

Buckhorn Isaac Cobb 8 Feb 1849; William Cobb 16 October 1852; Discontinued 17 October 1853; Joseph L. Hart 16 Sept 1856; Discontinued 20 January 5 (illegible 57?)

Burnt Stand
Robert A. Reid 16 September 1847; Repose Haralson Co. 21 February 1859.

Chanceville
Henry S. Chance 16 July 1857; Richard W. McKee 28 November 1859; Discontinued 28 September 1866.

Chevestown:
Zachary J. Allen 26 December 1882; Discontinued mail to Cheves August 6, 1883.

Gold Village
William P. Statmaker 14 January 1868; Discontinued to Villa Rica 2 November 188(?).

Hickory Level
James Baskin: 20 October 1837. Discontinued 27 June 1866, Reestablished 23 July 1866; James L. Baskin 23 July 1866; Discontinued 11 June 1868; Reestablished 19 June 1874; William M. Allen 19 June 1974; Discontinued 23 July 1877; John T.

Bryce 17 February 1881; (Reestablished 18 January 1886;) John W. Taylor 18 January 1886; William H. Bledsoe May 28 1886; James L. Baskin 20 November 1888; William T. Wynn 5 April 1899.

Temple
Joseph H. Allen 24 April 1882; Richard L. (S.) Rowe 15 October 1887; Miss Myrtie Craven 25 May 1892.

Simsville
Received mail once a week. George W. Autrey 20 July 1876; B. J. McCain; Discontinued 1883.

Villa Rica
James L. Adair January 6, 1831; B. Walker, B. Haynes February 16, 1831; S. C. Candler and J. Awrey May 15, 1837; Ezekiel S. Candler April 11, 1840; William H. Awtrey December 14, 1847; William B. Moss May 12, 1850; William B. Moss (Muse) 12 May 1851; Dennison B. Palmer September 29, 1851; Abbott M. McWhorter October 1, 1853; Valentine M. Hodgson December 7, 1854; George W. Awtry October 30, 1855; John B. Slaughter January 26, 1856; Thomas M. Hamilton December 6, 1856; Seaborn W. Noland February 3, 1866; William B. Candler November 16, 1868; Zachary T. Allen August 7, 1883; William B. Candler April 30, 1885; Zachary T. Allen March 30, 1889; Leanora R. Allen February 13, 1904.

Grand Lodge of Georgia 1854 -Villa Rica Lodge No. 72, Villa Rica, Carroll County
A. M. McWhorter, *W. M.; D. H. Witcher, S.W.; J. T. Slaughter, J. W.; John Mitchell, Treasurer; V. M. Hodgson, P.M., Secretary; L. H. Davis, S.D.; B. M. Witcher, J.D.; Benoni Fowler, Tyler;

Rev. J. Baskin; Rev. J. Bryce; Rev. D. Stripling, P.M.; John T. Chambers; W. Cartright; H. S. Chance; N. H. Gordon; Isaac Kinney; F. M. Little; E. B. McWhorter; G. W. McLarty; S. W. McLarty; A. N. McLarty; R. T. McCurdy;

R. N. Russell; T. Stokely, P.M.; Rev. T. Turner; J. H. Underwood; John B. Wick; William West; C. Polk; J. L. Hill; J. M. Bryant; W. C. Baskin; O. B. Bowen; T. L. Bowen; James Jacobs; and F. A. Wylds.

For the year 1854: Initiated 2; Passed 2; Raised 2; Rejected 1; Resigned 4; Deaths 2; Suspended 1; Expelled 1; Dues paid $29.25.

Regular Meetings of this Lodge are held on the 1st and 3rd Wednesday nights of each month. *W. M.—Worshipful Master; S. W.—Senior Warden; J. W.—Junior Warden; S. D.—Senior Deacon; J. D.—Junior Deacon; P. M.—Past Master; F. C. — Fellow Craft degree; E. A—Entered Apprentice degree; Tyler—guardian of the door, while the Lodge session is taking.

3

Gold Deposits in Villa Rica
and
Climatic Anomalies the Winter of 1827-1828

"Forsan et haec olim meminisse luvabit."
Perhaps some time it will be pleasing to remember these things.
Hart Cobb

The Gold Belt—Gold, Copper and Asbestos Mines

Land Lot #s 155, 165 & 166: Allen mine, Askew and Hart mines; 192; 193, Hick's (Hix's) mine; 194–Clopton mine; 195–Chamber's mine; and 206–Pine Mt. Gold mine. New evidence that settlers came to the Villa Rica area to mine for gold earlier than 1830 as reported in history books.

In *Georgia's Last Frontier*:
 . . . Carroll County's mining history began in 1830 soon after the county was settled. In that year gold was discovered at Pine Mountain, a short distance north of the future site of Villa Rica. This community was originally known as Hixtown, named for William Hix, who had operated a tavern and a general store there before 1830. By 1832 several hundred men were employed annually in the mines, which produced an annual average of 25,000 pennyweights of gold for the next few years. (A pennyweight was 1/20 of an ounce and valued at approximately one dollar.) The principal mining belt was situated on lots 155, 165, 166, 192, 193, 194, and 195 in the Sixth Land (6th) District. The ore-bearing veins were numerous varying from a few inches to several feet in thickness. These often expanded into pockets containing many tons of high-grade ore. The mining process used before the Civil War was the simple placer

method with hand rockers, in which unskilled labor was employed. Each hand averaged from two to twenty pennyweights per day.

Gold Deposits in Carroll County

Information from an 1896 geological book on gold deposits in Georgia reveals that only in two localities in Carroll County has gold been found in sufficient abundance to be of economic importance.

The more noted of these localities, lies in the Villa Rica region, in the extreme northern part of the county. Gold was discovered, here, near Pine Mountain, in 1830. Two years afterward, several hundred hands were regularly employed, in the mines, and produced, annually, for a number of years, more than twenty-five thousand penny-weights of gold. The entire output of the mine has been estimated by W. B. Candler who has been living at Villa Rica for many years, at $500,000."

The early workings, which consist both of placer and surface mining were confined chiefly to the narrow bottoms, along the small streams and the adjacent hill-slopes. The area over which gold has been found in paying quantities is limited to a narrow belt not over six miles in length and less than two miles wide."

The topography of the region shows an advanced stage of denudation. The numerous small streams are usually sluggish, while the surface, though occasionally broken, by low ridges and hills, has the general appearance of a plain. With the exception of the so-called Pine Mountain, a small hill, near the center of the mining area, none of the ridges or elevations attain a height, of more than seventy-five feet, above the surface of the streams. These topographical conditions have seriously interfered, in places, with surface-mining, owing to the difficulty, of conveying the water to the deposits, location on the hillsides. Ore was carried to the nearest stream to be washed. In most cases, this difficulty, however, has been met, and overcome, later by the use of engines, in elevating a water holding tank or, by hauling the earth, containing gold, to the nearest stream.

The rocks of this area are quite different, from any, hitherto examined. In immediate contact with the vein, the rock consists mainly of granite, which is usually such fissured, and occasionally, to such considerable depths, that the expense of mining the ore is reduced to a minimum. Associated with the granite, occur schists and other metamorphic rocks, consisting of masses of hornblende and of magnesian silicates, such as serpentine, talc etc.

The gold-bearing veins are numerous; but, only a few, so far, have been worked, with profit. They vary, from a few inches to many feet in thickness, and consist mainly of quartz, which usually appears to have been crushed and broken, by some movement of the rock-mass. These veins often expand into pockets, carrying many tons of high-grade ore. Instances are given, where several hundred pennyweights of gold have been taken, from one pocket, alone.

The vein-mining consists of open cuts, extending along the outcropping of the veins. Some of these excavations are many rods long, and from ten to thirty feet deep, the earth or decomposed granite having been removed by hand."

The principal part of the works, as well as the most favorable prospects, for further development, are located on lots 155, 165—Hart & Allen; 166—Askew & Hart; 192, 193—Hicks; 194—Clopton; and 195—Chambers, all in the **6th district**.

Land Lot #155, 6th District, Carroll County
Book B, page 321, Carroll County, 3 Apr 1832. JOHN ASBURY and WILLIAM THORNTON, Monroe County appoint John Brooks, Carroll County attorney to assign title to Land Lot #155, 6 district Carroll County. Attest: Phillip Chambers, Thomas Rabun J. P., 1 Nov 1833.

Book B, page 322, Paulding County, 15 Sep 1832 JOEL H. DYER, Paulding County to DAVID CLOPTON, Carroll County $33.00. 2/3 land lot #155, 6th district Carroll, except 10 acres in the N. E. corner. Attest: A. W. McBrayer, Samuel Wilkinson J. P., 1 Nov. 1833.

Book B, page 322, Carroll County, 4 Dec 1832. JOHN BROOKS, agent for JOHN ASBURY and WILLIAM THORNTON, Monroe County to JOEL H. DYER, $500.00. Land Lot #155, 6th district Carroll County except 10 acres, N. E. corner and one branch. Attest: Wm. Hics, Charles Hulsey, J. P., 1 Nov 1833.

Lot #155, Page 409, Book F, Paulding County, February 4, 1850. DAVID CLOPTON to THORNTON BURKE. Sum of $517.50 for land lot #155, in the 6th district of Carroll County. Also land lot #147, in the 2nd district (now Douglas County). The West half of land lot #175, in the 2nd District in Carroll County. Attest: W. E. Slaughter, Joseph C. Williams, J.P., April 28, 1851.

Land Lot #165 G. A. Allen Gold Mine (at Hart Town)
Location: Carroll County, 2.2 miles due west of the junction of Highway 78 and Georgia Highway 61 at Villa Rica. Immediately south of Highway 78; 6,340 feet FNL and 12,400 feet FWL of the Villa Rica 15-minute quadrangle.

According to S. P. Jones, 1909: The Chambers' Mine was operated prior before the Civil War and again in 1908. This consisted of open cuts, shafts, and surface mining. The shafts are now nearly filled and the open cuts considerably slumped and overgrown.

This mine was called the Allen mine because the Allen family lived there on this corner and had Allen's store there in the 1900's. (33°43'56.60"N 84°57'36.14"W)

Land Lot #165 The Hart Mine
This mine, lot 165, 6th district was worked extensively and has produced a

considerable amount of gold. The principal part of the works consists of an open cut, 75 yards long, about 20 feet deep, and several rods wide. Some two years ago (1892), work was renewed on the property; a shaft was sunk on a vein to the depth of 35 feet, the ore was taken out and milled; but, for some reason, the work was soon abandoned. There is now, to be seen in the open cut penetrating the decomposed granite, a quartz vein about 18 inches thick. The quartz is light grey, and carries at the point exposed, only a small amount of gold. Whether the exposed vein is a part of the main ore-body, or only an off-shoot from it, could not be determined. Unfortunately, the prospects on this property, as well as on the above named lots, were in no condition for examination. There are valuable gold properties in the vicinity of Villa Rica. However, they must be put in a better condition for inspection before any trustworthy report can be made. Not one of the various lots examined was sufficiently prospected to throw any definite light on the character or value of the ore-bodied. The works are generally old and well filled with earth or flooded with water.

The Hart Mine extended from the right corner of South Van Wert and 78 Highway to the left corner of South Van Wert Road and 78 Highway. In the 1900's Allen's home and store was on the left in front of this mine. (33°43'56.60"N 84°57'36.14"W) (33°43'50.31"N 84°57'41.20"W)

Another Hart Gold Mine was located 1/2 mile to the northwest of North Van Wert and 78 Highway, where the tower can be seen in this present day– (33°44'08.56"N 84°57'54.43"W).

Land Lot #165 6th District Carroll County
Land Lot #165 6th District Carroll County, Book B, page 444, January 2, 1830. CHARLES McCLAIN to DANIEL McDOWELL. Sum of $350.00. 1/2 of Land Lot# 165 6th district, Carroll County. Attest: John D. Richards, Jas. McDowell, Neil Stone, J.P., May 4, 1865.

Land Lot 165 6th district: Book F, page 46, Georgia, 28 Jan 1831, ANDREW KERR, JOHN KERR, JAMES HOPE and JOHN HOPE and ABEL HARRISON, $2,400.00. Land lot #165, 6th district Carroll County. Attest: David Waugh, Richard Allen J. P. 15 Oct 1847.

Book B, page 311, August 6, 1833. J. E. DENNARD, administrator to JOSIAH HATCHER (deceased), Wilkinson County to LEWIS BAILEAU of Carroll County, $600.00. Land Lot #165, 6th district Carroll. Attest :J. Chambers, Wm. G. Springer, J. I. C. 6 Aug 1833.

Book B, page 442, Carroll County, 1 Apr 1834, LEWIS BAILEAU Carroll County to PHILLIP CANSELLER. $1,000.00. Land lot #165, 6th district Carroll County. 202 1/2 acres. Attest: Nelson Allmun, George Swain.

Hart Town Environs

Book B, page 445, Philadelphia County, Pennsylvania, 1 Aug 1834, LEWIS BAILEAU, Philadelphia to AUSTIN BAILEAU. $1,100.00. Land lot #165, 6th dist, Carroll County. 202 1/2. Attest: William Yonker, Samuel Northrop, John Rupelt, J. P., 4 May 1835.

Book C, page 28, 5 Jul 1836. JOHN DEAN, sheriff to PHILLIP CANSELLER. $84.00. Land lot #165, 6th district Carroll. Sold to satisfy the suit of PHILLIP CANSELLER vs. LEWIS (sic) BAELEAU. Attest I. C. Cobb, William Beall J. I. C.; 30 Aug 1836.

Book C, page 71, August 19, 1836 PHILLIP CANCELLER to JAMES COLTHARP. Sum of $1,000.00 Land lot #165, 6th district Carroll County. 202 1/2 acres. Attest: John A. Jones, John Wright, J.P. January 21, 1831.

Book C, page 370, 11 Sept 1838, Cobb County. JAMES COLTHARP and GREEN McSPADDEN to ANDREW KERR, JOHN KERR, JOHN HOPE and JAMES HOPE (Kerr and Hope of Augusta, Georgia, Richmond County). Sum of $2,853.43. Land lot #165, 6th District Carroll County to secure debt. Also Land Lot #95 in 9th district of Carroll County. Also Land Lot# 245 in 9th district in Carroll County. Attest G. D. Rice and W. H. Tomlinson.

Book D, p. 167, Carroll County, 4 Feb 1840. MATTHEW REID, sheriff to KERR & HOPE (ANDREW KERR, JOHN KERR, JAMES HOPE, JOHN HOPE). $9.00. Land lot #165, 6th district Carroll County. Sold to satisfy a suit in Carroll County. Snoden and Shearer vs. JAMES COLTHARP AND GREEN C. McSPADDEN. Attest: A. H. Harrison, I. E. Cobb, J. I. C.; 10 Apr 1841.

Book F, page 37, Carroll County, 13 Mar 1844. ABEL H. HARRISON to NICHOLAS G. THOMAS. $1,500.00. Mining interest in Land Lot #165, 6th district Carroll County, also a portion of same lot, west of Youngs Ferry Road, south of the Tallapoosa Road, except the smith and joiners shop. Attest: Irvin Jones, Wilson Cartwright J. P. 30 Sep 1847.

Book F, page 290, 8 Mar 1848. ABEL H. HARRISON to M. C. AUTRY. $1,000.00 Land lot 165, 6th district Carroll County. 202 1/2 acres. Reserving 1/2 mining interest S. W. corner containing land owned by Dr. N. G. THOMAS, a blacksmith shop and a joiners, about 15 acres. Attest: R. N. Russell, Sm. C. Candler, J. I. C. 18 Aug 1849.

Book F, page 519, DeKalb County, 16 Dec 1850. CLAYTON WILLIAMS, Dekalb County to SAMUEL C. HART. $80.00. 1/2 South west corner land lot #165, 6th district Carroll County. 15 acres bounded on the east by Moores Ferry Road on the North by Jacksonville Road. Attest: John T. Hart, James Davis, J. P. 26 Apr 1851.

Book F, page 519, Carroll County, 4 Jan 1851. M. C. AWTRY to SAMUEL HART. $1,600.00. Land lot #165, 6th district Carroll County. 202 1/2 acres except 1/2 min-

ing interest and 1/2 of 15 acres in the S. W. corner, premises once owned by Dr. N. G. Thomas. Attest: J. M. Raburn, O. H. Hansen, J. P. 25 Apr 1851.
Land Lot #166 The Askew Mine (33°43'57.36"N 84°57'45.15"W)
   Part of the mines at Hart Town was the Askew Mine located 1/2 mile down Atlanta-Jacksonville Highway (today 78 Highway) on the southwest from the plantation.

Land Lot #166 6th District Carroll County
Book B, page 161, Carroll County, 1 November 1831, JESSE BOON to JAMES DICKSON Georgia. Sum of $1.00 for Land Lot# 166, 6th district. Carroll County 202 1/2 acres. 14 year lease. Attest: James Majors, Thomas C. Miers.

Page 163, Carroll County, 2 Feb 1832 JAMES DICKSON transfers lease rights to the branches to NELSON ALLMAN and BENJAMIN CHAPMAN reserving the right to mining veins on ridges for self. Attest: William Slate, A. G. Fambrough. 1 Mar 1832.

Land Lot #166,Page 158, Book B,Carroll County, February 23, 1832. John Brooks to Benjamin Boon of Morgan County. Sum of $2,186.00 for land lot #166 in the 6th district of Carroll County. Land lot containing 202 1/2 acres. Land lot drawn by Joshua Morgan of Wilkes County. Attest: Philip S. Allbritten, I.E. Cobb, J. C.

Land Lot #166, Page 362, Book B, Carroll County, February 20, 1834. Thomas Rabun to George Swain. Sum of $1,750.00 for land lot #166, in the 6th district of Carroll County. Reserving 1/2 mines and minerals and mining rights. Attest: Thomas Roddy, Phillip Canceller, April 28, 1834.

Land Lot #166, Book D, page 47, Book D, 20 Feb 1840 Paulding County. JAMES MAJORS to JOHN A. JONES. $1,500. Land Lot #s 166 & 167 in the 6th district, Carroll County. Each contains 202 1/2 acres. To sell land to satisfy a promisory note by J. & W. MAJORS to JOHN JONES, guardian of SEABORN JONES. Attest: Crawford Wright, John Y. Allgood, J. I. C. Paulding Co. 28 Feb 1840.

Book F, page 798, Paulding County, 7 Feb 1844. GEORGE SWAIN to THOMAS H. SPARKS. $1,000.00. Land lot #166, 6th district Carroll County. Attest: Warren Akin, J. C. York, J. P. 10 May 1852.

Book E, page 182, Carroll County, November 14, 1844. JOHN DEAN the Sheriff to THOMAS H. SPARKS, Paulding County. $11.00. Land Lot #166, 6th district Carroll County. Seized by virtue of writ of fifa, THOMAS H. SPARKS vs WILLIAM MAJORS, JAMES MAJORS and DAVID HIDEN. The property of DAVID HIDEN. Attest: John Long, George W. Hunt, J. P. 5 Nov 1844.

Book F, page 797, Paulding County, 10 Oct 1851. THOMAS H. SPARKS, Paulding

County to THOMAS W. BURTON. $1,000.00. Land lot #166, 6th district Carroll County. 202 1/2 acres except mining privileges of THOMAS RABUN. Attest: L. N. Weaver, Charles W. Denson J. P. 10 May 1852.

Book G, page 229, Carroll County, 13 Oct 1851. THOMAS W. BURTON to JAMES C. ECHOLS, Telfair County. $800.00. Part of land Lot #166, 6th district, Carroll County, except 39 acres where Pleasant Grove meeting house stands. 1/2 gold reserved to THOMAS RABUN. Attest: Gilbert Cole, Leonard Fulbright, Joseph L. Hart, O. A. Henson, J. P. 5 May 1853.

Lot #166, Page 616, Book E, District 6, Carroll County, Georgia. December 5, 1852. T. W. Burton to H. J. Hogue. Sum of $200.00 for 40 acres. Half of the interest claimed by T. Rabun. Attest: Thomas H. Hurt, James W. Hurt, J. Chambers, J.P. December 29, 1863.

Book G, page 612, Carroll County, 29 Dec 1853, H. J. HOGUE to LEONARD FULLBRIGHT. $30.00. Part of Land lot #166, 6th district Carroll County. Bound on the east by SAMUEL HART and J. F. YATES, on the north by J. F. YATES AND F. LUTHER. On the road from Atlanta to Jacksonville, by way of Villa Rica. Attest: Joseph Wynn, B. Cason, J. Chambers, J. P. 26 Dec 1854.

Book G, page 615, Carroll County, 22 Nov 1854. HENRY J. HOGUE to FREDRICK LUTHER. $300.00. Part of land lot #166, 6th district Carroll County. East of JAMES ECHOLS. Attest: Joseph Wynn, E. Cason, Jonathan Chambers J. P. 2 Jan 1855.

Land Lot #192, 6th District, Carroll County
Book B, Page 21, Campbell County, August 12, 1830. WINIFRED RODGERS to JOHN CARTER, JOHN HANVEY, THOMAS HAMILTON and ALFRED IVERSON of Jones County. Sum of $5,000.00 she was paid for land lot #192, in the 6th district of Carroll County. Land lot containing 202 ½ acres, with all mineral rights. Witness: John P. Speer, Martin, D. Rodgers, J. I. C., April 27, 1831.

Book D, page 79, May 18, 1832. ALFRED IVERSON, JOHN HARVEY, JOHN CARTER and THOMAS HAMILTON appoints Elijah Bryant, attorney to sell land lot #192. 202 ½ acres. Signature includes name of Peter Clower. Attest: Harvey Kindricks, Isaac Kindrick, J.P. Robert Dickerson, J.P. May 22, 1840.

Book D, Page 70, Carroll County, August 1, 1839. ELIJAH BRYANT, Agent for ALFRED IVERSON, JOHN HARVEY, JOHN CARTER, PETER CLOWERS to JONATHAN SANDERS. Sum of $500.00 for land lot #192, in the 6th district of Carroll County containing 202 ½ acres. Attest: S. C. Candler, E. S. Candler, R. V. C. Ruffin, J.P., May 2, 1840.

Book D, Page 71, Carroll County, October 1, 1839. MATTHEW REID the Sheriff to E. L. BRYANT. Sum of $505.00 for land lot #192 in the 6th district of Carroll County containing 202 ½ acres. Sold to satisfy a suit. E. L. Bryant vs. Jonathan Sanders. Attest: John Mehaffey, William G. Springer, J. I. C., May 20, 1840.

Book F, page 208, Carroll County, December 25, 1848. THOMAS H. ROBERTS to JOHN B. WICK. Sum of $25.00 for town lot #58, in the Villa Rica as laid out by Roberds of land lot #192, in the 6th district of Carroll County. Attest: John Coal, Saml. C. Candler, J. I. C. February 9, 1849.

Book G, page 442, Carroll County, 13 Jan 1854. THOMAS H. ROBERTS to MICHAEL GOODSON. $600.00. Part of east half land lot #192, 6th district Carroll County, except that sold to LARKIN H. DAVIS and JOHN B. WICK. 75 acres. Attest: William Rogers, Thomas Stokeley J. I. C. 10 Apr 1854.

Land Lot #193 William A. Hicks (Hix) of Hixtown
Land Lot #193, 6th District, Carroll County
Book B, page 289, Muscogee County, 5 Dec 1832. ALFRED IVERSON to DAVID CLOPTON, Carroll County $1,000.00. 1/8 interest in land lot #193, 6th district Carroll County. Attest: Lewis O. Allen, Ellwin E. Bessell, J. I. C., 20 Apr 1833.

Book C, page 255, Carroll County, 1 Jan 1833. JILES BOGGESS to JOHN A. JONES. $10.00. Interest of William Hicks, Land lot #193, 6th district Carroll. Sold to satisfy a suit in the Inferior Court of Coweta County, John A. Campbell vs WILLIAM HICKS. Attest: Thomas McGuire, Hiram Wright J. P., 18 Jan 1833.

Lot #193, Page 524, Book F, Carroll County, May 14, 1834. Joseph Chambers, Jesse H. Chambers and Clayton Williams, Benjamin Chapman, Robert Watson and Edmund W. Holland to David Clopton and Edward A. Broaddus. Land lot #193, in the 6th district of Carroll County known as **Gold Mine.** Parties agree to lay off 17 1/2 acres for a town in the Southeast Corner. The remaining be divided which was 83 1/3 to Clopton and Broaddus. Attest: Allen Talbot, Denizen B. Palmer, Charles Hulsey, J.P., April 29, 1851.

Book E page 147, Carroll County, 25 May 1842. EDMUND W. HOLLAND, agent for DAVID CLOPTON, EDWARD A. BROADDUS, EDMUND W. HOLLAND, BENJAMIN CHAPMAN, JOSEPH CHAMBERS, JESSE H. CHAMBERS, CLAYTON WILLIAMS to CHARLES B. HENTON, EZEKIEL S. CHANDLER, LEONARD C. HUFF, DENISON B. PALMER AND WILLIAM A. R. PATRICK trustees and their successors METHODIST EPISCOPAL CHURCH VILLA RICA. $1.00. 11/12 town lot in Villa Rica, land lot #193, 6th district Carroll County, Town lot #3. 70 feet in front, 250 feet back, 50 feet wide south end, 1/3 acres. To be used to erect Methodist Episcopal Church denominations, also to be used as a school house. Ed-

Hart Town Environs

mund W. Holland, agent for Villa Rica Town Co. Attest: John B. Wick, John Hilderbrand, J. P. 3 Sept 1844. (33°44'53.81"N 84°54'40.98"W)

Book G, page 463, Carroll County, 17 May 1854. LARKIN H. DAVIS to CHARLES V. CHAMBERLAIN and EDWARD W. BANCROFT, merchants of Charleston, South Carolina Promissory notes $2,139.86. Land lot #193, 6th district Carroll County. Ten acres bounded by the town of Villa Rica and JOHN B. WICK. Attest: Alexander Isaacs, Thomas Stokeley, J. I. C. 18 May 1854.

Land Lot #194 The Clopton Property

During the writer's examination of the locality, (in 1896) only one property, in the vicinity of Villa Rica, was being prospected. This is known as the Clopton property, located on lot 194, 6th district. The property was, then in the hands of a Boston company, who had recently made a number of open cuts, shafts and tunnels, along the outcropping of the vein; and had just completed the erection of a mill of recent patent, which was at that time, being perfected and put in running order. As the President of the Company had instructed the Manager of the works, not to give any information, whatever, concerning the value of the ore, or the process of extracting the gold, nothing was learned about the property, which would be of interest to the public. (33°45'.00.77"N 84°55'50.91"W)

Land Lot #194, 6th District, Carroll County

Lot #194, Page 408, Book A, February 21, 1828. William M. Bennett appoints Thomas C. Brown of Muscogee County lawful attorney in fact to sell land lot. Drawn by WILLIAM BENNETT. Attest: L. A. Jernigan, C. J. Jenkins Jr.

Land Lot #194, Page 409, Book A, June 8, 1830. WILLIAM M. BENNETT by attorney in fact THOMAS C. BROWN to JOSEPH D. McFARLAND. Sum of $500.00. Attest: John Rogers, William Darden, J.I.C. September 18, 1830.

Land Lot #194, Page 409, Book A, July 20, 1830. JOSEPH D. McFARLAND to ELI S. SHORTER of Putnam County. Sum of $4,000.00. Attest: John Rogers, William Darden, J.I.C., September 18, 1830.

Book A, page 410, Greene County, 13 Sep 1830. ELI S. SHORTER to ALFORD CLOPTON, JOHN WARRAN, JOHN E. MORGAN, WILEY W. MASON, JOHN J. BOSWELL, BENJAMIN FORT and JAMES M. DUNN and LYMAN BURNAPP, merchants. $1,000.00. Land lot #194, 6th district 202 1/2 acres. 1 & 1/2 tenths Alford Clopton, 1/10 John Morgan, 1/10 John Warran, 1/10 Dunn and Burnapp, 1/10. Attest: L. Q. C. Lamar, Adam G. Saffold J. I C. O. C., 18 Sept 1830.

Land Lot #195 Chambers Mine

Land Lot 235, 2nd District was sold to buy Land Lot #195—The Chambers Mine. The Carroll County deed book page 225 shows that James Dickson sold to Allmon—Chambers & Company February 7, 1832, for $700, Land Lot #235 2nd District of Carroll County (now Douglas). A Carroll land lot contained 202 1/2 acres of land. This land was traversed by Mud Creek and Regan Road and near the intersection with High Point Road in present day. After 1870, Douglas County Records show that land was selling in 1832 for about 1 to 2 dollars an acre: twice the price that Allmon—Chambers & Company paid for the land. They fully expected to find gold on the land. It is unclear if they knew how gold was retrieved in Carroll County. It is imbedded in rock and has required a tremendous amount of work and expense to extract, so much so that several years later most all gold mining in Carroll had ceased.

Land Lot #195, District 6: On November 1, 1832, Joseph Chambers and his son Jesse H. Chambers bought Lot #195, 6th District of Carroll, except 60 feet which was sold to William Dixon, John Sheppard and Allen Tolbert. This lot (202 /2 acres) was about 1 mile NW of present day Villa Rica and where the widow of James Dickson lived. They paid $3,000 to Jesse Lane, Oliver Clarke, Reuben Cone and William Ezzard of DeKalb County, Georgia for the land.

To pay for the land and equipment to mine the gold, Joseph and Jesse, his son, mortgaged Land Lot #235, 2nd District and obtained a promissory note for $3,500, filed with the court on January 21, 1832, Chambers to Lane et al. Attested by: George S. Moody, Denison B. Palmer, Charles Hulsey, JP. The gold mine was purchased and work was ready to begin. This Chambers' mine on Land Lot 195, 6th District, was west of Old Villa Rica by one mile. The present-day Villa Rica Community building at Gold Dust Park may have been built near the old Chambers Mine.

In an article written circa 1908 describing the Gold mines in Carroll County by an unknown mineralologist:

Chambers Mine: This mine, on land lot #195, 6th district adjoins the Jones' tract and was about one mile northwest of Villa Rica. Considerable mining has been prospected on the auriferous quartz vein at this locality and surface washing covering an area of a number of acres has been done. An open cut was made before the Civil War on the vein referred to and was enlarged in the course of more recent mining operations. Some shafts were also sunk on the vein. The cut is about one-hundred-fifty yards long. At one point where a small portion of the ground was left standing for passageway of limited exposure of the vein is to be seen. At this point it shows a thickness of about four feet. No work has been done on the vein for a number of years and it could not be ascertained what gold was obtained when mining operations were being carried on. . . .

These operations consisted in surface washing near the northwest side of the vein. The material was carried in a flume across the open cut and washed by machinery situated on the southeast side. Work had been suspended before the property was visited and it was not learned what success attended this mining. Near the southwest end of the cut surface washing was done years ago over an area of a number of acres.

Hart Town Environs

According to those who have worked at the locality, a number of small comparatively rich pockets have been found in the vicinity of the main vein. The gold in these is said to have been in very thin quartz veins, or quartzose layers in the decomposed rock.

A letter dated July 22, 1872, Villa Rica, Georgia from R. J. Gaines to Major Richardson:

I will commense with what is known in this county as the "Chambers Lead" some 5 miles in length, with outcroppings at various points. Copper has been cut on the Hill property at a depth of 95 feet disclosing a vein of yellow suphurete of copper some 8 feet in width. Adjoining this mine is the Chambers property, upon which has been sunk a shaft of about 100 feet with a similar result to that of the Hill shaft . . .

Carroll County Times, June 2, 1873:

Sale Day . . . At the Sheriff's sale at 11:00 o'clock the property of John T. Chambers was sold to B. M. Long for $230.

Carroll County Times, August 31, 1877:

Mr. John T. Chambers has discovered a very rich asbestos mine on his plantation one mile from Villa Rica on the road leading to Carrollton. We wish the old Captain success and that he will reap a rich harvest.

Approximately 20 acres was stripped of residum, exposing the underlying granitic and hornblende gneisses; much of this area is still bare, supporting only sparse vegetation.

Land Lot #195, 6th District, Carroll County
Book B, page 227, Carroll County, 1 Nov 1832. JESSE LAND, OLIVER CLARKE, REUBEN CONE and WILLIAM EZZARD, Dekalb County to JOSEPH CHAMBERS & JESSE H. CHAMBERS. $3000.00. Land lot #195, 6th district Carroll except 60 feet sold to William Dixon, John Shepard and Allen Tolbert. Attest: B. W. Hargrove, Charles Hulsey J. P., 25 Nov 1832.

Land Lot #195, Book B, page 227, Georgia, November 20, 1832. Henry P. Jones, by his agent Willis J. Brazel of Burke County to Reuben Cone, Jesse Lane, William Ezzard and O. Clark of Dekalb County. Sum of $600.00 for 1/2 of land lot #195, in the 6th district of Carroll County. Attest: Augustus R. Jones, John A. Jones.

Book B, Page 257, Carroll County, November 21, 1832. Joseph Chambers, Jesse Chambers to Jesse Lane, Reuben Cone, Oliver Clark and William Ezzard of Dekalb County. Sum of $5.00 for a part of land lot #195, in the 6th district, located in Carroll County. Land lot #235, in the 2nd district. Carroll (now Douglas) county, where the widow of James Dickson lives. . . . To secure promissory note, Sum of $3,500.00, Chambers to land, et al. Attest: George S. Moody, Denison B. Palmer, Charles Hulsey, J.P., January 21, 1833. (33°44'47.26"N 84°56'26.57"W)

Pine Mountain Mine

The Pine Mountain Mine was located on Land Lot #206, Stockmar Road at today's Stockmar Park.

The visibility of washing the saprolite material on the slopes of the mountain on a large scale has been considered. Water could be obtained by pumping from a creek about three-fourths of a mile distant. Gold is probably widely distributed over a considerable area at this locality, but if hydraulic mining on an extensive scale was undertaken a large amount of material carrying little or no values would probably have to be moved. From a few panning tests made from the saprolites a small amount of rather fine gold was obtained. Opportunity was not afforded, however, to make any extensive tests. (33°45'10.89"N 84°53'07.87"W)

Lassetter Mine

The Lassetter Mine was located on Land Lot #189 near Highway 101 and the Industrial Road.

Workings consist of a vertical shaft, 10 feet X 4 feet, now filled to within 12 feet of the surface, and a pit 10 feet in diameter, 6 feet deep; these are about 200 feet apart, aligned in a N. 70 degree E. direction.

A quartz vein exposed in the shaft is greater than 10 feet thick, colorless to milky, with a coarsely granular appearance due to fracturing. The vein is intensely shattered across its entire width. The quartz contains minor muscovite and feldspar; no sulfides were noted. The country rock is muscovite-biotite granite or granitic gneiss.

Approximately 0.25 mile to the ENE, on the same property, some residuum-alluvium has been worked. To the SW about 0.6 mile an old shaft has been filled and cultivated over. (33°44'28.89"N. 84°57'15.27"W)

Climatic Anomalies the Winter of 1827-1828

The land lottery for Georgia began in 1827. Some of those who drew land lots of 202 1/2 acres never lived on this acreage; they were sold for profit. The majority of drawers came as settlers to their new land. Many came because of the gold discovered there. Some families came to Carroll County to farm the land, raise their children and start a new life. The farmers cut trees to build log cabins and cleared and plowed the fields for early gardens and "put in a crop." They brought supplies and provisions with them, but these ran out. They depended on both a summer garden and a winter garden. Imagine the work that went into establishing a home and enough provisions to feed a family.

Then came an unprecedented change in the weather. The winter of 1827 was unseasonably warm which was to their advantage in growing vegetables. January of 1828 brought severe flooding and the spring brought a freeze never before seen in the south. This change in the weather, brought unbelievable hardship on these early pioneers when it came to having enough food to survive through 1828.

Data collected from newspaper articles, diaries, fur trapper accounts, and tree rings indicate that the United States and particularly the eastern United States experienced strong temperature anomalies among the most extreme known in historical records. The results of collected evidence reveals climatic impacts in the Southeast U. S., including widespread blossoming of fruit trees in mid-winter called false spring. From locations in Charleston, Nashville and Fort Jessup in mid December, afternoons temperatures ranged from 75-79 degrees.

From the *Pensacola Gazette* and *West Florida Advertiser*, January 11, 1828:

The Weather. If we may judge from the weather and the appearances of vegetation this is not Winter. Roses have been in full bloom here during the whole month of December—the trees are all budding and the weather is uncomfortably warm for winter clothing. Within the last ten days, the thermometer has been as high as 79. There has been no appearance of cold. On the 1st of January, a large watermelon which had grown in an open field without any protection from the weather was eaten in this City!

By mid-January, it was precipitation that played a prominent role on winter vegetation growth. There was so much rain that severe flooding in the Mississippi River Valley and heavy snowfall in northwestern North America occurred. "It has been raining, with but few days intermission since the 1st of December. *The Wheeling Gazette* conjectures that five feet of rain has fallen at that place within three months, and we believe the quantity has been quite as excessive over the general average, here. All have made up their minds not to expect fruit this year."

Fayetteville, Tennessee, February 22, 1828, *The Village Messenger* reported that "For the last two months it has rained almost every day. The water courses in this part of the country have been swollen, and the bottom lands inundated to an extent, and for a longer time, that we ever before witnessed."

Because plantations were a commercial enterprise, careful daily record-keeping was essential, providing detailed direct daily weather information for some geographic areas. Historical Societies and State Universities recorded this extreme weather. Newspapers provided verbal weather descriptions of these extreme daily weather events with useful information on rising and falling levels of rivers.

After the high temperatures in winter, called false spring, followed by severe rainfall, came a spring of unprecedented frost, ice and severe low temperatures. The last event in this series of extreme weather events became known as the "great killing freeze of April 1828."

The following description at Huntsville, Alabama, recounts a typical example of the killing frost that occurred in early April 1828: "On the nights of the 5th and 6th, instant, we had a freeze and frost here that has destroyed our gardens; and what is uncommon, the peas in the garden are entirely killed. Our corn that has been planted the 1st of March, and of some growing size, was killed into the ground; the wheat was in a common way, about eighteen inches high, it is killed to the root; I had one hundred and sixty acres sowed. All the fruit entirely killed that had bloomed. I discover a part of my apples not bloomed, and some few of the plum kind, such as the damson and other late plums and cherries. The ground was frozen three or four inches deep, and we had ice an inch thick. Such cold weather was never felt in Alabama in April."

An individual in Charleston, March 5, reported four days of ice. "Thermometer said to be 2 degrees below freezing—Ice said to be in the City, and was in fact at my house."

The major false spring event of the winter of 1827-1828 was largely distinguished by late and very prominent killing frosts over the Southeast U. S. in early April 1828, likely one of the most severe in the last several hundred years with no event approaching its magnitude since that time."

4

Intruders, Pony Boys and Slicks

...he was "frightened" of the 400 families of intruders who had settled in Carroll County (recently ceded by the Creek Indians).

Intruders came before the Land Lottery of 1827

Fayette County, Fort Troup.
July 11th 1825
To His Excellency,
 Sir,
 I have received information, (which I conceive my duty to communicate to you) that the Citizens of—[sic] are intruding and trespassing on the Indians, by taking and conveying off the corn and other property of General William McIntosh, together with other Friendly Indians. From a letter, I this day received from Colonel Wagnow of DeKalb County, and from the information of other persons of respectability, I am informed that the Whites citizens of this State are committing depredations, and in fact stealing and taking off the property of the Indians on the head of Talapousa [sic]. From my situation I have thought it the most advisable to communicate the above facts to your Excellency and elicit your opinion as to the most advisable plan for me to pursue against these intruders, as in my opinion I do deem it necessary that something ought to be done to put a stop to these plundering whites divested of every principle of right and Justice. I have sent on this by a friend of mine Mr. Jones, who was going to Milledgeville, and who will hand you this, and permit me to solicit your Excellency, to send me an answer by the bearer.
 With Sentiments of Esteem your Excellency,
 Obedient Servant,
 Alexander Ware

Like any good idea, vigilantism had its time and place. It outlived its usefulness or was corrupted in a hurry. Several have stated that the Pony Club itself started out as a movement of Slicks. Even Joel Leathers of the Carroll County Pony Club complained about all the vagrants and miscreants filling up the lands newly taken from the Creek Indians. One of Joel Leathers' first acts when he moved to Carroll County (1827) was to write Col. Montgomery of Indian Affairs in Georgia about intruders on Indian lands:

In the letter dated 1829, he wrote that he was "frightened" of 400 families of intruders who had settled in Carroll County. Leathers warned that these intruders were a lawless and unruly bunch of land grabbers.

Changes were in store for the Pony Club and the Indians in 1831 and 1832. Governor Gilmer's idea of seizing the mines for the state of Georgia lost to that of Wilson Lumpkin, who wanted another land lottery to distribute lots to deserving Georgians. The new Governor was a well-known friend of Senator Allen Fambrough and they were working on a solution to the Cherokee question. The Senator suggested that lands abandoned by Indians voluntarily leaving for the West should be rented to whites. Lumpkin picked up this idea and soon the Indian Country was teeming with renters. This ended the question of white intruders on Indian land; it could not be stopped. Special Agent for Cherokee Immigration, Benjamin Curry, had the task of enrolling Cherokee who chose to leave Georgia early; agents like William Hardin and William Cleghorn would sign up whites and collect rents.

Pony Club is Formed

New mining towns sprang up in Carroll and other counties in Georgia. Pine Mountain was a community of several hundred and Gainsville, in newly formed Hall County, became a gold producing town. Clarksville in Habersham County and two towns in what would be Lumpkin County were formed. Dahlonega, in Lumpkin County, became the county seat, named from the Cherokee-language word Dalonige, meaning "yellow" or "gold."

As soon as Carroll County was formed, the Pony Club moved in. With their border gone, they could either operate as bandits against the Creek if they moved west, or they could operate against the Cherokee from Carroll County. Eventually they would operate from several locations near Indian Country.

The Indians particularly suffered from the predations of the Carroll County Pony Club (Neenoskuskee in Cherokee), (especially Clean Town, Sand Town, Leathers' Ford, and Buzzard's Point or Buzzard's Roost).

Captain Slick

Shortly after the Red Stick War of 1813-1814, and the cession of the middle portion of Alabama Territory to the United States, white intruders began pouring into these new lands by the thousands. Until counties were set up with governments and land was sold legally, it was every man for himself. On several occasions, Return [sic] Meigs, the Indian Agent, was forced to send U. S. troops into Alabama to burn the squatters towns and destroy their crops to make them leave. It was, indeed, against the law to squat on federal land, but intruders were banking on the "law of preeminence" to assure them land no one wanted at a fraction of the cost. Amid all this anarchy, depredations on settlers and Indians were rife. As settlers had done in North Carolina and in South Carolina, they formed groups of regulators to punish the worst offenders in the territory. In every state, the regulators were different and Alabama was unique in producing the legend of Captain Slick.

Captain Slick probably never existed. He was a term used to describe what would happen to horse thieves and claim jumpers. They would be "slicked" or "sleeked;" that is, whipped and run out of the territory.

A man of that name lived a few miles across the Georgia line, who was ever ready to "slick" the pony club members. The term caught on and was also used in Georgia, Mississippi and even Missouri. In the final fight with the Pony Club in Carroll, Paulding and Polk Counties, the Slicks would emerge triumphant, having pushed the club out of contention for local power.

Slick punishment for stealing horses was usually thirty-nine or more lashes with hickory branches. Rather than hang horse thieves, it was common to give lashes for a simple reason: everyone had done it or was doing it. It also reflected Indian thinking of the jurisprudence assigned to borrowing livestock, a severe whipping. The Indians, who ushered in the idea of stealing wandering horses from one area and selling them in another, originated the laws of whipping horse thieves. Until their removal, and when laws were strengthened, the practice never stopped.

They formed Captain Slick's company and advertised for all honest men to meet at a certain schoolhouse in the neighborhood on a certain day. They met and bound themselves in certain matters, made rules and laws for the government of the company, and made strong friends who would quickly inform each other of their movements.

The Pony Club's success can be tied directly to its position of power in Carroll and later Paulding and Polk Counties. Beginning in 1827, members of this gang served on the Grand Jury. Not everyone on the jury was a member of the club, but there were enough to assure that members would not be indicted. They continued to appear on the Grand Jury and Petit Juries until 1832 when the "slicks" defeated them at the polls.

From Ray Henderson's *History of the Pony Boys* are the following excerpts:

From the *Georgia Journal*, Sept 29, 1828, page 3:

> Pony Club: In Carroll County, Georgia, we are informed by a gentleman who has recently passed thro' that place, of indubitable credibility, that there is a club, who makes profession of stealing horses as well from their own citizens as from strangers. There plans, from their contiguity

and intercourse with the Cherokee have been so judiciously executed as to elude detection. They do not, we understand, profess to take the life of a traveler, but only his horse, in order, it may be presumed that in cases of conviction their punctilious clemency may establish a contested principal in penal law, that there is a distance and tangible difference in value between property and life. This policy reminds of the reply of Judge Barnes, to the horse stealer, upon being asked what he had to say, why judgement of death should not be passed upon him and answering "that it was Hard to hang a man for only Stealing a horse," was told by the judge, 'man thou art not only to be hanged for stealing a horse, but that horses may not be stolen.' That punishment should be proportioned to offenses is just and politic we admit, but there is a lamentable deficiency in the justice and morality of this new county overlooking the alieni appetens which is so manifestly a nuisance to their neighbors and strangers is equally notorious."

Huntsville Advocate.

The Cherokee Phoenix added a little note to the same story which ran on September 24, 1828 (Vol. 1, No. 30, page 2):

We have frequently heard of this pony club. It is said by a traveller who passed this place some time since directly from Carroll, that this stealing association has become so dexterious (sic) in its profession, that if the devil had been in the shape of a pony, he would ere this have fallen a prey to its agility. "Pony Club" is but a limited name and will by no means give a correct idea of this neighboring combination—"cow club," "hog club," & c. may properly be added.

On one occasion where the Pony Club ventured into the Terrapin Creek area, the citizens fought back. Club Members Calloway Burke and James Upton (Philpot in-law) had just stolen cattle from John Goodlin and several Creek Indians. They were pursued by the Alabamians into Carroll County, Georgia where they stopped at the Home of a Mr. Almon, where the cattle were retrieved in his cane brake and driven back to Alabama by the Indians.

Letter to editor, *Carroll Times*, June 8, 1882.

Through fear of the Pony Club, Almon would not let them stay all night but loaned them a gun, and they started for Hixtown, now Villa Rica. . . . They met Burke and others, all armed. Goodlin's party was on the alert and each party soon detected the character of the other. Burke leveled his gun and Goodlin shot him dead.

This incident represents one of the few deaths of a Pony Club member in all the years they operated in the South. Calloway Burke was once employed by Carroll County to build the new jail in the new courthouse:" ...in May, 1830, the justices employed Calloway Burke to remove 'the gaol from the old court house' to the new county site. (County records 1830.)

In *Georgia's last Frontier*, the author described the life and downfall of the Pony Club in Carroll County:

> ... The principal rendezvous for this gang was on Hominy Creek (below Hickory Level on lot 22) near where it flows into the Little Tallapoosa, on a farm later owned by John D. Morgan. This was an area of swamps and dense thickets. Barnes Williams once reported seeing 'twenty-five or thirty' of these renegades sitting on a fence in the sunshine. Upon discovering the visitor 'they dropped like turtles off a log' and retreated to their lairs in the swamp.

Violence in Carrollton: The Pony Club

In the early 1830s a reckless gang of horse thieves and outlaws terrorized the county—as well as parts of Alabama and South Carolina—using their location on the wide-ranging Indian frontier to escape punishment. The gang operated from an area of swamps and thickets near where Hominy Creek flows into the Little Tallapoosa, below the community of Hickory Level.

Because well-placed gang members served on the Grand Jury and made the gang difficult to indict, local citizens who called themselves the "Slicks" banded together into two groups of vigilantes headed by Sloman Wynn and George S. Sharp. They caught and horsewhipped many of these thieves and ordered them to leave the country. In retaliation, the Pony Club in full force started a pitched-battle against the Slicks on the Carrollton square on election day, 1832. Although no guns and knives were used, the men on both sides fought desperately with fists, rocks and sticks. The law-abiding citizens, led by tavern owner Jiles Boggess, who was then sheriff, won the day. When the grand jury next met, some members of the defeated Pony Club charged Boggess and his Slicks with assault with intent to murder, but the jury praised them for ousting crime from the county.

George S. Sharp—Sharp was a "Slick"

George Spencer Sharp was born in Morgan County on August 29, 1818 and died April 17, 1903 in Carroll County. He was buried at the Sharp Family Cemetery off Highway 113 close to Center Point, two miles north of Carrollton. George's father was Hiram Jackson Sharp, who was born 24 April 1789 in Maryland and died in December 11, 1875 in Carroll County. George's mother was Sarah Ann Owens born in 1786 in Maryland and died on 12 March 1870 in Carroll County, Georgia.

George was mentioned in *Georgia's Last Frontier* as living in the north part of

Carroll County near the Indian Boundary where his family settled in 1828. Hiram was shown on the 1830 Georgia Federal Census with his family living among the early settlers near the Indian Trail, Alley's Trace. George payed taxes in 1844 and 1847 for District 6, Land Lot #15. His father, Hiram Sharp, Jr. paid taxes in 1844 and 1847 for District 6, Land Lot #16. Each had 202 & 1/2 acres. In 1840, 1850 and 1860, 1870 and 1880 George Sharp was a resident of Carroll County.

Hiram Jackson Sharp, Sr. fought in the War of 1812 as a Private in the 2nd Regiment, Thomas' Georgia Militia, Captain William Walker's Company. His son, George S. Sharp fought the Seminole Indian War in Florida in 1836 and returned after one fall.

George married Nancy R. Haynes on 29 July 1840 in Carroll County, Georgia. She was born 16 November 1823. She and George had children: William Franklin Sharp born 1843, died 1863; Phebe Jane born 1845; Victoria born 1849; and Martha A. Sharp (Muse) born 10 July 1853, died 1892.

Nancy R. Haynes Sharp died in 1857. On 16 December 1858, George married his second wife, Nancy Rebecca Hamrick who was born 20 October 1833 and died 8 March 1884. Their children were: Mary Ellen Sharp born 1862, died 1942; Hiram Thomas, known as "Fiddlin Tom" born 16 July 1863, died 7 September 1910; Nancy Rebecca Sharp McCalman born 1866, died 1929; and John Wilkes Booth Sharp born 1871, died 5 June 1885.

George fought in the Civil War for the Confederate States Army, 3rd Regiment Georgia State Troops, later changed to 7th Georgia Infantry Regiment, State Guard where he served as Captain.

Nancy R. Hamrick Sharp, George's 2nd wife died in 1884 in Carroll County. George married a third wife, Mollie E. Adams (1844-1908) in Haralson County on 6 March 1890. They lived in Harralson County before his death on 17 April 1903.

In 1890 George S. Sharp wrote several articles for the Carroll Free Press published in Carrollton, Georgia titled *Old Times in Carroll*. The following three articles published October 4, October 18, and November 1, 1895, bring alive the times in these early pioneer days:

Carroll Free Press—October 4, 1895

> About 1830 Aaron Jones bought the lot land that Reuben Reed and Joe McKenzie live on for two bed quilts from the Drawers. Other lands in proportion.
>
> In 1831-32 Majors & Coltharp sold goods near the banks of the little Tallapoosa river, one-half mile from Hart Town. Their goods were delivered on wagons from Augusta. All heavy goods cost high. We had to pay $5.00 upwards for a 200 pound sack of salt, Iron, steal and pot metal high. There were no stoves or parlor matches or gun caps. All plows, harness and swingle-free [sic] irons and horse shoes and wagon irons, gun barrels were forged out by country blacksmiths. Rifle guns finished up cost about $22.00, weight 12 to 14 pounds, flint and steel.

Hart Town Environs

The first patent axes I ever saw was about 1853, all before was made at home. I paid $5.00 for one of them. The first cotton gen [sic] and wheat thresh was put up about 1833 in this county. Picked seed from the cotton with our fingers to make our clothing up to that time.

In 1836 I volunteered to fight the Seminole Indians in Florida. Got back the same fall. Messrs Majors & Coltharp had moved to Hart Town. I bought a coat from them, paid $38.00 for it the first I ever wore, except those that were carded and spun on a wheel and wove on a Georgia loom. It was a clawhammer tail, brass buttons also a sham to cover my breast and bosom, tied around the waist and collar with ??ings, neck stock with big buckle. Just came from the war I would pull on those goods to meet my best girl in. You may imagine how large I felt pulled down 1?6, 18 years old. I'll desist from trying to give the style of my pants.

I want next to speak of some of our representatives in old times.

George S. Sharp.

Carroll Free Press—October 18, 1895

In 1832, Pap seeded ten acres in wheat with three-fourths of a bushel per acre in September. It seemed like the deer and turkey would eat it up as they were very numerous. I killed as many as we wanted. The next summer we saved one hundred and sixty bushels off said ten acres. Those days there were no fertilizers. Wolves, catamounts, foxes, pole cats, turkey and a few bear abounded those days. Pap killed a panther near the spring of water I am using from now, that had just killed a big hog of ours and had about finished his breakfast off it. I took a ten foot rail and measured him. He was just as long as the rail from tip to tip.

Violence in Carrollton
The Pony Club & Slicks on election day 1832

We were near the line dividing the Creek and Cherokee (i)ndians. They would call to see us occasionally. They were friendly and generally wanted to trade. They would not come any path or trail, if there was a dozen to the house. First seen of them would be peeping through cracks back of the house.

I will give a little of my experiences sowing wheat. Twice I have sewn in the same field, one half full moon in September, the other 1st of November. Each time the September sewing made fine wheat and the November wheat did not make. Just so with low land corn. If you want a sure stand plant soon as any. It is the surest plan to escape the bud worms. The corn will pass the stage before their time is to work.

When we first settled where I now live in 1828 the sand hill cranes and wild geese passed twice a year in the spring going north and in the fall going south. They were numerous at times flopping and hollering. Stock unacquainted with them would frighten as much as you ever saw them at a train. They kept diminishing every year until now you scarcely ever see one or hear them holler. There were several years that I never saw an old fashioned blue bird, or red bird. I was four or five years old before I ever saw a blackberry briar growing in Carroll. There were wood chucks and whipoorwills equal to Car?ters [sic] eats.

George S. Sharp
Find-A-Grave

Large dewberries grew promiscuously over the woods.

Carroll Free Press—November 1, 1895

MR. EDITOR—By your permission I come again. In the first settling of this county chestnut timber was plentiful in the fall until Christmas. I could soon fill my hat picking chestnuts from the ground. As soon as the leaves would fall and dry the Indians would fire the woods and burn the leaves to gather chestnuts, causing smoky weather for a while, which caused the name of Indian summer. There is but a small resemblance of the days now and the days then. Game would get fat on chinquapins. In 1840, when the forest and shrubbery grew up, settlers kept numbers of acres from burning, thinking it would be an advantage to the land. I have experienced this. Land wears out about as fast in the woods as in cultivation. In 1840 I cultivated five acres of new ground, and the poorest on the lot made five barrels of corn per acre. Now the best spots allowed to grow up in shrubbery, can't make half that amount. I am cultivating land now that has been in cultivation ever since 1830. Except where it has been allowed to wash off I can make five barrels per acre, and can't make as much on any I clear now.

In those old days I was about grown before I ever saw a pair of shoes that was put together with pegs or brads. They were all sewed together out of our own home-made leather: buck and coon hide for our upper leather.

Mr. Editor, those were the best of my days. We were allowed to wear shoes or go barefooted; school our children in such books as old Webster's, and procure them from whom we pleased, as cheap as possible, and our pa(s)pers [sic] were as well cared for as they are now, and taxes was not more than one-fifth what they are now. Where are we now. We miss our predecessors track, and I fear we are hasting back to thrones and kings on high.

I learned some time ago that there was a wire up from Atlanta to Buzzard Bay for Cleaveland to touch to set the Exposition to rolling. I expected from the goldbugs' literature over the country that it was a trick, and that the shock would not leave a piece of skin upon a silverite's heel this side of the sea. I will now close with my respects to the editor and our appreciation for his Atlanta letter.

George S. Sharp

Fiddlin' Tom Sharp
Courtesy Cathy Gibson and Don Sharp

5

Early Settlers of Hart Town & Pleasant Grove

From his service at the graveside, they could hear cannon fire coming from the battles west of Atlanta.

Hart Town

Early residents of Hart Town were James Coltharp, Will Driscoll, Samuel Hart, William Hart, Billy Hixon, J. G. W. Lassetter, John Long, James and William Majors, Alexander Green, and James, Joel and William Yates.

Majors and Coltharp Store

According to *Georgia's Last Frontier:*
In 1831, the firm of Majors & Coltharp sold goods at a little store on the headwaters of the Little Tallapoosa near Hart Town.
Majors & Coltharp Trading Station was on the headwaters of Little Tallapoosa River before 1832. After 1832, it had been moved 1/2 mile east to what was later known as Hart Town.

James Coltharp

James W. Coltharp (b. August 9, 1809, Jefferson County, Tennessee now Hamblen County, d. December 24, 1873, Edom, Van Zandt County, Texas), the son of John Coltharp, III (b. April 28, 1781, Virginia, d. May 28, 1867, Madisonville, Monroe County, Tennessee). James' mother was Susannah Horner (b. November 1, 1786, Washington, Tennessee, d. June 11, 1855, Monroeville, Monroe County, Tennessee).

James married Joanna Adeline McSpadden on March 11, 1828 in Monroe, Tennessee. Joanna McSpadden Coltharp (b. August 16, 1810, Kentucky, d. August 12, 1891, Henderson, Texas).

James and Joanna Coltharp had nine children, two born in Tennessee, five born in Georgia and two in Texas.

James and Joanna Coltharp

Abel & Marietta Colthrap

1) William Henry Coltharp (b. January 28, 1829, Tennessee, d. December 3, 1905, Tarrant County, Texas). William married Catherine Brown. His second wife was Ella B. Granberry; his third wife was Henrietta Kirkland. William served in the Civil War as 1st Lieutenant Company C. Griffin's Infantry Battalion in Texas.

2) Charlotte Elizabeth Coltharp (b. October 21, 1830, Tennessee, d. April 24, 1897, Edom, Van Zandt, Texas). While living in Carroll County, Charlotte married Augustus Chandler Beall.

3) Sarah Catherine "Kitty" Coltharp (b. April 24, 1833, Wilkes County Georgia, d. June 30, 1907).

4) Sophronia Adaline Coltharp (b. June 8, 1837, Georgia, d. September 14, 1869, Texas). While living in Carroll County, Sophronia married William M. Green.

5) Beety [sic] (b. 1840, Georgia).

6) Abel Bruce Coltharp (b. November 1, 1840, Carroll County, d. December 14, 1909, Henderson, Texas). Abel married Marietta E. Chandler.

7) Melissa Isabella (b. December 15, 1844, Carroll County, d. October 24, 1848 Georgia); Melissa died at the age of four.

8) Mary Cavendar (b. 1848, Texas, d. Texas).

9) Emily Caroline (b. 1851, Texas, d. 1863, Van Zandt County, Texas).

James Coltharp owned Land Lot #165 at Hart Town; in February 1840 there was a suit Snoden and Shearer vs James Coltharp and Green C. McSpadden, who was his father-in-law. James Coltharp was a partner in the Majors & Coltharp Store at Hart Town until about 1844. The suit was over payment for goods purchased.

As members of the New Hope Primitive Baptist Church, both James and Joannah appear in the New Hope church minutes as members. February 29, 1832, James Coltharp was received by letter from Chestau, Monroe County, Tennessee. On July 6, 1836 James (with six others) were listed on the church committee to find land and build a meeting house.

Joanna joined the church "Received by Letter" December 31, 1836 and was baptized in the Little Tallapoosa River.

In August of 1844 James and Joanna were "Dismissed By Letter" from New Hope Baptist Church. They moved to Attala, Mississippi; in 1848, this family lived in Van Zandt, Texas; and on the 1850 Federal Census, James and his family lived in Hamburg, Van Zandt County, Texas.

Alexander Porter Green

Alexander Porter Green, son of William Mercer Green and Nancy Porter Green was born 19 May 1818 in Haywood, North Carolina. Alexander married Eliza Ann Chappell on 23 November 1843 in Carroll County. Eliza Ann was (b. November 26, 1824, Georgia, d. June 9, 1906, Villa Rica). They lived close to Hart Town near the intersection of Atlanta-Birmingham Road and North and South Van Wert Road. The Green family first lived in a log cabin on Land Lot #158.

Alexander Porter Green bought full lots of 202 1/2 acres or half which was 101 1/4 acres to partial acreage of Land Lot #s 90, 114, 123, 137 and 1848 to 1852:

Deed book F, Page 172 Carroll County, 7 Mar 1848. ALEXANDER P. GREENE and HILBURN S. HULSEY, Adm. estate of WILLIAM GREENE, deceased to ROBERT A. GREENE, highest bidder. $300.00. South half, lot #152, 6th district Carroll County. 101 1/4 acres. Attest: G. W. Hiden, Gilbert Cole, M.A. McRae, J.P. 6 Nov 1848.

Deed book F, Page 200 Carroll County, 7 Mar 1848. ALEXANDER P. GREEN and HILBURN S. HULSEY, administrator estate WILLIAM GREEN to WILLIAM N. DAVIS, highest bidder. $802.50. Land lot #137, 6th district Carroll County. Attest: Gilbert Cole, Thomas Green, W. A. Cole, M. A. McRae, J. P. 27 Jan 1849.

Deed Book F, Page 769 Carroll County, 5 Nov 1850. BENJAMIN F. TIDWELL, Putnam County, administrator of estate JOSIAH TIDWELL, deceased to ALEXANDER P. GREEN, Carroll County. $250.00. 1/2 land lot #123, 6th district Carroll County. Attest: G. W. West, Joseph C Williams, J.P. 11 Mar 1852.

Deed book F, Page 770 Carroll County, 23 Feb 1850. SILAS LAWRENCE, Gwinnett County to ALEXANDER P. GREEN. $700.00. Land lot #90, 6th district Carroll County. 202 1/2 acres. Attest: R. Y. Higgins, Wm. N. Taylor, Henry S. Chance, J.P. 11 March 1852.

Deed book F, Page 770 Carroll County, 5 Nov 1850. BENJAMIN F. TIDWELL, attorney for MARY E. McLEARY, Barbour County to ALEXANDER P. GREEN. $83.33. 1/6 land lot #123, 6th district Carroll County. 33 1/3 acres. Attest: G. W. West, Joseph C Williams, J.P. 11 Mar 1852

Deed book F, Page 772 Floyd County, 22 Jul 1851. ARCHIBALD DAVIS to ALEXANDER P. GREEN. $50.00. 1/6 land lot #123, 6th district Carroll County. Attest: George MT. Ware, Will A. Moore, J.P. 11 Mar 1852.

Deed book F, Page 771 Carroll County, Georgia, 30 Jan 1852. THOS W. GAR-

NER to ALEXANDER P. GREEN. $802.00. Land lot #114, 2nd district Carroll [now Douglas] County. Attest: William B. Height, Joseph C Williams, J. P. 11 March 1852.

Alexander Green fought for the Confederate States Army in the Battle of Atlanta and was killed in 1864. When his wife Eliza Chappell received word of his death and that he had been buried in a shallow grave beside the Chattahoochee River, she went with help to retrieve his body. She brought his body back, traveling in a wagon. His burial was at Pleasant Grove Cemetery. During his service at the graveside, they could hear cannon fire from the battles west of Atlanta.

Alexander left Eliza Ann with nine children.

1) Antoinette J. Green (b. February 10, 1848, Villa Rica, d. 1923, Villa Rica). She married John Jethro Velvin.

2) James Walter Green (b. April 20, 1850, Villa Rica). James married Sarah Margaret Sykes.

3) Virginia Caroline "Jennie" Green (b. January 4, 1858, Villa Rica) married Thomas Frank Sykes.

4) Martha Lula Talloolar Green (b. January 14, 1855, Villa Rica, d. 1942, Villa Rica) married John Walker.

5) William Henderson Green, a twin, (b. July 5, 1857, Carroll County, d. 1904) married Hallie Snellgrove.

6) Jesse Mercer Green, a twin, (b. July 5, 1857, Carroll County, d. 1891).

7) Mary Carrie Gorder Green (b. November 23, 1859).

8) Tommie Lorena Green (b. April 6, 1864, Villa Rica, d. 1925, Villa Rica) married John Fain in 1887.

9) Nora Elizador Green 1861, d. 1888.

Eliza Ann Chappell Green was buried at the Pleasant Grove Baptist Church Cemetery.

About 1876, the second child, James Walter Green, built a large two-story Victorian style house with the balcony-porch on the family land: 202 1/2 acres of Land Lot #158 just across from the Hart House. About the same time, the family built a very large barn, known as the largest barn in Carroll County. The Green family lived here for several generations, then, the house and property were sold. This beautiful home and the barn still exist today. (33°43'54.79"N 84°57'14.28"W)

William Hart

There were several William Harts: one was listed on the Carroll County 1830 Census as the head of a family as a free white persons between ages 20–29, living with a free white female between ages 15–19.

Also, Samuel Hart had a brother William M. Hart, born in 1788 in Hancock County. A listing of marriage records from Hancock County, shows that William Hart married Nancy Beall on January 26, 1819. William and Nancy Beall Hart had one child, a daughter, Mary, (b. May 25, 1831, Scott, Johnson County, d. August 12,

David & Mary Hart Beasley and Daughter, Sophronia

1897, Johnson County). On May 1853, Mary Hart married David Redding Beasley (b. August 10, 1823, June 11, 1901). They had several children including a daughter, Sophronia.

Some historians believe William Hart, who lived in Hart Town in 1830 and was a Justice of the Peace, was the "Judge" Hart who built the Hart House and started the mining village of Hart Town well before Samuel Hart arrived sometime about 1843-44. For more on the Hart family see Chapter 11.

The Abraham "Abram" Leathers' genealogy book tells that as a 16-year-old in 1840, Abram worked for "Judge" Hart, building a porch, hauling stones and hoisting timbers. At the end of the week, he walked home and told his mother that "one day I will own that fine house." See Abraham Leathers' story, also in Chapter 11.

William W. Hart fought in the War of 1812 and was granted a land lottery even before 1827. Among those who were also granted land was his sister Mary's father-in-law William Coolbaugh, Sr. Image below. For more on the Colbaugh (Coolbough) family, see Chapter 10. William and Nancy Hart moved to St. Clair, Illinois as did two of his brothers. In the Hart Family Cemetery in Taliaferro County at Crawfordville there is a tombstone for an infant William M. Hart, (b. 1842, d. December 21, 1842); the parents are unknown.

For the bounty and relief of which he has petitioned, this 25th of January, 1826.

War of 1812: James Elliot, George H. Bingham, James Watts, Henry Trope, Elenezer [sic] Mann, Nathan Coon, William Keeter, Daniel B.—, Isaac Sutton, Henry Wyatts, John Northroup, Abraham Foster, J. C. Powell, S. Myers, William B. Foster.

J. M. Piollet, Simon Kinney, George Scott, James P. Bull, John N. Weston, J. Woodruff, Wm Shelley, Burrt Ridgeway, Nathn N. Pitts, Rupel Fowler, *William Coolbaugh, 2nd, William W. Hart.*

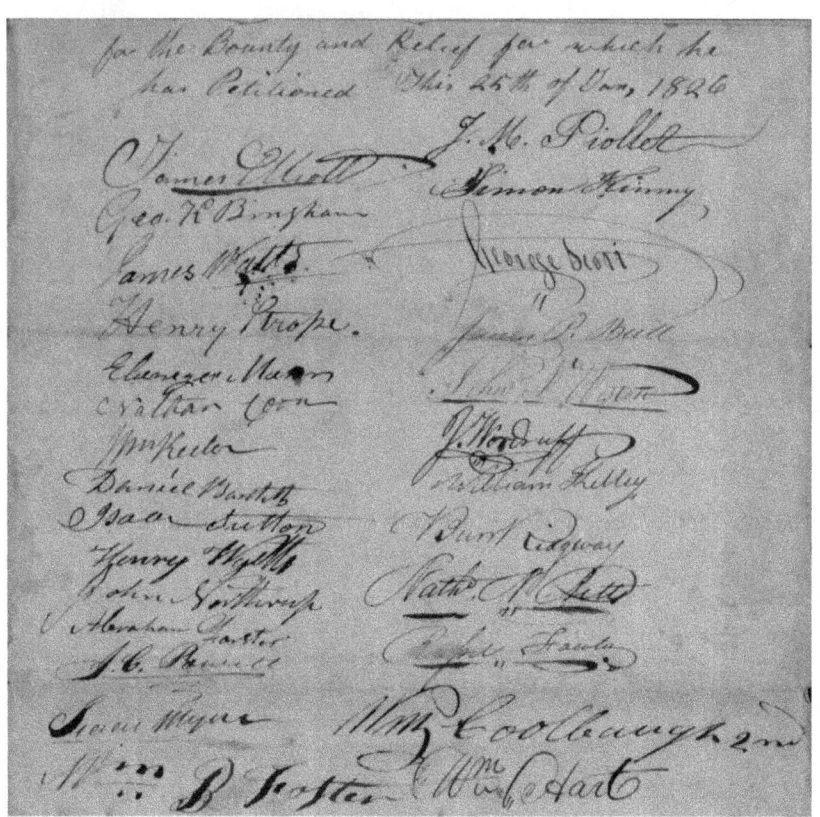

William "Billy" E. Hixon of Hart Town

Billy Hixon (b. February 23, 1819, Georgia, d. June 16, 1896, Carroll County). In 1850, he lived in Green County, Georgia. Billy married Emily Elizabeth Echols on November 23, 1843 in Taliaferro County. Emily (b. June 3, 1823, Georgia).

They moved to Carroll County before 1860, as they are shown on that census as well as the 1870 and 1880 U. S. Federal Census Records. The Georgia Property Tax Digest for 1873-1877 shows Billy Hixon paid taxes on LLs 150, 154, 162 and 166, each of which were 202 1/2 acres. According to the family, over the next generation, he gave each of his children a hundred acres and a house, most of which were in the Pleasant Grove Community.

His family grew up in a large two-story home, that was about 1/4 mile west of the Hart House, facing the Birmingham-Atlanta Highway (33°44'03.66"N

84°5815.36"W). This plantation style home was located on Land Lot 166. The family lived here for two generations. Billy and Emily Hixon had a daughter and three sons.

1) Sarah Elizabeth Hixon (b. 1845).

2) James Crawford Hixon (b. December 1847, d. 1915) married Emily J. Chambers (b. 1845, d. 1883) on December 22, 1871. James and Emily had two sons: Oscar W. Hixon (1872-1909) and Olin Hugh Hixon (1878-1959). James' second wife was Mary Elizabeth Witcher (1852-1914) whom he married August 9, 1887 in Fulton County.

3) Elijah Franklin Hixon (b. December 27, 1849, d. April 18, 1931) married Margaret J. Davis (b. February 23, 1856, d. July 9, 1883). They had two children: Ada O. (b. October 22, 1874, d. 1971). Ada married Robert Atticus Yates. Howard M. Hixon (b. August 12, 1882, d. July 15, 1883).

James, Emily, Oscar and Olin Hixon
Find-A-Grave

Elijah's second wife was Susan M. "Susie" Cagle (b. 1864, d. 1941). They married on March 10, 1887 in Fulton, County, Georgia. Elijah and Susie had one child, Ethel Hixon Wilson (b. 1891, d. 1961).

4) John Thomas Hixon (b. September 28, 1861, d. December 27, 1931) married Lula E. Cheves (b. 1868, d. 1938) on August 12, 1886 in Carroll Co. She was the daughter of Allison Cheves and Mahaley Anne Shinn of Chevestown.

John Hixon was a merchant, politician, legislator, religious leader, and Sunday School Superintendent at Pleasant Grove Church for more than 40 years. He died in church while performing his duty.

John and Lula Hixon's children:
1) Annie (b. August 1887, d. 1975) married Walter McMichael;
2) Era (b. January 15, 1889, d. 1955) married W. L. Steadham;
3) Horace (b. December 2, 1890);
4) Eva (b. circa 1891);
5) Johnnie Lou (b. February 1893) married Hoke Lyle.

Billy Hixon, father of Sarah, James, Elijah and John Hixon married again after his first wife, Emily died. Billy's second wife, Elizabeth Hixon, (d. August 20, 1885, Villa Rica). Both are buried at Pleasant Grove Baptist Church Cemetery.

Many of Billy and Emily's children and grandchildren continued to live in Carroll County in the Hickory Level community as they are shown on the 1900, 1910, 1920 and 1930 U. S. Federal Census Records. Many of these family members are buried at Pleasant Grove Baptist Church Cemetery.

John George Washington "Jack" Lassetter

John George Washington Lassetter (b. July 2, 1858 in Carroll County, d. October 26, 1956, Carroll County was the son of William Cheadle Lassetter and Mary Parthenia L. Brown Lassetter. On the 1870 U. S. Federal Census Record, this family lived in District 5 of Carroll County; in 1880 this family lived in District 729 of Carroll County; Jack was 21 and worked on his dad's farm.

Jack Lassetter married Mary E. Barnett in 1884. On the 1900 Federal Census, they are shown with two children and a niece, Mertie Neal, age 22, living in District 642, Surelwats Street, Villa Rica. In 1920, 1930 and 1940, they lived on Temple Road in District 642 in Carroll County. His occupation was that of farmer on all the census records.

Jack and Mary had two children:
1) Erie Lassetter (b. August 26, 1885, d. September 5,1886); she died at one year old;
2) William Casper Lassetter (b. August 31,1887, d. 1962).

After his first wife, Mary, died in 1909, Jack married Addie Mae Green (b. 1878). She was a teacher at Villa Rica School. Jack and Addie had children: James Green Lassetter, Marion Annette and John George Washington Lassetter, Jr.

John George Washington "Jack" Lassetter, Sr. owned a gold mine on Land Lot# 189 in Villa Rica. For those details see Chapter 3 on Gold Deposits in Villa Rica.

Jack died in 1956 and Addie died in 1962. Both are buried at Pleasant Grove Baptist Church Cemetery.

James B. Majors

James B. Majors, a twin, (b. 1797, Rhea County, Tennessee, d. October 25, 1879, Palestine, Anderson County, Texas) was co-owner of the Majors & Coltharp General Store. James' parents were Peter Majors (b. 1773, d. 1844) and Mary Wright Majors, (b. 1788, d. 1880). James' wife was Jane Upton (b. June 2, 1802, Kentucky, d. December 21, 1875, Palastine, Texas).

James and Jane Majors had four children in Tennessee before coming to Carroll County. Children: Pleasant Henry (b. April 3, 1821, d. October 1, 1873); Isaac Barton (b. 1823); Mary Ann (b. 1825); James W. (b. 1828, d. January 15, 1858, Anderson County Texas).

James Majors became a member of the New Hope Primitive Baptist Church on March 1829, "Received by Letter." He became the pastor in May of 1829. On November 22, 1834, James Majors was "Dismissed by Letter." It is unknown if he requested termination of his job as pastor, but records show that the family continued to live in the area.

While living in Carroll County, James and Jane Majors had five more children:
1) Marshal Lee (b. 1832);
2) Mablean (b. 1833);
3) Martha Jane (b. 1837);
4) Emaline (b. May 2, 1838, d. October 28, 1872, Texas);
5) Peter Lafayette (b. October 5, 1842, d. October 17, 1875, Palestine, Anderson County, Texas).

This family left Georgia and on the 1850 Federal Census were shown in Tippah, Mississippi. Here they had a daughter, Amanda, born in 1845.

In 1860 they lived at Kickapoo, Anderson County, Texas. In 1870, they lived in Palestine, Anderson County, Texas where they both lived until their death.

Jane Upton Majors died in 1875 and James B. Majors died in 1879.

William B. Majors

William B. Majors, the twin of James B. Majors, (b. 1797, Rhea County Tennessee, d July 1863, Jefferson, County, Arkansas) was the son of Peter Majors (b. 1773, d. 1844, and Mary Wright Majors (b. 1788, d. 1880).

On March 16, 1818 in Knox County Tennessee, William Majors married Susannah Scaggs. William and Susannah had six children. Elbert was born in Tennessee, the others in Carroll County:
1) Elbert Lee, (b. March 22, 1823, d. 1909);
2) Alexander W. (b. 1825, d. 1861);
3) James W. (b. 1829, d. 1873);
4) William J. (b. March 18, 1832, d. 1909);
5) Augustus A. (b. 1836, d. 1862);
6) Martha (b. 1838).

William was "Received by Letter" into the New Hope Primitive Baptist Church on September 25, 1830. By November 30, William was a trustee of the church when two acres on the NE corner of Land Lot 145, Second District was proposed to be given to the church. On August 15, 1832, William was ordained to become a deacon in the church, by the reverend, and brethren Kelley and Dykes. On November 20, 1835, William and his wife requested dismissal from his job of deacon of the church. A little over a month later on December 26, 1835, he withdrew his request and both remained members.

On July 6, 1837, William was appointed, along with others, to a committee to select the place to build the meeting house. On July 23, 1837, this committee reported that the church house would be built near the camp meeting ground near Charles Sheetes' place.

After the death of his first wife, Susannah, William Majors married Mary Brightwell on May 13, 1838 in Steward County Georgia. On July 27, 1839 William

A. Majors and Mary Majors were dismissed by letter. The reason is not known.

It appears that William and his twin, James B. Majors (see above), had a sister Nicey Majors, 1824-1906, who also came with them to Georgia, for she was "Received by Letter" into the church on January 1, 1832 from the Baptist Church of Christ in Rhea County, Tennessee.

In 1850 the William Majors family was back in Rhea County, Tennessee. After Mary's death he married Sarah McColphin on October 5, 1852.

On the 1860 Census this family was living in Jefferson County Arkansas. They lost two sons to the Civil War: Alexander W. Majors was killed at Pea Ridge Arkansas on March 3, 1862. Augustus A. Majors was killed on April 6, 1862 at the Battle of Shiloh in Hardin Tennessee.

William Majors died in July of 1863 in Jefferson County Arkansas.

James Yates of Hart Town

James and Tabitha Yates were both born in Virginia circa 1785. They migrated to South Carolina where Joel Pinckney Yates was born on May 25, 1825. In the 1820 census of Pulaski County, Georgia, James Yates was shown with his family. In 1830, he was listed on the Census in Fayette County, Ga. and in 1840, in Campbell County, Ga. They came into Carroll County circa 1842.

By the 1850 census, James and Tabitha had no children living at home, but an Elizabeth Mason, born in 1779 in Virginia, was living with them. Elizabeth may have been a sister to one of them. James Yates, James F. Yates, a physician, William Harrison Yates, and Joel Pinckney Yates bought lots 197, 198, and 220 in the 6th District of Carroll County, being close to Hart Town.

Joel Pickney Yates

Joel Pickney Yates (b. May 25, 1825, South Carolina, d. October 10, 1890, Carroll County) son of James and Tabitha Yates (above) married Martha Jane Stewart on On December 11, 1845. Tabitha (b. October 28, 1828 in Carroll County, June 25, 1913 Carroll County). In the next 28 years, seventeen known children were born to them. Their second child, Mary, died and was buried in the Hart Town area along with Joel's parents James and Tabitha Yates. Elizabeth Mason also was buried there.

The 1880 Census of Carroll County shows Joel and Martha Jane Yates had moved south of Bowdon to the New Mexico militia in the Ninth District. Carroll County's 50th Post Office was established June 29, 1885, being called Joel. It was the custom back in those days to always name the post office after the postmaster. In this particular case, it was being named for Joel Pinckney Yates, for the post office was on his land and he was the postmaster. He ran this until his death on November 10, 1890. His family continued to run the post office there until it was closed in 1904.

Joel Pinckney Yates and Martha Jane Stewart Yates had seventeen children.

1. Lydia Elizabeth Yates (b. November 18, 1846, d. November 29, 1916) married Fabius Maxwell Thornton on January 15, 1870.

2. Mary Yates was born circa 1847 and died at an early age. She was buried near Hart Town.

3. Tabitha Yates (b. September 30, 1850, d. March 16, 1934) married George Anderson on April 26, 1867. They raised their family and were both buried around Elmore County, Alabama.

4. Sarah Jane Josehene "Josie" Yates (b. November 18, 1849, d December 01, 1934) married Doctor Porter Chambers on December 31, 1868.

5. Hannah Catherine Yates (b. February 21, 1851, d. September 10, 1900 married James Madison Wood on November 11, 1877.

6. Georgia Ann Caroline Yates (b. February 18, 1852, d. February 12, 1890 married Milton R. Chambers.

Milton & Georgia Ann Yates Chambers
Courtesy Roger Smith & Frank Duke

7. William E. Yates (b. September 3, 1853, d. June 20, 1935 married Eliza L. Bishop on December 23, 1880. He was buried at Oak Grove Baptist Church in Joel, Georgia.

8. James M. Yates (b. circa 1855) married a Sheets and was buried around LaGrange, Georgia.

9. Joel L. Yates (b. March 23, 1857, d. June 5, 1884).

10. Joseph E. Brown Yates (b. May 5, 1858, d. November 3, 1930 married Mollie Bishop on July 24, 1884.

11. Harrison P. Yates (b. circa 1859), married Itura and they raised their children near Phoenix City, Alabama.

12. Rufus M. Yates (b. circa 1861) married Carrie Willingham. They raised their family in Rocky Branch, Alabama and were buried there. .

13. Synthia Lenore Yates (b. circa 1863) married John N. Wood on August 10, 1881. They raised their family near Wedowee, Alabama and are buried near there.

14. Martha "Mattie" Slaughter Yates (b. February 6, 1866, d. March 18, 1926) married Guss F. Knight on March 27, 1887.

15. Eller Lenora Yates (b. June 23, 1868) married Warren Spencer Lowery on December 10, 1894.

16. Willis Alvin Yates (b. circa 1869) married Octavia Moon on December 20, 1895. They raised their family around Jasper, Alabama and were buried there.

17. Sallie Adella Yates (b. October 16, 1873, d. June 9, 1954) married W. H. Brand on December 25, 1887.

Joel Pickney Yates died in 1890. Tabitha Stewart Yates died in 1913 at age eighty-four. Both were buried at Pleasant Grove Baptist Church Cemetery as are their children: Lydia, Sarah Jane, Georgia Ann, Joel L., Joseph, Martha, Eller, and Sallie. This cemetery was near Joel, Georgia where he was the postmaster.

Book G, Page 383 Carroll County, 8 Sep 1853. LEONARD C. HUFF to JOEL P. YATES and JAMES YATES. $400.00. Land lot #197, 6th dist. Carroll County. Attest: A. H. Harrison, F. M. Little, J.P. 19 Jan 1854.

Book G, Page 589 Carroll County, 11 Feb 1854, WILLIAM K. HURT to J. F. YATES and W. H. YATES. $1,000. West half land lot#197, 6th dist. Carroll County plus 7 1/2 acres land lot #198. Attest: Joel G. Yates, F. M. Little, J.P. 5 Dec 1854.

Book G, Page 589 Meriwether County, 18 Dec 1854. CHARLES B. ZUBER to WILLIAM F. YATES, and JOHN F. YATES. $1,000. Land lot #220, 6th dist. Carroll County. Attest: Henry L. Thomas. Thomas Walton, J.P. 5 Dec 1854.

Book G, Page 590 Carroll County, 2 Mar 1854. JAMES YATES to JOEL P. YATES. Love and affection. East half land lot #197, 6th dist. Carroll County. Reserving life estate for self and wife, TABITHA YATES. Attest: Samuel C Candler, F . M. Little, J.P. 5 Dec 1854.

Book G, Page 612 Carroll County, 29 Dec 1853. H. J. HOGUE to LEONARD FULLBRIGHT. $30.00. Part of land lot #166, 6th dist. Carroll County. Bound on the east by SAMUEL HART and J. F. YATES, on the north by J. F. YATES and F. LUTHER. On the road from Atlanta to Jacksonville, by way of Villa Rica. Attest: Joseph Wynn, B. Cason, J. Chambers, J.P. 26 Dec 1854.

Pleasant Grove

Early settlers of the Pleasant Grove community included: Willis Bagwell, John Conner, Abel Embry, Frances Marion Fielder, Henry Haynes, Jonathan Haynes, James Reeves, Parker Rice, Luke Skinner, J. O. Stone, T. F. Sykes, T. H. West, and Robert Atticus Yates.

Henry Haynes

Henry Haynes (b. October 17, 1797, Henry County, Virginia, d. March 1877, Hope, Hempstead County, Arkansas) was the youngest son of William and Sara Haynes. His family moved to Burke County, North Carolina and settled along Pigeon Creek where he and his brothers William, John, James, Ephraim, Edward, Johnston, Jonathan and two sisters were raised. The family moved to Missouri in 1818 and remained there until 1825. Henry married Phoebe Eaton. They had three children: Sarah (1820), Mary (1822) and Nancy (1823), all born in Missouri.

The entire family became involved in the Primitive Baptist movement in western North Carolina and northeast Georgia. William and John helped establish

Providence Primitive Baptist Church in Habersham County. Henry was ordained a minister by his brother William in 1829 while he was a member of Providence Primitive Baptist Church.

Henry and his family, along with his brothers Johnston, Edward and Jonathan and their families, moved to the newly opened Indian Lands in Carroll County, Georgia. They all became part of the New Hope Primitive Baptist congregation. Henry preached at both New Hope and Concord Baptist churches in 1830 and 1831. The minutes of the respective churches indicate his participation in the establishment of these churches. The Church split over the question of missions and Henry moved to the Poplar Springs Primitive Baptist Church, which he had helped build. He remained there as minister until 1857.

Henry's first wife Phoebe died in 1838 or 1839. She had ten children and only two of them survived past the Civil War: Elizabeth, who married Gilbert Cole and probably last lived in Carrollton, Georgia; George, who was a teacher at the school located near the Concord Baptist Church, north of present day Villa Rica, Georgia on state highway 101 (Yorktown Road).

Phoebe was buried at New Hope Cemetery or Poplar Springs Church Cemetery, in an unmarked grave. Henry Haynes married his second wife Elizabeth Goodson, on her twenty-first birthday in 1839. She was born on June 26, 1818 in Lincoln County, North Carolina. She bore him eleven children.

Sometime in the 1840's, Henry had traveled to Arkansas and was well known for his devotion to the church and its mission. He participated in the Primitive Baptist Convention in Arkansas in 1847 and preached the opening sermon for this convention.

On May 30, 1850, Henry sold his 202 1/2 acres land lot #154 of 202 1/2 District 6 to James Echols. Later, he and his family asked for and received dismissal from the Carroll County, New Hope Primitive Baptist Church; then, transferred to Colombia County, Arkansas in 1857. He was to establish and administer to churches in Pike and Hempstead Counties, Arkansas. In 1877, he died at age 80 on his farm near Hope, Hempstead County, Arkansas.

Jonathan Haynes

Jonathan Haynes, older brother of Henry and son of William & Sara Hill Haynes of Virginia, North Carolina and Missouri; then, Habersham County, Georgia; then, Carroll County, Georgia, settled and stayed in Carroll County to raise his family. Jonathan (b. November 17, 1795 in Henry County, Virginia, d. 1880, Bartow County) married Cynthia "Synthey" McDowell on August 25, 1818. Cynthia (b. 1801, Haywood, North Carolina).

He and his brothers, Edward, Johnston and Henry moved their families to Carroll County in 1830. They, along with others, came together to form the New Hope Primitive Baptist Church. Minutes of the meetings have already been shared in an earlier chapter. Jonathan was appointed to a committee to purchase land for a new meeting house. He was elected as a trustee and as a brother to assist in laying the new church's foundation on November 27, 1830. According to the minutes, the committee did not finish the job and some harsh (but polite) words were exchanged. The outcome was that the new church, named New Hope, was built east of the town that is now known as Villa Rica, Georgia, near the present-day Atlanta Highway, US 78, and the old Pumpkintown Road crossing. The church was obviously not completed by February 1, 1834, because church services were held at Jonathan's home.

While living in Habersham County, Jonathan drew Gold lottery land lot #138 in the 19th district. On January 16, 1832, he was appointed to the Road Commission for Carroll County, and then appointed Justice of the Peace and performed several marriages. On June 3, 1833, he was appointed to the Grand Jury for two terms. On February 3, 1835, he was appointed as County Road Commissioner. On June 1, 1835, he was appointed to the Grand Jury. On February 3, 1835, he was appointed Road Commissioner of the 642nd Militia District.

In 1837, 1838 and 1839 Jonathan Haynes was elected to the Georgia State Senate. During the 1830s and 1840s, the Georgia Senate consisted of one elected citizen from each county. In 1837, he opposed William Springer in the race for the position and won. The main issue was the building of a state railroad from Augusta, to Carrollton, via Macon. The road was to continue on to Chattanooga, Tennessee. He won the election on the basis that the railroad would destroy one of the main sources of revenue and income for the area, the hauling of goods and freight by oxen-drawn wagons to the mines, merchants and farmers in Carroll, Cobb and Douglas Counties from Augusta and Macon. Paulding County was not yet constituted, although there were many people living in the area. Jonathan owned a fleet of these wagons and was protecting his interests by opposing the railroad construction in this part of Georgia

The wagons that hauled the goods from Savannah, Augusta and Macon were pulled by large teams of oxen. The teams were made up of from four to eight braces of oxen: a brace being two oxen yoked together, although some writers have referred to a brace as being four oxen yoked together. The drivers (drovers) of these teams used long, black, woven whips that were snapped over the heads of the oxen, thus inducing the oxen to pull the heavily loaded wagons. The drovers were very proud of their skill at cracking their whips and the number of braces they could control. They became famous over the Southland and were known as Crackers.

Jonathan was successful and able to purchase 400 acres at or near Hickory Level. He lost his bid for reelection as by 1839, attitudes of the people living in West Georgia were changing about the need and demand for a railroad. Jonathan became a full-time farmer, had a large farm and a goodly amount of children. The 1840 & 1850 census shows Jonathan Haynes & Lief (later died), Lucinda; William Henry Haynes; Elizabeth; Riley; Cynthia, Arminda; Lafayette, John Monroe Haynes and Sarah.

His father William died in Villa Rica, Carroll County in 1846. His mother Sara Hill Haynes died in Villa Rica in 1850. By 1850, Jonathan's 400 acres was reduced to 75 acres. Abstract books C, D show that Jonathan and his family lived on Land Lot 158 toward in the Pleasant Grove Community.

The 1870 census shows that Jonathan, age seventy-five and Cynthia, age sixty-nine, lived on a 101 acre farm in the Van Wert district of Polk county, Georgia, near Rockmart, Georgia. In 1880 he was age 84 and lived with his daughter Lucinda Kinney and her children in Polk County. He died 1880 in Bartow County. Cynthia later lived with her daughter, Sarah Haynes Brown in Bartow County, Georgia. It is unknown where either are buried.

Darling Franklin Sykes

Darling Franklin "Frank" Sykes (b. February 13, 1830, North Carolina). His wife, Sarah Ann Frances Cochran Sykes was born January 13, 1835 in North Carolina. Darling Sykes enlisted in the Confederate Army in 1862 and was killed in the Battle of the Wilderness in Spotsylvania, Virginia on May 6, 1864.

Sarah Ann Frances Sykes was left with children:
1) Frank Sykes (b. 1835);
2) Mary Sykes (b. 1855);
3) Sarah Sykes (b. 1857);
4) Hariet Sykes (b. 1859);
5) Stephen Alexander Sykes (b. 1862).

Sarah Ann married Nathan Vincent Stallings who was born in 1834. Their children in the coming years were:
6) John Wesley Stallings (b. 1866);
7) Eliza Ann Stallings (b. 1867) married John Conner;
8) Robert E. Stallings (b. 1872;
9) Festus Harrison Stallings (b. 1874);
10) Charles Eugene Stallings (b. 1876).

Thomas Franklin Sykes

Thomas "Frank" Sykes (b. December 16, 1853, Lee County, d. July 6, 1939, Villa Rica) moved to Carroll County with his parents, Darling and Sarah Ann Cochran Sykes. Frank married on December 28, 1875 in Carroll County to Virginia Caroline "Jennie" Green, (d. April 15, 1926, Villa Rica) of Villa Rica. Jennie Green was the daughter of Alexander Porter Green and Nancy Green.

Frank and his wife tried farming in Texas, traveling there in a covered wagon in 1878. After two years, they gave up and returned to Georgia by train with their three small children:
1) Walter C. Sykes (b. December 23, 1876, Villa Rica, d. May 9, 1917);
2) Annie Belle Sykes (b. June 6, 1882, Villa Rica, d. March 2, 1973), who married James Henry Pope;
3) Lois Sykes (b. February 20, 1899, Villa Rica, d. August 12, 1967). Lois married Marvin Eugene Stephens.

Thomas "Frank" Sykes was a prominent farmer, a very active member of Pleasant Grove Church, and Postmaster for a term at Hickory Level. He was also a Mayor of Villa Rica.

Thomas Frank Sykes
Courtesy Villa Rica Masonic Lodge Members

On the 1860 Census, his value of real estate was $800 and his value of personal estate was $2,020. In 1910 the family lived on Simmons Street close to Sweetwater Street in Villa Rica. Shown was Thomas 55, Virginia 56 and another head of household Ms. Lula Walker age 65. In 1920, they lived on Sweetwater Street in Villa Rica. In 1930, Frank was age 76, and was living with his daughter Lois age 38 in Etowah Alabama. Frank and Jennie Sykes were each buried at Pleasant Grove Baptist Church Cemetery.

Thomas "Frank" Sykes served for several years as Worshipful Master of the Villa Rica Masonic Lodge, #72. From his obituary:

He was initiated into Villa Rica Lodge #72, July 9th, 1898, passed to the degree of Fellowcraft August 13, 1898, and raised to the sublime degree of a Master Mason September 10, 1898, and after a long life of faithful service was called from labor on July 6, 1939. He served 17 years as Worshipful Master of his lodge.

We need only two simple words. We say humbly and with reverence that he was truly a "Christian Gentleman." . . . A gentleman in that he was courteous, thoughtful, and considerate in all his relations with his fellow man. He was indeed 'One of God's Noblemen.

Robert Atticus Yates, Teacher at Pleasant Grove School

Robert Atticus Yates (b. April 9, 1869, d. May 24, 1909, Carroll County) was son of Elijah Matthew Yates (1838-1906) and Martha Matilda Steed Yates (1844-1916) of Campbell County and Carroll County. In December 1894, in Carroll County, Robert married Ada O. Hixon (b. 1874, d. 1971) the daughter of Elijah Franklin Hixon and Margaret Davis Hixon of the Pleasant Grove Community.

Robert Atticus Yates was a teacher in 1892 at the Pleasant Grove School and Ada Hixon was a student in the senior class. Catherine Yates West, age 90 who is the granddaughter of Robert and Ada Yates, tells the family story that the teacher-pupil romance developed over time; they waited until she graduated to admit their feelings to each other or to anyone else. They married when she was twenty.

Robert Atticus Yates remained a teacher for many years at Pleasant Grove

School which was across the road from the Pleasant Grove Baptist Church and about a half mile further southeast—on the left of Pleasant Grove Church Road. (33°43'21.00"N 84°58'00.60"W)

The U. S. Federal Census Record shows that Robert and Ada lived in District 642 Carroll County in 1900.

They had four children:
1) Myrtie Mae (b. March 2, 1896);
2) Minnie Kate (b. January 4, 1899);
3) William Raymond Yates (January 17, 1902;
4) Margaret Alene (b. May 12, 1905).

Robert Yates died in 1909 and Ada died in 1971. Though she was just five years younger than her husband, she outlived him by sixty-two years. Both were buried at Pleasant Grove Baptist Church Cemetery as were their children and many Hixon and Yates relatives.

Robert & Ada Yates and Family

6

Early Settlers of Hickory Level

The old timer said, "We gits too soon old and too late smart."
George Bell, age 94, from Villa Rica, now Greatfalls, Montana

Early residents of Hickory Level included: Larkin Allen, Alcimus Allen, Henry Arney, Jacob Awtrey, Rev. James Baskin, David Brock, J. M. Bryce, Walter Dorough, Jessie Gray, Ned Gresham, Billy McCain, Wright Majors, Peter Mosteller, Newton Pierce, Rev. Thomas T. Powell, Honest Smith, Bob Stephens, David Stripling, Billy Taylor, Slomman Wynn and James Upton.

Alcimus Harris Allen

Alcimus Harris Allen (b. October 1, 1824, Houston County, d. July 28, 1868, Carroll County) was the son of Alcimus Harris Allen, Sr. (b. 1779, Anson, North Carolina, d. 1828) and Cynthia Kilgore Marcus Threadgill (b. 1787, Georgia, d. 1840). Alcimus, Jr. married Jane Moore McCain on December 19, 1844 in Troupe County, Georgia. Jane (b. 1826, Georgia, d. May 28, 1894).

In 1850 this family lived in Troupe County, Georgia District 697. The 1860 Federal Census shows them living at Hickory Level in Carroll County.

Their children were:
1) William Marcus (b. 1847, d. 1916);
2. James Harris (b. 1849, d. 1887);
3) Cynthia Elvira Allen Brooks (b. 1851, d. 1920);
4) John A. (b. 1854);
5) Robert H. (b. 1855);
6) Adeline Martha Jane Steele (b. 1860, D. 1939).

In 1860, Alcimus Allen's real estate value was $1,580 and his personal estate value was $2,000.

Tragedy struck Alcimus's sister's family in 1853 and ultimately affected

Alcimus Allen

Alcimus and his family. Mary Francis Allen, Alcimus's sister, and her husband Henry Ledbetter Threadgill lived in Chambers County, Alabama in 1850 with six children raging from ages six months to fourteen years old. Mary and her family were struck with Typhoid Fever in the summer of 1853. The parents and two small children, Thomas, 3, and Martha age 2, died from the fever.

On November 7, 1853 Alcimus Allen became guardian of Mary and Henry Threadgill's four surviving children: Eliza Ann, 17; Harriett Virginia, 10; Eugenia, 8; and Alcimus, 5. Alcimus Harris Allen himself was just 29 and his wife Jane was just 27.

The Allen and Threadgill family attended the Concord Methodist Church, the Allen's being charter members.

Alcimus Harris Allen served in the Civil War for District 649 Georgia Military District, Carroll County. He enlisted in Company I, 5th Georgia Infantry on September 25, 1862. While he was away, his two young sons and a nephew ran the farm. In 1862, when the father left, William was age fifteen; James was thirteen; and Alcimus Threadgill was fourteen: three teenagers on a farm trying to raise enough food to keep this large family fed while the father was away at war. Alcimus Allen mustered out on April 26, 1865 at Greensboro, N. C. (Roster of Confederate Soldiers).

On July 28, 1868, tragedy struck the Allen/Threadgill family again, when Alcimus Allen, then 43, was accidentally killed by his nephew, Walker Gray, while deer hunting. After the death of the patriarch, the Allen and Threadgill family struggled but sought out their opportunities to face changes in farming and work and stay in the area.

Both Jane and Alcimus Allen were buried at the Concord Methodist Church Cemetery as many members of this family were also buried there.

In 1936, a newspaper article on a family reunion stated "the Threadgill family of Carroll County had seventeen grandchildren and eleven great-grandchildren. There has been five generations of the Threadgill family in Carroll county since 1853."

Reverend James Baskin

James Baskin known as "Uncle Jimmy" in his later years, (b. August 18, 1800 in Abbeville, South Carolina, d. March 4, 1888, Carroll County) was the son of Wil-

Hart Town Environs

liam (b. 1768, Virginia, d. 1838, Gwinnett County). James' mother was Isabel Cowan Baskin (b. 1768, Abbeville, South Carolina, d. 1820 Gwinnett County).

James married Henrietta Williams Harrison on March 17, 1825 in Gwinnett County. Henrietta (b. June 1800, Laurens, South Carolina, d. January 10, 1872, Carroll County). They moved to the area that became known as Hickory Level in Carroll County in 1825, even before the county had been named. James named this unsettled, wilderness area Hickory Level because of the flat terrain and the large amount of hickory trees. He donated land for the Concord United Methodist Church. He was the first postmaster in this developing community.

He and his wife, Henrietta, lived and raised their family here. They are shown on the 1830, 1840, 1850, 1860, 1870 and 1880 Federal Census Records for Carroll County. Their children were:

1) William Jasper (b. January 19, 1826);
2) James Lawrence (b. July 22, 1827);
3) Mary Ann Elizabeth (b. March 25, 1829);
4) Virginia J. (b. November 14, 1830);
5) Walter Colquit (b. October 18, 1832);
6) Margaret J. (b. January 22, 1835);
7) Clark W. (b. December 26, 1836);
8) Martha (b. 1839);
9) Sarah E. (b. July 24, 1841);
10) Thomas W. (b. 1844).

James Baskin's wife, Henrietta died in 1872 and was buried at Concord United Methodist Church Cemetery.

James married again, on November 4, 1872, in Carroll County to Rhoda Chandler (b. 1835, d. 1899).

A testimony by James:

I, James Baskin of Hickory Level, Carroll County, Georgia was born in Abbeville District South Carolina in 1800, 18th day of August. Was moved to Jackson County, Georgia the same year. Grew up to manhood and when about 20 years of age professed religion, joined the Methodist Church in September, 1821. I was appointed class leader at Mt. Zion Church, Gwinnett County, Georgia in 1821. In 1825, I moved to Carroll County and was again appointed Class leader. (I) Was licensed to exhort in 1835, P. Glover, preacher in Charge. Was licensed to preach July 1837, Rev. J. W. Glenn, P. E. I was set apart for the office Parson in the Methodist Episcopal Church South the 18th day of December 1846, by Bishop James O. Andrew at Athens, Georgia on December 18th, 1857, I was set apart and ordained Elder by Bishop Hubbard H. Kavannaugh, at Rome, Georgia. Signed: James Baskin

P. S. This is for my Grand-daughter, Alice Baskin Turner.

Reverend James Baskin

Reverend James Baskin died in 1888 at Hickory Level and was buried in the Concord United Methodist Church Cemetery. He was a friend to humanity. A devoted husband, a kind father and a true Christian.

David Nelson Brock

David N. Brock (b. June 7, 1829, Georgia, d. March 17, 1899, Meredith, Henderson County Texas) was the son of Waddy Brock and Sarah Easterwood Brock. Waddy Brock was born in Kentucky and fought in the War of 1812, enlisting when he was in Tennessee. Sarah Easterwood Brock (b. 1802, South Carolina, d. March 11, 1877, Georgia).

In 1852, David Brock married Mary Elizabeth Davis in Tennessee. Mary (b. November 19, 1833, Tennessee, d. June 6, 1910, Tolbert Texas).

David N. Brock

On the 1850 Federal Census David Brock lived in *Division 11* Carroll County with Martha Brock and Sarah Watson. He was 22 and a laborer. In 1860, he and Mary lived in District 6 and his occupation was a miller. His real estate value was $200.

On June 22, 1861, David N. Brock enlisted June 22, 1861 as a Private in Company I, 19th Georgia Volunteers Infantry Army of Tennessee Confederate States of America, the Gold Diggers. He was captured at Winchester, Virginia on December 2, 1862 and paroled there on December 4, 1862. Records show that he was paid at James Island, South Carolina for cummutation of rations on December 17, 1863 for the time he was on sick furlough from March 4 to April 3, 1863 and from June 20 to July 19 1863.

In 1870 The Federal Census of Carroll County at Villa Rica list his occupation as a miller and his real estate value was $400. The 1880 Federal Census shows him in District 649 Villa Rica. David was 51; Mary was 48 and his occupation was that of farmer.

David and Mary Brock had eleven children, ten boys and one daughter:
1) George William Brock (b. December 2, 1852, Carroll County);
2) John Cannon (b. 1856, Alabama);
3) James Waddy (b. April 5, 1857, Villa Rica);
4) Aaron Madison (b. May 4, 1859, Carroll County);
5) Sarah Jane (b. 1861, Carroll County);
6) Marion Jackson (b. June 4, 1866, Carroll County);
7) Robert Lee (b. March 9, 1869, Carroll County);
8) Eli Walker (b. December 12, 1870, Carroll County);

9) Charles Albert (b. March 17, 1872, Carroll County);
10) Thomas Franklin (b. September 30, 1873, Bibb County, Georgia);
11) Rufus Wilburn Brock (b. October 20, 1875, Carroll County.

The oldest son of this family, George William Brock was shown on the 1900 Federal Census Record as living in Henderson County, Texas. Since David, the father, died in Texas in 1899, and so many of the other sons died in Texas, most of the family members likely moved there between 1880 and 1899. Mary, the mother of this large family, died in Texas also.

James Fulton Bryce

James Bryce (b. January 18, 1806, North Carolina d. February 23, 1880, Carroll County) was the son of William Bryce, (b. December 12, 1773, Irvine, Ayrshire, Scotland, d. 1841, Carroll County, Georgia) and his wife Mary Ellen Orr (b. June 4, 1774, Ayr, Ayrshire, Scotland, d. June 1, 1841, Carroll County, Georgia).

On May 14, 1829 in Carroll County, James F. Bryce married Eleanor "Nellie" Ray Sharp, the daughter of George S. Sharp. Nellie (b. November 25, 1812, Morgan County, d. February 17, 1879 in Carroll County).

James and Nellie Bryce had thirteen children:
1) Sarah Jane Bryce Smith (b. February 16, 1830, d. 1911);
2) William Hiram Bryce (b. February 19, 1832, d. 1874);
3) James Young Bryce (b. March 31, 1834, d. 1892) became a minister;
4) Mary Eleanor Bryce Wynn (b. May 6, 1836, d. 1880);
5) George Robert Bryce (b. May 23, 1838, d. 1908);
6) Private John Fulton Bryce (b. December 2, 1840, d. November 25, 1934);
7) Nancy Ann Elisa Bryce Aldridge (b. March 21, 1843, d. 1909);
8) Emily Margaret Bryce Chambers (b. November 15, 1846, d. 1899);
9) Felix Sloman Chalmbers Bryce (b. July 5, 1849, d. 1931);
10) Henrietta Mahala Bryce Shell (b. August 5, 1851, d. 1945);
11) Parthenia Ann Elizabeth Bryce Greer (b. December 18, 1853, d. 1944);
12) Ira Bascomb Bryce (b. April 28, 1855, d. 1934);
13) Joseph Bryce (b. Mar 22, 1857, died as an infant in 1857).

James E. Bryce and Family

James Bryce was listed on the Carroll County Federal Census in 1830; in 1840 he was listed in District 642 Carroll County; in 1850, he was in *Division 11* Carroll County where his real estate value was $1800; in 1860, he and his family lived in District 6 Hickory Level and his occupation was Methodist Clergyman.

August 28, 1863 James Bryce enlisted as Corporal, Company E, 9th Georgia Battalion, Cavalry, State Guard, Confederate States Army in Buchanan to serve under Captain W. J. Walton. He was 57. His son, John Fulton Bryce served as Private Company F, Cobb's Legion Infantry in the Confederate States of America.

On the 1870 Census for Carroll County, James Bryce and his family are shown as living in Hickory Level, his real estate value was $600 and his personal estate value was $700.

James died in 1880; Nellie died in 1879; both were buried at the Old Villa Rica Cemetery in Villa Rica.

Thomas H. Chandler

Thomas Chandler (b. February 24, 1804, Franklin County, d. October 31, 1890, Carrollton) was the son of Joseph Chandler (b. 1769, d. 1853) and Sarah Farmer (b. 1770, d. 1851).

Thomas Chandler moved to Carroll County in 1827 from Franklin County, Georgia. He married Mary Bell Jackson on November 16, 1829; she was also from Franklin County, born there on December 22, 1805. Thomas was the first lawyer in Carroll County and lived first at Old Carrollton near Sand Hill until 1830. He bought Land Lot 167 in District 6 at the intersection of Hart Town.

Thomas Chandler also bought Land Lot 129 in the 10th district on which part of Carrollton is situated. He built a small cabin near a spring which became a park.

He went to work farming and practicing law and early on was elected Tax Receiver of the County. His duties required him to ride from one end and one side of the county to the other and travel Indian trails which were almost the only kind of roads at that time. He rode from the line of the Cherokee County to West Point, Georgia and from the Alabama line to the Chattahoochee River. His salary per year was thirty dollars. There were only about 600 voters in the county and the population was 3,400.

Thomas Chandler was a member of the Legislature in 1843. He owned a considerable amount of land when the Civil War began in 1861.

He enlisted as Private on June 24, 1861; discharged, disability, June 9, 1862; appointed 2d Corporal of Co. B, 7th Regiment Confederate Cavalry, June 16 1862. The roll for August 1864, last on file, shows him present. During the war, Thomas served with General Robert Toombs; they were close friends ever after the Civil War.

Thomas and Mary had three sons:
1) Marion who married Francis Stephens;
2) Newton J. who married Harriet E. Chandler;
3) Thomas H. who married Emma Josephine Peteet and went to Texas in 1866.
Thomas' daughters were:

Hart Town Environs

4) Dorothy who married J. Gilbert Wright;
5) Rhoda who married a Bledsoe then James Baskin;
6) Martha who married Hiram Miles Mathas;
7) Mary Ann who married Joseph William Thrower;
8) Harriet "Hattie who married Thomas W. Baskin.

Mary Bell Jackson Chandler died September 12, 1880 in Carroll County. "Uncle Tom" died on October 31, 1890 at the age of 86 years. He was always a temperate and moral man. He was buried in a Carrollton Cemetery in Carroll County.

Edmond "Walter" Dorough

Walter Dorough (b. March 12, 1882, Heard County) was the son of George Herschel Dorough (b. February 29, 1856, Carroll County, d. April 8, 1886, Carroll County). Walter's mother was Lucinda Caroline Baughman Dorough (b. April 6, 1852, Carrollton, d. November 12, 1930, Carroll County).

On the 1900 U. S. Federal Census Record, Walter, 18, was living in Carroll County, District 649 and was listed as single, hired hand.

Walter married Florence Eufala Taylor on December 1, 1901 in Carroll County. She was the daughter of Private John Walker Glenn Taylor (b. 1840, d. 1900) and Theodosia Carolyn McEachen Taylor (b. 1846, d. 1934) of Carroll County. She was the granddaughter of William Harvey Taylor (b. 1798, d. 1873) and Eliza H. McKinley Taylor (b. 1805, d. 1884).

Walter and Florence lived on a large farm on Hickory Level Road, (Villa Rica Road, later called Dorough Road). They are shown there on the 1910, 1920, 1930 and 1940 Census. They raised nine children:

1) Florene (b. October 19, 1903, d. 1996) married Lovick Eugene McWhorter;
2) John Wesley (b. May 15, 1907, d. 1958) married Hattie B.;
3) Edmond Herschel (b. May 5, 1909, d. 1982) married Willie Elsie Henry;
4) George Preston (b. November 15, 1911, d. 1998);
5) Carrie Louella "Lula" (b. January 2, 1913) married Arling Williams;
6) Robert Merle (b. October 30, 1918, d. 1956);
7) Carrie Lee (b. November 27, 1919, d. 1951) married a Brown.
8) Maggie Lee (b. November 27, 1919, d. 1951);
9) Charles Grady (b. January 23, 1928) married Virginia Hembree.

The land lot that has been associated with the Dorough family for several generations was granted to William Harvy Taylor in 1836. The property remained in the Taylor family until it was deeded to Florence Taylor Dorough, wife of Edmond Walker Dorough, in 1907. The Dorough family lived at Hickory Level on this farm of 196.31 acres of the original land lot of 202 1/2 acres. The property has been farmed continuously since it was granted to William Harvy Taylor in 1836. The main crops were wheat and oats, but other crops, such as peanuts and cotton, were produced.

Three tenant families lived in the Dorough place and helped on the farm. Six to eight mules were used to aid in the farming process. It was during this time

Dorough Round Barn

that many of the outbuildings were constructed. The farmhouse and other structures created a farm complex which enabled the Dorough family to successfully operate a dairy and farm.

But the "heyday" of the farm existed at the time the Round Barn was built in 1917. Edmond was encouraged by the Carroll County Agent to began a dairy barn. In 1916, he sought the easiest method of tending a herd of dairy cattle. Following a trip to Arkansas, he hired Floyd Lovell to build a "Round Barn" in an attempt to introduce new methods of increasing productivity of dairy products. This unique design allowed for more utilized floor space and a central silo which would enable the farmer to store large amounts of feed in a small, ready accessible location.

The Round Barn construction cost was $7,500; and the additional cost of a silo in the center. The round barn was a fourteen-sided structure of oak board-and-batten construction. The two-story structure had a diameter of ninety feet and was forty feet tall. The foundation was of reinforced, poured concrete. The 150 ton silo was held together with steel rods. On the first floor, feed bins circled the silo and stalls for dairy cattle were located on the outer wall.

The Dorough Dairy Operation began shortly thereafter in 1917. Farming had continued during the construction of the Round Barn and silo, but then in 1919 the boll weevil ruined all but three bales of cotton. Soon the farming was secondary to the dairy business which existed until about 1925-26. The dairy operation failed because long hauls to the creamery were not practical, dirt roads became impossible during rainy season, and the winter season proved to be hazardous to the infant dairy operation.

Hart Town Environs

The farmhouse located a short distance from the barn was a nineteenth-century, one-and-one-half story frame structure with the rear of the house built in the early nineteenth century. The roof was pitched with a high central gable and the central entrance was flanked on each side by windows. A shed porch, supported by four square wood columns, was attached to the front of the house. Also located on the property was over the years: a carriage house behind the farmhouse, privy behind that, a tenant house, a small barn and a well house. In the earlier years, several other tenant houses and barns were on the property. At one time the property belonged to Edmond Hershel Dorough, (1909-1982) Walter and Florence Dorough's son.

In 1980 the Round Barn was placed on the National Register of Historical Places. Neither the round barn nor the early nineteenth-century home exist today.

Book C, Page 2 Campbell County. 14 Mar 1836. HENRY PEEPLES, Jackson County, to WILLIAM H. TAYLOR. $500. Land lot #72, 6th dist. Carroll County. 202 1/2 acres. Attest: John McLeuratt, T. W. Garner, J. P. 29 March 1836.

Asa Griggs

Asa Griggs (b. December 1827, Putnam County, d. 1900, Chambers County, Alabama) was the son of Judge William Griggs and Louise C. Griggs. He was already attending doctor courses when he married Rebecca Elizabeth Davenport in Heard County in 1848. He moved to Carroll County with his family. His neighbors were the Witcher's, Larkin Davis, and Martha Candler and family in the Hickory Level District.

He became the Principal of the Villa Rica Male and Female Institute when he was 23. This was an Academy before the Castle on the Hill. It was opened for only a very short period of time before Asa Griggs left to attend to his studies.

Shown in Abstracts: Page 438, Book E, 25 July 1850: PARKER M. RICE to ASA W. GRIGGS. $700.00. East side land lot #193, 6th district Carroll County, bounded on the west by S. CANDLER, north by MRS. JARNIGAN, east by Mr. WICKS and south by the town of Villa Rica. Also four town lots, #1, #2, #4, #6, containing 34 acres. Attest: S. H. Davis, Lamb W. McGarity, Henry S. Chance J.P. 6 Aug 1850.

Asa Griggs was educated at the University of Georgia and graduated from the University of Tennessee. He was a professor at Oglethorpe Medical College, Savannah, Georgia. He filled the surgery position there as well. He also filled the "chair" of the Medical Peachtree in Atlanta Medical College until 1878; he was made Emeritus of the same college with the honor he shared until a year before his death. A year before the Civil War, his wife died in 1860 at West Point. He remarried a few months later to Lois McCants so his children would be looked after.

As the Civil War started, he noticed the shortage in doctors. He enlisted and was appointed Surgeon of 33 Regiments of Alabama in 1861; then he was promoted to Chief Surgeon of Central Hall Hospital in Atlanta, Georgia. Afterward transferred to the command of General Forrest at Murfreesboro, Tennessee.

When the war was over, he stayed in Alabama and for 20 years he held his practice in Chambers, Alabama until he became ill. He died in 1900.

Wright Majors

Wright Majors, the younger brother of William and James Majors, was born in Jefferson City, Tennessee on December 5, 1805. He came to Carroll County Georgia about 1828, lived on Land Lot #105 about four miles south Hart Town, attended Concord Methodist Church at Hickory Level for a period of time, died about two years later, an untimely death.

He died in Carroll County in 1830, age 25, and was shown on the 1830 Census. His wife was Susan Upton Majors; they had five children. Their children were Calvin, Caroline, James M., Wright, & William W. A bond of $1,300 was given by James Upton, Thomas J. Bryce and Alexander Hogan. On September 3, 1844, James Upton was the guardian for the children. The cause of his death is unknown.

Wright Majors, deceased, estate: Return through 1843 by James Upton and James Majors, Administrators. Mentioned: James Upton, Upton & McPherson, Y. J. Long, James & W. Bryce, J. Long, Hogan T. Roddy, Hiden, McRea, Walker, Monk, John Robinson, Mr. Moony, Benjamin Merrell, James Mehaffey, J. S. Boggess, John Whisenhunt, James Baskin, M. McRea, James Poe, J. Gilley, E. McPherson, S. Mulwee, J. J. Young, D. Hiden, H. Mehaffey, J. Coltharp, A. Hogan, Jas. Coltharp, W. N. Davis, Jas. Baskin, Irwin Pollard, J. D. Chapman, E. P. Hogan, Widow Majors.

Book G, page 299, Carroll County, 26 Sep 1851. GREEN HICKS, guardian of the person and property of WRIGHT W. MAJORS, a minor to ANDREW J. BUTRAM, highest bidder. $203.50. 83 acres land lot #105, 6th district Carroll County. Estate of WRIGHT MAJORS, deceased. Attest: Willis Smith, John W. Palmer, J. P.

Francis Marion Richards

Francis Marion Richards (b. 1803, Tennessee, d. February 27, 1859, Carroll County) was the son of John Richards (b. 1774, died 1838) and Elizabeth Fowler (b. 1780, d. 1855). Francis married Angelina Mahala Hale (Hail) in 1823 in Tennessee. Angeline was born in 1805.

Francis Marion Richards migrated from Tennessee to Alabama, and came to Carroll County around 1827. He was shown on a juror's list for inferior court in 1827 and 1829. Court documents indicate that he was very civic minded. He served on the petit court and the grand jury in 1829 and 1833. He was a road commissioner in Carroll County in 1831, 1833 and 1834.

Francis Richards was shown on the

Angelina Richards
Courtesy Pauline Roberts

Francis Marion Richards, Jr.
Courtesy Pauline Roberts

1830 Federal Census for Carroll County. In 1840 the U. S. Federal Census shows him in District 649; in 1850 he was in *Division 11*; and in 1860, 6th District Hickory Level all in Carroll County, Georgia.

Francis and Angeline had thirteen children, the first four of whom were born in Alabama. The rest were born in Carroll County, Georgia.

1) Arminda Amanda (b. circa 1823, Alabama, d. 1880). She married on April 19, 1840 in Carroll County to James C. Leathers, (b. 1820, South Carolina, d. 1882).

2) William Milburn (b. December 7, 1826, d. March 19, 1910) married Margaret Mary Williams on December 18, 1845 in Carroll County. Margaret (b. June 15, 1834, d. May 30, 1904, Carroll County).

3) Elizabeth A. (b. 1828) married James H. Roberts on March 10, 1844 in Carroll County.

4) Susan Idelia (b. May 1830, d. 1910, Sand Hill, Carroll County) married in Carroll County to Thomas Willis (b. September 1848, d. July 21, 1880, Carroll County).

5) John W. (b. 1831, d. December 15, 1880) married Alice Summerline on March 17, 1867 in Carroll County.

6) Eliza Jane (b. February 01, 1833, d. circa 1910) married Isaac Crayton Hicks on December 10, 1848 in Carroll County.

7) James C. Richards (b. circa 1835) married Sarah C. Hesterly on September 12, 1856 in Carroll County. He enlisted as a Private on March 4, 1862 with Company I, 19th Regiment Georgia Volunteer Infantry "Villa Rica Gold Diggers" Confederate States Army, Carroll County. He was captured at Frederick, Maryland on September 12, 1862 then exchanged at Aiken's Landing, Virginia on November 10, 1862. He was later killed at the Battle at Fredericksburg, Virginia, on December 13, 1862.

8) Francis Marion Richards Jr. (b. January 18, 1837). He married Mary C. circa 1865. He enlisted on July 23, 1861 at Benton, Arkansas, as a Private in the Confederate States Army, Company E, 11th Arkansas Infantry. He was captured April 8, 1862 at Island 10, Missouri and sent to Camp Douglas in Illinois and exchanged at Vicksburg, Mississippi on September 4, 1862. He served until the end of the war. He died August 28, 1931 and was buried at the Whitesburg City Cemetery in Carroll County, Georgia.

9) King Henry Richards (b. January 15, 1839).

10) Amanda V. "Eva" (b. circa 1840, d. 1910). On December 27, 1861, in Carroll County, she married Sterling Montgomery Hesterly (b. October 15, 1841, Coweta

County, d. Texas, 1914).

11) Emily Mahala (b. March 15, 1840) married Richard Carnes on September 29, 1853 in Carroll County. Emily died in 1917 and was buried at Bearden, Arkansas.

12) Joseph Denman was born circa 1843 and died December 13, 1862 at the Battle of Fredericksburg, Virginia. The family history was that Joseph died the same day as his brother James C. (above), also in the battle of Fredericksburg.

13) Andrew Jackson Richards was born circa 1847. He married Nancy Odessa "Susie" Summerlin. Andy Richards owned a circus and came to the Carroll County area periodically to put on shows and visit relatives. This family of the Richard's Brothers Circus performers put down just below New Georgia Baptist Church in a clump of trees in Paulding County.

Andrew Jackson Richards
Courtesy Pauline Roberts

There were four generations of Richards Brothers' Circus performers—husbands, wives, and children—from this family who traveled the U. S. putting on shows. After they trained animals for the Ringling Brothers, this last generation settled down in Texas. Andrew Jackson Richards died in 1934.

Francis Marion acquired land in Paulding County (eighty acres) and owned a great deal of land in Carroll County. Beginning in 1832, he acquired land near Ithica Gin Road in Carroll County, Georgia and built a large home there. Abstracts below show that he acquired 709 acres in District 6, Carroll County in the Ithica Gin Road and Hickory Level area, between December 1832 and March 1849.

He was a farmer, a businessman, and probably a bonded whiskey distiller. He built a store and a grist mill. He died at age 56 on 27 February 1859.

After he died, William Hembee was hired to administer the estate and did so for ten years. Angeline Richards also took over the function of running their large farm on Ithica Gin Road after her husband died. She passed away seventeen years later in 1876.

Francis Marion was buried at the Richards' Cemetery, on Ithica Gin Road near Van Wert Road.

Book B, Page 367 Jasper County, 20 Dec 1832. HENRY ELLIS to FRANCIS M. RICHARDS. $700.00. Land lot #69, 6th dist. Carroll County. 202 1/2 acres. Attest: Green B. Walker, Drury Wilkins, J.P. 20 May 1834.

Book D, Page 148 Carroll County, 26 Dec 1837. JAMES A. ATCHISON, Troup County to FRANCIS M. RICHARDS. $500. Land lot #91, 6th dist. Carroll County.

Attest: Edward Haynes, William Haynes.

Book D, Page 348 Meriwether County, 19 Jan 1838. ISHAM A. FREEMAN to FRANCIS RICHARDS. $150. 1/2 land lot #70, 6th dist. Carroll County. Attest: A. J. McAfee, Lewis Williams, J.P.; 27 Oct 1842.

Book E, Page 189 Carroll County, 13 Jan 1844. SIMEON FREEMAN, Newton County to FRANCIS M. RICHARDS. $170.00. Half of land lot #70, 6th dist. Carroll County. 101 1/4 acres. Attest: Francis M. Little, Thos Rabun, J.P. 25 Dec 1844.
Book E, Page 225 Carroll County, 20 Mar 1849. BENJAMIN C. BURNS to FRANCIS M. RICHARDS. $200.00. Land lot #60, 6th dist. Carroll County. Attest: Wm. W. Merrell, J. C. Benson.

7

The Civil War Affects Families: Candler, Chambers & Haynes

*Company I was organized under a large oak
tree in front of Dr. Slaughter's Home (later S. T. Haynes' home).*

A Nine-Year-Old Boy in a Covered Wagon
J. A. Roberson, Centennial Edition of the *Carroll County Times*, Thursday, October 13, 1927:

> It was a drab November day in 1860 when first I set foot on Carroll County soil, coming with my father and family from DeKalb County, Georgia, a distance of about 70 miles in an ox-drawn caravan of bow-covered wagons loaded with our household effects, and followed by a herd of cattle, a drove of hogs and two cur dogs. The 70 mile journey was negotiated in about four days.
> My first impression was that Carroll was a wild and wooly region and to a considerable degree it was just that. On our journey almost through it, we had occasion jocularily to name a number of places by some odd sight, or by some eccentrictity observed among the scattered inhabitants. One settlement, as I recall, we gave the name of 'suck-bully' because a little bull yearling tried to follow our cattle and the lady of the house ran after it calling "suck-bully!" "suck-bully!!"
> My father and mother daily preceded the caravan in the family "carryall" and carried the baskets of rations that had been prepared in advance of starting. They drove ahead each day and established both noon and night camps. My father cut logs of wood and built big fires and bought water, and my mother boiled large pots of strong coffee and had it ready to refresh the other travelers upon their arrival with the caravan. It was at the last noon camp of the journey that I saw the first thing in Carroll County that especially pleased me. That thing was a large cotton

basket full of red mellow apples which my father bought for the travelers from old Mr. Matthis, whose home was first beyond the creek a few miles east of Carrollton. It was the first thing I saw waiting on us as we approached the last noon camp and I was the first to get to it, for I was as hungry as any nine year old boy can get. I ate and ate and a few hours thereafter I ached and ached. That was my first Carroll county pain, and I didn't like it then, nor have I yet learned to like it. . .

Let me say that our method of traveling in those days, though primitive, was by no means unusual, indeed, we had no other. There were no railroads in the county then, nor highways. The best roads consisted of two beaten ruts with grass growing between. They served to lead us to our destination if we could negotiate the hills, scramble over the rocks, mud holes, and stumps. . .

Well, after lunching on cold boiled ham, cheese, eggs, coffee and bread at our last noon camp at the creek, we set out on the last lap of our toilsome journey, and in the course of time, rolled into Carrollton, then a kind of ramshackled frontier village, composed, in large part, of log huts with sagging doors, and looking considerably weather beaten. I thought it was a hick town, and it was because there was a man in the south end corner of the public square proclaiming it. He was as drunk as a 'billed owl' and said 'hick' each time he opened his mouth! . . .

Six miles further to the west brought us to our destination well after darkness had settled upon us. To save my life, I could not get enthusiastic about our new home! It just seemed to me that there were better countries on this earth where we might as well have moved and I had the nerve to tell my father so! He replied 'Go bring me a turn of wood to put on the fire!' I went.

J. A. Roberson tells of the coming of the Civil War:

J. A. Roberson lived in Carroll County for 35 years. The *Carroll County Times*, Thursday, October 13, 1927 published an article by J. A. Roberson:

The following year, 1861, rumblings of the Civil War began and in a short time, soldiers were seen marching, marching. Carroll County sent forth her valiant sons to the slaughter, which drew nearer and nearer until eventually by 1864, the alternately rising dust from the marching columns of friend and foe was practically perpetual. Sorrow and wailing was everywhere. Even defenseless Carrollton fell a victim to the vindictive torch of relentless federal soldiers who were brave and chivalrous enough to burn a bark shelter from over a sick woman. Really, the future of town or county did not exist in prospect. As old Joe Harper said, "everything was terribly batter-whanged."

But eventually there dawned a day of promise. Carrollton began to

Hart Town Environs

slowly rise from the ashes and the county began to discover a star of hope. The sufferings and deprivations endured during war times had taught the people many lessons in economy—even that irish potatoes can be eaten without salt. An unselfish community spirit began to grow and the people went to work with a will to repair the damage and recover their homes. The Carroll County which to me had seemed wild and wooly was being redeemed from under such odium. Carroll County which had once been a band of horse thieves, known as "The Pony Club," developed a citizenry that was known for its honesty and uprightness.

The churches and school houses in pioneer days were constructed of split logs and seated with the same kind of slabs into which holes were bored and pieces of saplings driven for legs, which tar oozed out to stick a boy fast to his business. These have long ago been supplanted by neat frame buildings, clad in immaculate white, and significantly proclaim the advancement of an enlightened citizenry.

It was a mistake that Carroll County did not begin to conserve the wonderful natural resources so abundantly distributed throughout the county.

I remember when there were herds of nimble-footed deer (that) could be seen bounding through the open forests of the finest timber, and wild turkeys could be seen in large flocks. Other small game, such as birds, squirrels, etc. were abundant everywhere. All were ruthlessly destroyed in the main for no more than the doubtful pleasure of shooting them. Now we have in their stead the boll weevil and numerous other pests which that same would have fed upon to produce more game.

The "Gold Diggers"

Gold Diggers was the nickname for the men of Company I, 19th Georgia Regiment during The Civil War. This was an appropriate nickname since members of Company I came from the gold mining town of Villa Rica.

Company I was organized under a large oak tree in front of S. T. Haynes home (33°45'16.50"N 84°56'23.46"W) (now at the intersection of Punkintown and Dallas Highway, #61) in Old Villa Rica, with John T. Chambers serving as Captain. The company mustered into the Confederate cause in June 22, 1861, as part of the Nineteenth Georgia Infantry Regiment C. S. A. with John T. Chambers serving as Captain. The 19th Georgia Infantry companies were raised in Henry, Jackson, Coweta, Carroll, Mitchell, and Bartow Counties comprising of 900 men. The unit was sent to Virginia and placed in the Potomac District. In 1861 Company I was sent with the 19th to Virginia, where a measles epidemic spread throughout the regiment. During the war, it served under the command of Generals W. Hampton, Archer, and Colquitt. It was in Hoke's Division Anderson's Core.

In 1862 the 19th fought in the following battles: Seven Pines, Mechanicsville, Richmond, Cedar Mountain, Second Manassas, Antietam, Sharpsburg, Warrenton and Fredericksburg. The 19th Georgia Infantry fought in many battles, then moved to Charleston, S. Carolina, and later Florida where it took part in the conflict at Olustee.

In 1863 the 19th Regiment was assigned to the famous "Colquitt Brigade" and fought at Chancellorsville. In 1864, the 19th and other Georgia Regiments headed south to Florida. In was in Northern Florida, where the 19th along with other battled-hardened Georgia Regiments earned for Brigadier General Colquitt the nickname of "Hero of Olustee" for defeating the Northern Troops at the Battle of Ocean Pond. John T. Chambers mustered out on April 26, 1865 as a Captain Assistant Quarter Master.

In April, 1864, the 19th regiment returned to Virginia and continued the fight at Drewry's Bluff and Cold Harbor and in the Petersburg lines, south and north of the James River. This regiment lost 32 killed and 157 wounded during the Seven Days' Battles, 13 killed and 76 wounded in the Maryland Campaign, and 3 killed and 40 wounded at Chancellorsville. It sustained 96 casualties at Olutee Florida.

In 1865 the unit participated in the North Carolina Campaign and surrendered with the Army of Tennessee.

Carroll County furnished 2,560 soldiers for the Confederate Army, more than 50% of the white male population.

Samuel Charles Candler

Samuel Charles Candler, Sr. was born December 6, 1809 in Columbia County, Georgia, the son of Daniel Candler who was born in 1778 and died in September 1816. His mother, Sarah "Sally" Slaughter, was born in 1784, the daughter of Samuel Slaughter from Wilkes County, Georgia, who had served as a Revolutionary Soldier; she died June 1, 1865 in Villa Rica, Georgia.

Samuel Candler

Samuel Candler's father died when he was seven and he was raised by a relative, Ignatius W. Few. Though Samuel had a large extended family, he learned to make his own way in the world.

Samuel Charles Candler married on December 8, 1833 in Cherokee County, Georgia to Martha Bernetta Beall, the oldest daughter of Noble Peyton Beall (1799-1878) and Justiana Dickinson Hooper (1802-1880). Martha Bernetta was born on December 6, 1819 in Franklin County, Georgia.

After Samuel and Martha married, they lived for short time in Cherokee County where Samuel served in the Georgia Legislature representing Cherokee County in 1833.

When Samuel and Martha moved to Carroll County, they brought with them a wedding gift from her father: an Indian pony named Picayune. The young Candler couple built their family home two miles to the northeast of Hart Town on land lot #196. The site of the former Candler home is today at the east end of Lake Paradise Road, one-fourth mile down from Highway 101.

Samuel had 300 acres watered by several streams. It was the ideal land to farm. They first built a "dog-trot" style log cabin on the crest of the hill in a grove of oak and hickory trees, with large rooms that opened onto a hallway. There were large porches on the front and back of the cabin. Following the custom of the time, one large room, warmed by a fireplace in winter, doubled as a dining room and sitting room. The kitchen was a separate building.

They raised eleven children, eight sons and three daughters:

Martha and John Candler

1) Milton Anthony Candler (b. January 11, 1837, d. 1909) became a lawyer;

2) Ezekiel "Zekie" Samuel Candler (b. December 6, 1838, d. 1909) who also became a lawyer;

3) Florence "Fanny" Julia Candler (b. December 22, 1842, d. 1926);

4) Sarah "Jessie" Justina Candler (b. January 14, 1845, d. 1921);

5) William "Willie" Beall Candler (b. January 28, 1847, d. 1928);

6) Noble Daniel Candler (b. January 29, 1849, d. 1887);

7) Elizabeth "Lizzie" Frances Candler (b. July 4, 1850, d. 1922);

8) Asa Griggs Candler (b. December 30, 1851, d. 1929) was the inventor of Coca-Cola and founder of the Coca Cola Company;

9) Samuel "Charlie" Charles Candler, Jr. (b. March 13, 1855, d. 1911);

10) Reverend Warren Akin "King Shorty" Candler, Sr. (b. August 23, 1857, d. 1941) who became a bishop in the Methodist Church and was President of Emory College at Oxford that was later moved to Atlanta and became Emory University;

11) John Slaughter Candler (b. October 22, 1861, d. 1941) who was a Judge for the State Supreme Court of Georgia. All of their children but the first son was born in Carroll County while they lived at the old home place.

The Georgia Federal Census shows the family resided in District 642, Carroll County in 1840; *Division 11*, Carroll County in 1850; District 2 in 1860 and Villa

Martha Candler and Seven of Her Sons

Rica, Carroll County in District 2 in 1870. In 1850, Samuel C. Candler was listed as a Merchant with a real estate value of $2,000. In 1860, his real estate value was $5,700 and personal estate value was $13,250. In 1870, he was listed as a farmer with a real estate value of $2,500 and personal estate value of $3,500.

Samuel C. Chandler served as sheriff of Carroll County and served two terms as state senator from his district in Carroll County. Samuel was an early postmaster in Old Town.

When Gold was found in the Villa Rica area, it was acceptable for landowners, to build a house and farm the land, but it was permissible for them to sell the mineral rights to a person who could then mine for gold. All shared in the use of the land as long as the farmer stayed clear of the mining.

Samuel Chandler was an agent for the stockholders of those who sold mineral rights. Acting as the agent for a group of Macon investors who leased out gold prospecting rights on land they owned in the area, Candler received ten percent of the rents he collected.

Samuel was one of the very earliest merchants in the area. He and his son W. B. Candler were cotton merchants in Old Town. Candler borrowed $1500 to open a store in the town and was successful enough to repay the sum promptly. This general store—Villa Rica's first— usually contained $2,000 in stock. Miners came to the store with gold dust that they packed in goose quills for safe-keeping; thus the storekeeper became a small gold dealer. Through these and other investments, Samuel

Candler became one of the most prosperous men of his region. When the railroad came through in 1883, Samuel C. and his son W. B. Candler literally moved the store building farther toward the new Villa Rica. With several partners, he developed the site that became the town of Villa Rica.

Because he could afford the best acreage, he undertook commercial agriculture and speculated in land: in 1847 Samuel owned 7,800 acres in Carroll and Paulding counties.

On the 1864, District 642, Villa Rica, Carroll County, Georgia "Re-Organizing the Georgia Militia" Samuel C. Candler was listed as a 54-year-old farmer.

During the Civil War, the northern troops came to Samuel and Martha's home to arrest him because he was a prominent politician in the area. According to oral history, he and others were hiding in Alden's swamp.

> The family legend entitled *Gr-Gr-Gr-Grandma was a Spitfire* tells that when General Stoneman's Union Cavalry pounded up to the door of the Candler household looking for Samuel Candler, the horse soldiers found Martha Candler instead. When she refused to tell where her husband had fled, the officer in charge asked, "Don't you know I can blow you to hell?"
>
> To which she reportedly replied, "There's not room enough in hell for me; it is too full of (damned) Yankees." She then told the soldiers exactly where they could go and how to get there. Historians say their intent was to arrest him and not to hang him. The soldiers were trying to scare her into revealing his location but to Martha, she was protecting her husband's life.

Samuel C. Candler died November 13, 1873 and was buried at the Hillcrest City Cemetery in Villa Rica. His wife Martha Beall Candler died in July 3, 1897 at Cartersville in Bartow County, Georgia at her daughter's home. She was buried at Hillcrest Cemetery in Villa Rica, also.

Joseph Washington Chambers
Joseph Chambers (b. June 18, 1778, Virginia, d. July 23, 1840, Villa Rica) married circa 1800 to Sarah Elizabeth Moody (b. December 20, 1782, Haw River, Chatham County, North Carolina, d. September 5, 1860, Villa Rica).

> Colonel A. T. Davidson spoke at the Lyceum, Friday Night, November 7, 1890 and said:

> Joseph Chambers, who moved to Georgia about the first of the opening and discovery of the Carroll County gold mines, say about 1831 or '32. He was a man of more than ordinary character, led in public affairs, raised an elegant family for the times; his daughters marrying well. They

were splendid ladies, and their descendants belong to some of the best families in Georgia. His wife was a sister of John and Reuben Moody.

The family manufactured all their wearing apparel, tanned their own leather, made their axes and plows, and, in short, bought nothing from the stores except iron. In fact, they had nothing to buy with. There was but one post office in the county.

All the necessaries of life were procured from the markets in Georgia and South Carolina. It was a three week's trip with a wagon to Augusta, Georgia. For this market the neighborhood would bunch their products, bring their forces together and make trips to Augusta, loaded with bacon, peltries and such other marketable articles as would bear transportation in this simple way. The return for these products was sugar, coffee, salt and molasses and happy was the family on the return of the wagons to be able to have a jug full of New Orleans black molasses; and how happy the children were to meet their fathers and brothers again, and have them recite the many stories of the trip.

It was interesting to see the people meet to get from the wagons their portion of the return load; and happy was the small family that got a half bushel of salt, 50 cents worth of coffee and a gallon of molasses. There was general rejoicing, all going home satisfied and happy, content with their small cargoes, and satisfied that they had enough to do them for the next year or until the next trip. . . . Joseph Chambers, of whom I have spoken, represented the county for three sessions in the legislature.

On February 7, 1832 Allmon—Chambers and Company bought Land Lot #235, 2nd District of Carroll County (now Douglas) for $700. Allmon was most likely Nelson Allmon, Joseph's son-in-law. Joseph's name appeared in Carroll County when he attested the sale of land between Thomas Ruben and John Brooks on October 29, 1832. A few days later on November 25, 1832, Joseph and his son, Jesse Chambers, purchased Land Lot #195, 6th district, Carroll County, except for 60 feet sold to William Dixon, John Sheppard and Albert Tolbert.

Joseph's occupations were miner, farmer and State Senator (Haywood County N. C.). Of Joseph and Sarah's eleven children, all lived to maturity. They were all mentioned in his will. Joseph, realizing his life was short on earth, wrote his will on June 17, 1839, just seven years after arriving at the Villa Rica gold field. His will was recorded July 23, 1840. He was not listed on the 1840 United States Federal Census of Carroll County, but his wife, Sarah Chambers was listed.

Joseph was probably the first person to be buried in the Chambers "Burying Ground" as it was known by for nearly a hundred years. The cemetery was used by other families and grew in size until about 1932 when the City of Villa Rica, Georgia took it over. Today it is known as Hillcrest Cemetery and is the largest cemetery in the Villa Rica area. Sarah and other family members are buried there.

One of the old Chambers home places is thought to be just above the cemetery on the high ground to the south, near the old rock graves at the highest point. After Sarah died in 1860, John T. (her son) as executor, filed a petition with the Ordinary Court in Carroll County for "leave to sell land belonging to the Estate of Joseph Chambers deceased . . . be granted to John T. Chambers the Executor of the last will and said deceased to sell . . . to wit: four tenths of the undivided one fourth of said half of lot of land No. 195 in the 6th District of said county including all mineral and mining privileges therein. The December 1, 1884. R. L. Richards, Ordinary. C. C." This sale probably ended the Chambers mining era.

Joseph Chambers and Sarah Elizabeth Moody Chambers had eleven children: John Thaddus; Jesse H.; Nancy A.: Nicholas F.; William K.; Elizabeth; Mary C.; Hannah; Martha; Joseph W.; and Sarah L. Chambers.

Some of their eleven children are described below.

John Thaddus Chambers

John Thaddeus Chambers was the son of Joseph and Sarah Elizabeth Moody Chambers. John Thaddus (b. April 25, 1803, Jonothan's Creek, Buncombe (now Haywood) County, North Carolina). On April 2, 1829, John T. Chambers married Lucinda Malvina Hawkins in Buncombe County, North Carolina. Lucinda (b. April 25, 1809, Buncombe North Carolina) was the daughter of Benjamin Hawkins (b. 1762, d. February 21, 1827) and Sarah Hannah *Chambers* Hawkins (b. 1769, d. October 15, 1827).

John T. and Lucinda "Lucindy" had two small children when John and his father decided they would all move to the "gold fields" of Carroll County. John was 29 and Lucindy was 23. They would have 12 more children after they arrived in Georgia. When John's family arrived in Carroll County, they probably lived with his father and mother's family on Regan Road on Land Lot 235, 2nd District. Joseph had purchased the 202 1/2 acre plot of land. John and Lucindy later moved to the plot of land just above the present Hillcrest Cemetery at (new) Villa Rica. Abstract land records show Captain John Thaddeus Chambers drew Land in the 1827 Land Lottery in District 11, Lot 13, Carroll County Georgia. At some point he moved and lived on Land Lot #158 District 2 in Villa Rica, about one mile east of Hart Town.

John T. Chambers was a farmer, gold miner, owned a tannery and was a State Senator from Carroll County before the Civil War. On the 1850 Census, his occupation was listed as "mechanic" and real estate value was at $4,000. On the 1860 Census, his real estate value was $7,000 and his personal value was $6,700.

John T. was known as "Honest John." On August 25, 1839, he was appointed Clerk at the New Hope Primitive Church which was three and a half miles east of Hart Town.

From the *Carroll Historical Quarterly*, 1968

John Thaddeus Chambers volunteered for enlistment May 21, 1836 to fight in the Creek Indian War of 1836. He was a member of the 74th Regiment of Georgia Militia Infantry Creek Indian War in Wood's Battal-

John T. & Lucinda Chambers
Courtesy Roger Smith

ion, 3rd Brigade, mustered roll dated May 21, 1836 at Carrollton, Carroll County, Georgia. He served from a Private to a Major. The company consisted of 66 enlisted men and 12 officers and was known as the Thomas Bonner Company. On June 6th, 1836, the first night out of Carrollton going to the war, the regiment camped at Camp Odum, about 4 miles SE of Carrollton (now Blandenburg Road) in the Carroll County, Georgia . . .

It was at Girard, near Columbus, the place named as rendezvous for all the troops, that the army of ten thousand gathered. There were seven companies of infantry organized into a battalion with William Wood of Heard County as Lt. Colonel; John Chambers of Carroll County as Major. John had signed a six month enlistment. The Creeks were defeated and moved out of Georgia in 1836.

The Cherokees were removed in 1838. William W. Merrell volunteered and was appointed 1st Sergeant. His account is from his "Personal Notes of William W. Merrell 1880:

> . . . his school days were then brought to a sudden close by the breaking out of the Seminole & Creek Wars. He volunteered in Capt. William L. Parr's Company of 'Carroll volunteers' as first sergeant about the 1st of June, 1836, to serve in the regiment of Georgia Militia Volunteers commanded by Col. Calhoun, Battalion commanded by Major John T. Chambers. We marched to West Point, Georgia and were there mustered into the United States service for the term of three months and were stationed near that place on the state line of Alabama, where we remained in said service until about the 27th of August, 1836, when we were honorably discharged, for the reason the Government of the U. S. no longer needed our services.

Hart Town Environs

In 1842, John Thaddus Chambers paid taxes on Land Lots #158–101 acres; #159–202 1/2 acres; #162–6 acres; #166–202 1/2 acres and 50 acres of Land Lot #195, all in the 6th district of Carroll County. The 1840, 1850, 1860, 1870 and 1880 United States Federal Census shows the John T. Chambers family living in Villa Rica. At age 58, John Chambers led the 1st volunteers for the Confederates from Carroll County to the Civil War in 1861. He organized Company I known as the "Villa Rica Gold Diggers" and served as their Captain until October 3, 1862 when at age 59 he resigned because of failing health. His rank was listed as Captain Assistant Quarter master.

John and Lucinda Chambers had fourteen children. The 1850 Census lists Mariah Jordan, age eighteen, born in Georgia. She may have been a neice or may have been adopted. Jordan may have been her surname. On the 1860 census there was Abraham who was shown as 15, putting his birth date as 1845. Their children:

1) Nicholas Franklin Chambers (b. March 13, 1830);

2) Joseph Washington Chambers (b. October 20, 1831);

3) Sarah Ann Elizabeth Chambers (b. December 29, 1833);

4) Jesse Harrison Chambers (b. October 27, 1835, Villa Rica, d. March 10, 1918). Jesse lived with his parents and helped farm until he was 25 years old. On April 11, 1861 he married Tabitha Sarah Jane McCarley. She was born December 5, 1839 in Campbell County, the daughter of Moses McCarley and Lydia Yates. Also in 1861 Jesse enlisted in the Confederate States Army from Carroll County. He was assigned to Company G, 19th Ga Volunteer Infantry at Villa Rica. At one time he served in Company E & F, Floyd's 1st State Troops. Jesse left the command October 1, 1864, at Richmond, Virginia, sick with the measles. He was sent to Rome and then home in 1864, as he had typhoid fever.

After the war and on the 1870 census, Jesse and Tabitha Sarah Jane lived in Villa Rica next door to his parents. The 1880 census shows they lived in the 1259 Connor's Militia District in the Dark Corner area of Douglas County. For a while, they lived in Cullman County Alabama. After retiring from farming in Alabama and before 1910, Jesse and Sara returned to the Brownsville Community near the Sweetwater Baptist Church.

Jesse had a cancer on his eye in his later life and lost his sight in that eye. When he passed away in 1918, his obituary read: Mr. Chambers was 82 years old, a Confederate veteran, a Baptist, and a Mason. Tabitha Sarah Jane died February 17, 1931 in the Brownsville Community of Paulding County. Both are buried at the Sweetwater Baptist Church Cemetery.

5) William Posey Chambers (b. October 2, 1837,Villa Rica, d. August 23, 1885, Carroll County.) He married Emily Margaret Bryce on September 12, 1866 in Carroll County. Emily (b. November 15, 1846, Georgia, d. March 13, 1889, Carroll County).

6) Robert W. Chambers (b. August 20, 1839, Villa Rica, d. May 1, 1840). He was buried at the Hillcrest Cemetery.

7) James L. Chambers (b. May 20, 1841, Villa Rica, d. March 25, 1875). On

February 15, 1872 he married Mary Mote; she was born circa 1852.

8) Benjamin D. Chambers (b. August 20, 1842, Villa Rica). He was wounded at Mechanicsville, Virginia on June 26, 1862 while serving in the Civil War; he was in the 4th Georgia Hospital at Richmond, Henrico County, Virginia; he died on July 28, 1862 in Richmond, Virginia.

9) Merrill Columbus Chambers (b. November 28, 1844, Villa Rica). He enlisted as Private with the Villa Rica Gold Diggers on June 22, 1861. He died near Camp Winder, Richmond, Virginia on May 31, 1862.

10) Doctor Porter "Doc" Chambers (b. October 30, 1846, Carroll County, d. February 17, 1929, Carroll County). On December 31, 1868, he married Sarah Josephine "Josie" Yates (b. November 18, 1849, d. December 1, 1934, Carroll County).

11) Milton Rice Chambers (b. June 2, 1848, Villa Rica,) On February 22, 1872, he married Georgia Ann Caroline Yates who was born on February 18, 1852 in Georgia Military District, New Mexico, Carroll County, which is close to Tyus. She died there on February 12, 1890 and was buried at Pleasant Grove Baptist Church Cemetery in Carroll County.

In December 1891, Milton Rice Chambers married Martha Kansas "Mattie" Stephens. Milton Rice Chambers died on October 28, 1927 and was buried at Pleas-

1st row: Blanche Meek, Alta Arnold, Roland Meadows, Clara Clonts, Irene Clonts,
2nd row: Jessie H. Chambers, T. Sarah J. Chambers, Glen C. Clonts (kneeling).
3rd row: Bob Meadows, Lawton Sewell, Grace Meadows, Horance Clonts (baby), Mertie Clonts.
4th row: Foster Meadows, Lem Meek, Will Arnold, Newt Meadows, Hugh Meadows, Georgia Malone.
5th row: Pearl Meadows, Fame Meadows (baby), Bessie Meek, Maybell Meek (baby), Amy Sewell Arnold (2nd wife of Will Arnold), Vene Chambers Meadows, Lou Arnold, Floy Watson.

Courtesy Roger Smith

ant Grove Baptist Church Cemetery in Carroll County.

12) Francis Marion Chambers (b. May 4, 1850, Villa Rica, d. November 13, 1920) married Mary Rosanna "Rosie" Sykes on November 12, 1871. Rosie (b. June 28, 1855, Georgia, d. July 25, 1938) was buried at Pleasant Grove Baptist Church Cemetery. Francis died in Georgia Militia District—New Mexico—Carroll County.

13) Hannah Minerva Chambers (b. June 27, 1852, Villa Rica, d. January 18, 1891, Morgan County, Alabama). On July 27, 1872, she married James "Jim" Knox Polk McCarley (b. September 17, 1849, Villa Rica, d. April 5, 1911, Los Angeles, Los Angeles County, California).

14) Nelson Josephus Chambers (b. March 29, 1854, Villa Rica, d. February 22, 1938, at New Mexico, Carroll County). Nelson was buried at Pleasant Grove Baptist Church Cemetery in Villa Rica. Nelson Chambers never married.

Jesse & Sarah Chambers
Courtesy Roger Smith

Two of John Chambers' sons died from wounds while fighting in the Civil War. John brought them back to Villa Rica, from Virginia, in a wagon, with their bodies covered with lime to be buried in the family cemetery: 5th Sergeant Benjamin D. Chambers and Private Merrill C. Chambers. They were buried in a common grave in the Chambers' Burying Ground now known as Hillcrest Cemetery, Villa Rica.

Lucinda, wife of John Thaddus Chambers died on April 3, 1880 in Villa Rica. Old Captain John Thaddus Chambers died on August 4, 1890 in Villa Rica. Both are buried at the family cemetery, known as the "Chambers' Burying Ground." In 1932, this former "Chambers' Burying Ground" was donated to the city of Villa Rica as a public cemetery and renamed Hillcrest Cemetery.

The old home place was near the old rock graves at the highest point of the present day Hillcrest Cemetery.

Jesse H. Chambers

Jesse H. Chambers, son of Joseph and Sarah T. Chambers, was born on March 13, 1805 in Buncombe County, North Carolina. On October 24, 1829, he married Margaret Woods, in Buncombe County, N. C. She was born about 1810 and died before 1837. His second wife was Catherine D. Steed who was born March 13, 1809 in Georgia.

Jesse H. Chambers bought land on November 1, 1832 in Carroll County with his father Joseph. They moved their families from North Carolina to a Carroll County in order to mine for gold in the newly discovered gold field near Hart Town. On March 23, 1839, Jesse was received into the New Hope Primitive Baptist Church at Villa Rica by emersion [sic]. Catherine was received by letter to New Hope on May 25, 1839. Jesse was ordained a deacon at New Hope, April 24, 1841.

Jesse H. and Catherine Steed Chambers had two daughters: Mary Elizabeth Chambers born in 1841 and Minerva Adeline Chambers born in 1848.

On February 26, 1842, Jesse was dismissed from New Hope Church by letter. Catherine was dismissed by letter from New Hope in 1851. In 1850 they lived in Forsyth County, Georgia. By 1860, they were living in Tyler, Smith County, Texas.

Catherine died April 15, 1875 in Tyler, Smith County, Texas. Jesse died on November 29, 1881 in Smith County, Texas and was buried at the Ebenezer Cemetery.

Hannah Chambers

Hannah Chambers, daughter of Joseph and Sarah Chambers, was born March 10, 1818 in Jonathan's Creek, Haywood County, N. C. and died October 03, 1882 in Acworth, Cobb County, Georgia. She married Abel Hill Harrison on January 6, 1835 in Carroll County. Abel was born March 31, 1805 in Turkey Creek, Buncombe Co, N. C. and died March 29, 1883 in Cobb County.

Sarah L. Chambers

Sarah L., the last child of Joseph and Sarah Chambers was born in 1824 in Haywood Co., N. C. and died in 1850 in Carroll County. On September 4, 1842, she married Merrell C. Awtrey. Sarah was named in Joseph's will to inherit $800 at her mother's discretion when she came of age.

John Monroe Haynes

John Monroe Haynes

John Monroe Haynes the tenth child of Jonathan and Cynthia Haynes was born near Hickory Level, Carroll County, Georgia on 11 October 1842.

When John Haynes was nineteen, he volunteered in June of 1861 to serve in the Confederate Army. When in Company I of the 19th Georgia Infantry Regiment, he was elected Corporal. Company I was known as the Villa Rica Gold Diggers. This Company was organized under an oak tree in the front yard of the home of young Doctor Slaughter, who at the time lived on the north corner of present day Highway 61 (then called Old Town Road) and Herrell Road (then Peggy Cole Bridge Road). This property was later purchased by John Haynes' son, Samuel Tilton Haynes, and has stayed in the Haynes family to the present time.

While serving in the Confederacy, John was wounded in the right elbow at the battle at Chancellorsville, Virginia on 3 May 1863 and was placed in General Hospital at Richmond, Virginia. The bullet fractured his elbow leaving

Haynes House
Courtesy Sarah Pitts

it stiff and inches shorter than his left arm; according to his pension application his right arm was then "substantially and essentially useless." He was discharged from the Army in the rank of Corporal on 4 August 1864. He also received the Confederate metal for Valor and other service metals which were donated to the Kennesaw Battlefield Museum, at Kennesaw, Georgia after his death by his daughter Estoria Haynes Shaw.

After John came home from the war, he married Mary Louisa "Mary Lou" Bomar in 1863. She was born in 18 April 1841 in Carroll County, the daughter of John Bomar and Sarah Tittle.

According to family stories Mary Lou was a very small woman which was to her advantage on occasion during the Civil War. Grown women were restricted and could not be out and about on the streets without fear of molestation or insult by Yankee soldiers who may have been in the vicinity. Children, on the other hand, were free and could go about the streets unrestricted. She was small enough to dress in children clothes and shorter skirts of a small girl not be bothered by any troops passing through the area.

John Monroe Haynes and his young bride, Mary Lou, moved to Polk County, Georgia along with his father and his sister Lucinda. They each purchased land near the Aragon township, north of Rockmart, Georgia. John bought 101 1/4 acres which he farmed.

John and Mary Louisa Haynes had six children: Leonidas P. born 1865, died 1923; Sarah "Sallie" Jane born 1868, who married a Hawkins; John Bomar Haynes born 1870, died 1941; Estoria born February 1873, married Frank Shaw, died 1958;

Samuel Tilden "Sambo" Haynes born December 1875, died 1933; and Jonathon Ephraim Haynes born 1878, died 1949.

John did not have full use of his right arm because of his injury; nevertheless, he found a way to plow his acreage. He could clamp a plow line between his arm and body and with a special loop he designed, control and work a team of mules. His grandchildren said that he could draw water from a well by clamping the rope to his body with the right arm and pull the windless with his left hand.

On the 1870 Federal Census, this family lived in Polk County. On the 1880 Census they are shown in District 1271, Douglas County, Georgia. Sometimes after 1880, John sold his farm in Polk County and moved back to Villa Rica. He bought a farm about one quarter mile north of the crossroads of Ledbetter Hill Road and Peggy Cole Bridge Road.

In 1920, John and Mary Louisa lived with their son, Samuel T. Haynes—the home originally owned by Dr. Slaughter, (who by then lived next door on the other side of Herrell Road which was once known as the Peggy Cole Bridge Road). This home was where the young men came to enlist under the tree to become Confederate soldiers Co. I the Gold Diggers.

As family stories tell, about 1930 the oak tree, which by then was a very large oak tree, was hit by a lightening bolt that knocked out the top of the tree. The limbs hit a wrought iron fence which stood in the front of the house between the yard and road. The fence was destroyed and the tree died and was cut down. Many still remember the decorative iron fence and the large tree at the intersection of the now Highway 61, Punkintown Road and Herrell Road.

Mary Louisa Haynes died 23 September 1923 in Carroll County. John Monroe Haynes went to live with his daughter, Estoria, in Morgan County, Alabama. He died in Alabama, on December 2, 1923. Both he and his wife were buried at Hillcrest Cemetery outside Villa Rica.

See Appendix B in the back of the book for the Muster Roll of Company I, 19th Regiment, Georgia Volunteer Infantry, Army of Tennessee C. S. A. Carroll County, Georgia "Villa Rica Gold Diggers."

Samuel Tilton Haynes

Samuel Tilton Haynes was born Christmas Day, 1875—the son of John Monroe and Mary Louisa Haynes, (see entry above). Sam was born in Polk County, and then the family moved back to Villa Rica to a farm near Ledbetter Hills crossroads. At the crossroads of Ledbetter Road and Peggy Cole Bridge Road (today's Herrell Road) there was a church on the northeast corner (33°46'17.86"N 84°54'49.03"W) and a school on the southwest corner (33°46'16.17"N 84°54'50.19"W). Samuel attended this school. The teacher there was Miss Elsie Shaw, the daughter of Frank Shaw, who married Sam's sister Estoria.

As a twenty-five-year old in 1900, Sam obtained his "seed money" to build his first store by planting, cultivating and harvesting an acre of cotton, which usually amounted to a bale of ginned cotton. He used these proceeds to open his first store on Sally Hughes Road (Old Town Road) (today Highway 61/Dallas Highway) in 1900. He renovated either a barn or an old carriage house that stood on the east side of the Wick's Tavern to become a store.

On March 2, 1902, Sam married Nancy Amelia "Mele" Norton; she was born on New Year's Eve, 1876. She was the daughter of John Marion Norton who was the pastor of the Methodist Church which was built in the center of where Punkintown Road intersects with Highway 61. This land was donated for a church by Sam's father John Monroe Haynes.

Sam and Amelia "took rooms" (lived) in Wick's Tavern which had become a hotel. They lived there for a while until Sam needed a larger building for his store. They moved into the two room house that was Dr. Slaughter's former home (on the corner of then Peggy Cole Bridge Road and Sally Hughes Road (Old Town Road) —today the corner of Herrell Road and Highway 61. On the same property was Dr. Slaughter's old hospital, which Sam Haynes converted into the Haynes Store.

Amelia Haynes contracted typhoid fever which made her very ill. While she was sick, she lost her hair. Her beautiful blond hair regrew as black.

Samuel and Amelia had five children:
1) Ruby (b. December 14, 1904) who married Ray Holsenbeck;
2) William Randolph (b. March 16, 1905);
3) Mary Lou (b. 1910) who married William H. Hulsey;
4) Hallie (b. 1912) who married James Buckelew;
5) Josephine Haynes who married C. Ermon Wallis.

As the family grew, Haynes enlarged the house by adding four more rooms to the original two-room house which was built about 1847. In construction, it was discovered that the timbers in the attic were connected with wooden spikes, not nails or bolts. A large milk porch was added to the back. A screened-in porch was added and served as a dining room during the summer.

The old hospital building that was converted into the general merchandise center became the main supplier for the mines and a hangout for the local miners. Reportedly, the miners sometimes came in drunk, told lies and had a few fights. Sam owned the only gold weighing scale in the area. The mine owners and the miners would bring their mined gold ore for weighing before sending to the United States Mint in Dahlonega, Georgia. The store prospered far beyond expectations.
(33°44'53.81"N 84°54'40.98"W)

A family story, passed down through the generations, tells that Amelia—"Mele" liked to sit on the porch in her big rocking chair in the cool evenings. On one occasion, she held a .44 Colt pistol in her lap. A rowdy miner came over the hedge and over the wrought iron fence. She was ready. She called out a warning, but he kept coming. She shot at him to defend herself. He was hit in the leg. Everyone ran out of the store to see what had happened. Mele was never bothered again.

Another family story tells how Gypsies traveled through the area from time to time to peddle their handicrafts and sometimes trade with the merchants. They would arrive in their colorful wagons with their beautifully dressed women and children. When they made their annual visit to the area, they pitched their camp in a pasture owned by Uncle Frank Shaw, just east and across the road from the store.

A group of them were in the store one evening when they tried to pull the old "separate-and-keep-the-proprietor-busy" trick while others shop-lifted merchandise. Sam reached for his shot gun, and it accidentally discharged into the ceiling. Needless to say, the store was cleared out post haste and there was no more trouble with the Gypsies. They left the next day, but the hole in the ceiling was never patched.

Sam became prosperous and purchased land and several farms. Many of these farms were occupied by tenant farmers. He purchased the Austin farm that was across the road from the Sulfur mines; he became the owner of the property that contained the old Methodist church and the Yellow House. The church was also used as a school at one time, then abandoned, so the church/school then became Sam's barn and lean-tos were added to store tools and stable the animals. The church/school/barn burned in the fall of 1940 (33°44'53.81"N 84°54'40.98"W). There was a fire in the house and repairs were made.

Sam died March 1,1933, after an illness with diabetes, which resulted in him losing toes, then having a foot amputated. Sam left his children property and farms; family members still own the property at the intersection of Punkintown Road and Highway 61. Amelia "Mele" Haynes died May 6, 1969. Both Samuel Tilton and Nancy Amelia "Mele" Haynes were buried at Villa Rica City Cemetery (Hillcrest Cemetery).

8

Early Settlers
of Old Town—Hixtown & Chevestown

*The mines were rough, whisky was freely drank and free fights of
the fists and skull, rough-and-tumble sort, were common.*
                                        The History of Villa Rica

Hixtown

William A. Hicks came to the gold mining area of Villa Rica very early and bought two land lots #s: 208 and 193. He built a house close to where these two lots joined. In part of his house, he had a store referred to as Hick's storehouse. Most of the very early miners came to Hick's storehouse (just east of today's Herrell Road on Highway 61) for their supplies. Here Hicks also had the first tavern. This hub of Hixtown was about one and a half miles east from what was later to become "new" Villa Rica. These land lots were situated on a east-west ridge dividing the Little Tallapoosa River and Sweetwater Creek.

The settlement of Hixtown was laid out on 17.5 acres of Land Lot 193. Each of these 60 "town lots" was 60 feet wide to the front and 200 feet deep. The first town lot began just east of today's Herrell Road and Highway 61. The main street was then known as Sally Hughes' Road, later referred to as Old Town Road and today is Highway 61. Taverns, general stores, and homes were built on this street.

A traveler in the 1830s, leaving Hix's Storehouse and going west toward what was later "new" Villa Rica, would see a Methodist Church located where Punkintown Road is today. This church was also used as a school and later Samuel Tilton Haynes' barn. Just across from the church/school/barn was a small house where Dr. Slaughter lived. He built the first hospital beside his house. These early structures were located on the right corner of today's Herrell Road (Peggy Cole Bridge Road) and Highway 61. Later Samuel Tilton Haynes bought the property, enlarged Dr. Slaughter's house and turned the hospital into Haynes' store. On the left corner (across Herrell Road) was Dr. Slaughter's larger, newer home and a larger hospital. Traveling west (toward new Villa Rica) was Wick's Tavern on the left.

Hicks' (Hixtown) Storehouse, and the beginning of Hixtown Town Lots, faces today's Highway 61. (33°44'54.14"N 84°54'43.39"W)

The *Atlanta Constitution*, Friday September 28, 1887 published an interview with Appleton Mandeville on the early days of Carroll County:

> The Cherokee Indians had about all left for other climes, but few and far between were the white settlements. Mr. Mandeville says in going to Villa Rica about four or five settlements were about all that were passed. There was a small settlement where Judge V. B. McClure now lives and Rev. James W. Baskin occupied his present homestead near Concord M. E. Church. He says he traveled forty miles into Alabama and only came to six or seven settlements. Carrollton and Villa Rica were the only towns in the county and Villa Rica at that time was the metropolis. The gold fever had broken out . . . and that had given Villa Rica a boon which had given her the start . . .

From the *History of Villa Rica*:

> Pioneer gold miners began operations at several different locations as early as 1826. Then came William Hix who built a tavern and general supply store on what later became Main Street (Old Town Road—originally Sally Hughes Road.) By 1832 there were some three hundred men working in the mines. As a matter of fact, practically half of the population of the entire County was to be found within a two mile radius of the new settlement at this time. Up to this time, the place was called Hixtown.

Old Town Merchants

The Southern Business Directory in 1854 lists several Merchants of Villa Rica, then made up of Hixtown & Chevestown which was later referred to as Old Town. The merchants in 1854 were J. M. Bryant, Harris and Hargraves, Harrison & Russell, Little & Holland, Underwood & Mitchell.

Book B, Page 55, Carroll County, 8 Jul 1831. ALLEN G. FAMBROUGH to WILLIAM HICKS. Land lot #208, 2nd district Carroll County. Attest: William Burk, D. W. Parr, J.I.C.

Book B, Page 255, Carroll County, 01 January 1833, JILES BOGGESS to JOHN A. JONES. $10.00. Interest of William Hicks, land lot #193, 6th dist. Carroll. Sold to satisfy a suit in the Inferior Court of Coweta County, John A. Campbell vs. WILLIAM HICKS. Attest: Thomas McGuire, Hiram Wright J.P., 18 Jan 1833

Early settlers formed a stock company, buying and laying off the lots on which the town was afterwards built. An attorney, Edmund W. Holland, was hired to represent

Hart Town Environs

the newly formed stock company composed of David Clopton, Edward A. Broddas, Benjamin Chapman, Joseph Chambers, Jesse Chambers, Clayton Williams and Robert Watson of Monroe County, formerly of Carroll County. Gold lots were $500 per acre, compared to $2 per acre for land elsewhere in the county. Buyers sometimes bought a fraction of a lot to obtain the mineral rights. Each fraction was twenty feet wide in the front facing Old Town Road and 200 feet deep. This entire area was rich in the purest gold found in the country. There were at least 19 active gold mines at the time.

There were 60 town lots, 60 feet X 200 feet with the frontage facing Old Town Road, then the Sally Hughes Road, today Highway 61; the numbering began close to the intersection of Herrell Road and Highway 61 and alternated, the odd numbers on the southwest, the even numbers on the northeast.

Names from the original deeds of these town lots: 1 & 2 - Huff; 3 - Trustees of the Methodist Episcopal Church; 4 - Leonard Huff; 5 - Roberts; 6 - Jacob Awtry; 7 - Williams; 8 - Margaret Jarnigan; 9 - Anderson, Jefferson and John Wick; 10 - Margaret Jarnigan; 11 - Walker; 12 - Needham Jarnigan; 13 - Walker; 14 - Margaret Jarnigan; 15 - Walker; 16 - Margaret Jarnigan; 17 & 18 - Awtry; 19 - Holland; 20 Candler;

21 - Huff; 23 - unknown; 24 - Samuel Candler; 25 - unknown; 26 Candler; 27 - Watson; 28 - Awtry; 29 - Watson, Awtry, Cameron, Phillips; 30 & 31- Candler; 32 - Needham Jarnigan; 33 - Williams; 34 - Candler; 35 - Edmund Holland & John Wick; 36 - Unknown; 37 - Watson; 38 - unknown; 39 - Watson; 40 - unknown;

41 - Roberts; 42 - Candler; 43 - unknown; 44 - Candler; 45 - unknown; 46 - Candler; 47 - Witcher; 48 - Candler; 49 - Roberts & Witcher; 50 - Bone; 51 - unknown; 52 - Williams; 53 - unknown; 54 - Williams; 55 - unknown; 56 - Williams; 57 - unknown; 58 - Roberts; 59 & 60 unknown.

The following are some of the original abstracts to deeds; some are being sold:. Lot #193, Page 255, Book B, Carroll County, January 1, 1833. Jiles Boggess to John A. Jones. Sum of $10.00 the interest of William Hicks, for land lot #193, in the 6th district of Carroll County. Sold to Satisfy a suit in the Inferior Court of Coweta County, John A. Campbell VS. William Hicks. Attest: Thomas McGuire, Hiram Wright, J.P., January 18, 1833.

Lot #193, Page 524, Book F, Carroll County, May 14, 1834. Joseph Chambers, Jesse H. Chambers and Clayton Williams, Benjamin Chapman, Robert Watson and Edmund W. Holland to David Clopton and Edward A. Broaddus. Land lot #193, in the 6th district of Carroll County known as Gold Mine. Parties agree to lay off 17 1/2 acres for a town in the Southeast Corner. The remaining be divided which was 83 1/3 to Clopton and Broaddus. Attest: Allen Talbot, Denizen B. Palmer, Charles Hulsey, J.P., April 29, 1851.

Lot #193, Page 223, Book B Carroll County, March 17, 1835. David Clopton, Edward A. Broaddus, Benjamin Chapman, Joseph Chambers, Jesse Chambers, Clayton

Williams and Robert Watson of Monroe County, formerly of Carroll County appointed Edmund W. Holland attorney in fact to sell town lots in Hicks (Hix) Town on lot #193, in the 6th district of Carroll County. Each having a different fraction of the lots, Attest: William C. Williams, R. V. C. Ruffin, J.P. February 1, 1838.

Lot #193, September 3,1835. District 6, Carroll County, Georgia Edward W. Holland power of attorney for David Clopton, Edward A. Broaddus, Benjamin Chapman, Joseph Chambers, Jesse H. Chambers and Clayton Williams To Abel H. Harrison. Sum of $45.83 1/3 for 11/12 of a town lot —which was #28 sixty feet in front back in 200 feet.

Lot #193, Page 295, Book B, Carroll County, June 29, 1837. Edmund W. Holland the attorney for David Clopton, Edward A. Broaddus, Benjamin Chapman, Joseph Chambers, Jesse H. Chambers, Clayton William and Edmund W. Holland to N. Jarnagin. Sum of $45.83 1/3 for town lot #12, in Villa Rica formerly Hix town, in lot #193, in the 6th district of Carroll County. Lot containing 1/3 acres. Attest: Isaac H. Underwood, R. V. C. Ruffin, J.P., June 11, 1838.

Lot #193, Page 284, Book E, July 27, 1842. Sarah Chambers to Leonard Huff sum of $80.00. Part of land lot. 33 11/12 acres .Beginning at S. E. Corner, running west along Chapman and Watkins line to the town reserve. Gold reserves and mining privileges. Attest: John T. Chambers, Jesse H. Chambers, Joseph C. Williams, J.P. November 11, 1845.

Lot #193, Page 39, Book E, September 2, 1843. Watson and Cannon to Noah Phillips of Newton County and Phillips and Dearing of Newton County. Mortgage for factory yarn $252.00 and $162.00. Lot in Villa Rica known as Canons house. Attest: Robert A. Watson, John Hilderbrand, J.P. November 8, 1843.

Lot #193, Page 403, Book E, February 14,1845. Larkin Johnson to John B. Wick. Sum of $200.00 for Villa Rica #9, southeast side of street 60 feet front, 200 feet deep, 1/4 acres. Attest: John F. Dobson, J. C. Williams, J.P. September 28, 1846.

Lot #193, Page 207, Book F, Carroll County, September 13, 1846. Edward W. Holland, Agent. David Clopton, Edward A. Broaddus, Edward W. Holland, Joseph Chambers, Benjamin Chapman, Jesse H. Chambers, Clayton Williams, to John B. Wick for the sum of $35.00 for 11/12 of town lots: #37, #39, in Villa Rica the south side of the main street. Located in the land lot #193, in the 6th district of Carroll County. Land lot runs to the line of Dr. Thomas Roberds. Attest: Madison Wallace, R. V. C. Ruffin, J.P. February 9, 1849.

Lot #193, Page 438, Book F, Carroll County, July 25, 1850. Parker M. Rice to Asa W. Griggs. Sum of $700.00 for the east side of land lot #193, in the 6th district of Carroll County. Bounded on the west by S. Candler, north by Mrs. Jarnigan, east by M. Wicks and south by the town of Villa Rica. Also four town lots #1,#2, #4, #6, containing 34 acres. Attest: S. H. Davis, Lamb W. McGarity, Henry S. Chance, J.P. August 6, 1850.

Lot #193, Page 589, Book F, Carroll County, January 9, 1851. Margaret Jarnigan to Thomas H. Roberds. Sum of $650.00 for 5 lots of Villa Rica, Georgia. North Side of the main street. Lots: #8, #10, #12, #14, #16. Attest: Samuel C. Candler, Joseph C. Williams, J.P., October 22, 1851.

One mile south lay a tract of land known as Chevestown, owned by Allison Cheves.

Cheves Town (Chevestown) (Cheevestown)

Chevestown was an early town located at the end of what is today, Magnolia Street, where there was a store, a tavern and the home of Allison Cheves. (33°44'13.55"N 84°55'33.27"W)

William Allison Cheves

Allison Cheves (Chevees) (Cheaves) (b. February 13, 1814, Walton County, Georgia, d. February 3, 1881, Villa Rica) was the son of James L. Cheaves (b. 1780, North Carolina, d. 1830, Walton County). Allison's mother was Elizabeth Alford Cheaves (b. 1780, d. 1843, Georgia).

William Allison Cheves married Lucy Hitchcock circa 1838 in Walton County, Georgia. Lucy Hitchcock (b. 1818, d. 1857, Carroll County). Their first child, Sarah Elizabeth Cheeves was born on June 17, 1839 in Walton County.

Allison Cheves, his wife Lucy, and daughter Sarah, left Walton County and went to Villa Rica to join the prospectors mining for gold in this newly discovered gold belt. Some prospectors were here as early as 1826. Between 1830 and 1840, as much as 20,000 pennyweights of gold were found yearly.

Sarah Elizabeth (Cheeves) Noland

The 1840 Federal Census record shows this family was living in Villa Rica and Allison's occupation was listed as a miner. In 1850 Allison's occupation was that of a miner.

The Georgia Property Tax Digest shows Allison Cheves in District 6 #642 Section 5 paying taxes for 202 1/2 acres Land Lot #161. In Villa Rica, Allison and Lucy had three more children: 1) Jesse (b. 1840, Villa Rica); 2) William A. (b. March 10, 1844) who married Amanda M.; and 3) Martha (b. November 16, 1846, Carroll County) who married Leonidas Roberts. Lucy, their first child, later married William Aubrey Noland.

Lucy Hitchcock Cheves, Allison's wife, died in 1857 and was buried at Pleasant Grove Baptist Church Cemetery in Carroll County.

After the death of his first wife, Allison Cheves married Emily Jerusha Awtrey on February 23, 1858 in Carroll County. She was born in 1820. Their first son, Earnest Jacob, was born March 14, 1859.

The 1860 Federal Census lists Allison's occupation as a farmer with a real estate value of $500 and a personal estate value of $500. He lived in the second district of Carroll County. His son Merrell A. was born August 1861.

William "Allison" Cheves enlisted as a Private on June 22, 1861. He was appointed Sergeant and elected 2d Lieutenant on August 31, 1862. He was wounded and captured at Fredericksburg, Virginia on December 13, 1862. He was paroled on December 14, 1862. On August 19, 1864, he was captured at Weldon Railroad, Virginia. He was sent to Washington, D. C., on August 24, 1864, received at Fort Delaware on August 29, 1864 and released there on June 17, 1865.

On October 3, 1864 Allison's 2nd wife Emily Jerusha Awtrey Cheves died.

Allison Cheves' third wife was Mahala Ann Shinn, (b. February 25, 1841, d. 1914). Allison and Mahala's children:
1) Mary Ella (b. February 13, 1866);
2) Lula E. (b. December 25, 1868); she married John T. Hixon;
3) John A. (b. February 18, 1871;
4) Daniel Scott Mead Cheves (b. March 8, 1874); he married Adeline Smith;
5) Dora E. (b. December 1876);
6) Addie Eugenia (January 13, 1880, d. 1883).

In 1870, Allison Cheves' real estate value was $1,000 and personal estate value was $300. In 1880 this family lived in District 642; he was listed as a farmer. William Allison Cheves died in 1881 in Villa Rica at the age of 66 and was buried at Pleasant Grove Baptist Church Cemetery outside of Villa Rica.

Jacob Awtrey

Jacob (Autrey) Awtrey (b. April 22, 1789, Green County, d. November 22, 1859, Carroll County) was the son of Absalom James Autrey, a Revolutionary Soldier (b. 1750, North Carolina, d. 1834, Henry County). Jacob's mother was Mary Lucy "Mollie" Naomi Camp (b. 1746, d. 1818).

On 12 October 1809, Jacob married Nancy Hill in Jackson, Georgia. Nancy (b. January 3, 1793, d. July 25, 1852, Carroll County).

On the 1820 Census Jacob Awtrey was shown in Green County Georgia, Captain Awtrey's District; in 1830 he was listed in Carroll County; in 1850 the Federal Census Record shows this family was living in *Division 11*, which includes all of Carroll County. Their value of real estate was $2,000.

On February 22, 1834, Jacob Awtrey was listed as an original member of New Hope Primitive Baptist Church, east of Villa Rica. The church minutes, 1829–1869 has an entry from July 6, 1837: Church appointed brothers Jacob Awtrey, Charles Sheets with five other men as a committee to select where the meeting house shall be built. Charles Sheats later became Jacob's son-in-law when he married Jacob's daughter, Susan in 1851.

Jacob and Nancy Hill Awtrey had the following children:

1) William Hill Awtrey (b. June 15, 1813, Jackson, Georgia, d. January 4, 1875, Villa Rica). On October 22, 1849, William married Louisa Dodson (b. October 22, 1821, d. August 6, 1897). William Hill Awtrey was the Post Master in Villa Rica, appointed December 14, 1847.

2) Merrell C. Awtrey (b. July 18, 1816, Jackson County, d. June 16, 1890, Acworth, Georgia). He married Sarah Chambers on September 5, 1842. He was buried at the Liberty Hill Cemetery in Acworth.

3) Emily Jerusha Awtrey (b. July 17, 1820, Jackson County, d. October 3, 1864, Carroll County). She married Allison Cheves on February 22, 1858 in Villa Rica. See excerpt above.

4) Isaac Awtrey (b. April 16, 1823, Jackson County, d. October 16, 1827, Carroll County).

5) Elizabeth Albina Awtrey (b. June 3, 1825, Jackson County, d. October 23, 1847, Carroll County) married on April 27, 1845 to Felix Denham.

6) Adeline M. Awtrey (b. August 10, 1827, Jackson County, d. May 3, 1908, Carroll County) married Henry Farmer Merrell on December 20, 1855. Henry (b. July 30, 1820, d. July 7, 1870).

7) George W. Awtrey (b. May 29, 1829, d. May 23, 1882, Carroll County). On September 8, 1852, he married Martha Embrey (b. March 16, 1835, d. December 18, 1915).

8) Susannah "Susan" Fitzalin Awtrey (b. September 5, 1831, Jackson County, d. 1907, Carroll County). On January 23, 1851, she married William H. Sheats (b. January 20, 1824, d. November 5, 1907). Susan was buried at Westview Cemetery in Fulton County, Georgia.

9) Sarah Awtrey (b. May 7, 1834, d. September 7, 1867, Paulding County). In May of 1857, she married Newman Beall who was born February 11, 1829.

10) Lucy Naomi Awtrey (b. September 19, 1836, Carroll County, d. January 19, 1918, Carroll County). On September 2, 1856, she married William Washington Merrell (b. September 16, 1815, d. May 21, 1900, Carroll County).

Both Jacob and Nancy Hill Awtrey were buried at New Hope Primitive Baptist Church Cemetery.

Book A, Lot #191, Land lottery 1827, Newton County, Jacob Autrey land lot containing 202 1/2 acres.

Book B, Lot #191, Page 147, Carroll County, 16 May 1831. PATRICK B. CONALLY, Jefferson County to JACOB AWTREY, Carroll. $200.00. 1/2 of land lot #161, 6th dist. Carroll, containing 101 1/4 acres. Attest: John A. Jones, Thomas R. H. Poteet.

Book B, Page 246, Lot #191, Carroll County, August 26, 1831. Jacob Awtry to William C. Osburn of Harris county. Sum of $700.00 for 1/2 of land lot #191, in the 6th district of Carroll County, North half. Witness: James Simpson, Richard Speaks, James Dickson, J.P., January 1, 1833.

Book E, Page 275, Carroll County, 24 Jul 1844. JACOB AUTREY to HIRAM McKINNEY. $75.00. 50 acres, south east corner land lot #191, 6th dist. Carroll County. Autrey reserves mining rights. Attest: Hendon B. Palmer, R. V .C. Ruffin, J. P. 8 Oct 1845. Book G, Page 31 Carroll County, 28 Jan 1852. JACOB AUTREY to D. H. WITCHER. $200.00. S.W. comer land lot #191, 6th dist., Carroll County. Attest: John Mitchel, Jos C Williams, J.P. 23 Aug 1852.

John Hicks' Store
Courtesy Pauline Roberts

John Columbus Hicks

John Columbus Hicks (b. May 6, 1865, Paulding County, d. June 1, 1924, Fulton County). His father, Isaac Crayton "Crate" Hicks (b. April 22, 1830, Haywood County, North Carolina, d. May 4, 1887, Carroll County). Isaac served in the Civil War as a Private in Company I, 56th Regiment, Georgia Volunteer Infantry, Carroll County. He enlisted May 20, 1862; he mustered out 25 November 1863.

John Columbus Hicks' mother was Eliza Jane Richards (b. February 1, 1833, d. 1910, Carroll County). She married Isaac Crayton Hicks on December 10, 1848.

John Hicks' grandfather was Matthew Hicks born in 1795 in North Carolina and died March 1871 in Cleburne County Alabama. John's grandmother was Sarah "Sally" Green Hicks born around 1790 in North Carolina and died in 1840 in Carroll County.

Sarah Green Hicks' parents were Kizziah Stroud Green (b. 1763, d. August 1, 1849, Carroll County) and William Green (b. February 22, 1762, d. March 22, 1837).

Hart Town Environs

John C. Hicks
Courtesy Pauline Roberts

Matthew Hicks and the Green family relocated from Haywood County, North Carolina to Hickory Level, Carroll County, in 1850. Sarah Green's father, William Green was a soldier in the Revolutionary War from North Carolina.

The 1850 Federal Census Records lists John C. Hicks as a boy living with his family in *Division 11* Carroll County. In 1860 this family was shown on the Hickory Level Census. In 1870 and 1880, they were in Cains, Paulding County, Georgia.

John Columbus Hicks first married Lizzie L. Doyal. After she died, he married Mary Winnie Lula Leatherwood on March 15, 1896. Mary Lula (b. October 9, 1877, Georgia, d. October 1961, Fulton County).

In 1900, the Georgia Federal Census Records shows that John and Mary Lula lived on Surelwats [sic] Street in Villa Rica and his occupation was that of landlord. In 1910, they lived on Villa Rica Street and he was listed as a merchant, owning a general store. His store was located next to the cotton warehouses, just off Main Street and North Avenue, near the First Methodist Church in Villa Rica. In 1920, they lived on College Street and his

**John C. Hicks - tallest man on back row. Right hand on mother, left hand on wife.
Occasion: 1897 Leatherwood Reunion** *Courtesy Pauline Roberts*

occupation was listed as Salesman, Dry Goods. His mother Jane, age 75, lived with them. They owned a home on College Street, presently known as North Avenue, in Villa Rica, Georgia. Several relatives from the New Georgia Community in Paulding County, lived with John during the week to finish their education in Villa Rica.

John and Mary Lula raised children: 1) Lillie born 1897, 2) Lennie 1898, 3) Wallace 1903, 4) Johnie 1904, 5) Ernest 1908, 6) Mary 1911, 7) Helen 1915 and 8) Robert 1916.

John C. Hicks was involved in politcs, serving on the Villa Rica City Council. He also assisted the local doctor in many surgeries which were performed in his store. He relocated to Atlanta, about 1921. He died in 1924 in Atlanta, and was buried at Crest Lawn Cemetery in Fulton, County.

Captain John "Jack" Anselm Jones

John A. Jones, an early settler of the Hixtown—Chevestown area, built a house at 110 Magnolia Street and lived in Villa Rica for many years. He was the son of Judge John Anselm Jones, Sr. (b. June 6, 1791, Augusta, d. August 1880, Rockmart, Polk County). John Anselm Jones, Sr. spent many years in Rockmart as a Judge. John Jr.,'s mother was Martha Walton Jenkins (b. 1795, d. 1850).

John "Jack" Anselm Jones, Jr. (b. July 3, 1814, Baldwin County, d. February 28, 1893, Baldwin County) married Susan C. Williams on June 20, 1850; Susan (b. 1828, d. 1906) was the daughter of Peter Jones Williams and Lucinda Parks. In 1860 and 1870 the couple lived in Milledgeville; in 1880 they lived in Atlanta, Fulton County.

John's brother, Colonel "Bat" Jones (b. 1836, Villa Rica) was a lawyer and influential citizen in western Georgia and in Polk County, where his father was a Judge for many years.

In *The History of Villa Rica*, John A. Jones and his wife Susan came to Villa Rica during the Gold Rush. He eventually owned 6,000 acres in fifteen counties and was Carroll County's largest land owner. He deeded land, then on Temple Street now known as Main Street, for 99 years for a new First Baptist Church to be built.

During the time of the Mexican War, Captain Jack Jones carried a company of about fifty men into war, most of whom enlisted from Villa Rica. The company never engaged in battle, but disease thinned the ranks until only six lived to return safely home.

He was the State Treasurer during the Civil War under Governor Joe Brown. Jack and Susan escaped to Nova Scotia with the state's federal money ($44,000). He returned to Villa Rica and was a one time member of the Pony Club, reformed.

John Anselm Jones and his wife were buried at the Memory Hill Cemetery in Milledgeville, Baldwin County, Georgia. A marker at his graveside reads, "Honest Jack, former treasurer State of Georgia." They had no children, thus leaving no heirs.

Peyton Noland, of Old Town, Died a Tragic Death

Peyton Noland, son of George Avery Noland (b. 1763, Virginia, d. 1818,

Walton County) and Alice Elsy Jane Noland, (b. 1765, Virginia, d. 1839, Mississippi), was born in Wilkes County, Georgia in 1793. He served in the Georgia Militia during the War of 1812 along with his brother-in-law, Samuel Gathright Moseley.

Peyton Noland married Sarah "Sallie" Mozley (Moseley) (b. 1795, d. 1856), daughter of Edwin Moseley and Sarah Gathright, in Walton County, Georgia on December 30, 1821.

Peyton and Sarah "Sallie" had seven children:
1) Annie Pathon Noland (b. 1821);
2) George R. (b. August 23, 1822, d. 1870);
3) Edward Moseley "Edwin" who married Orie Jane Owen;
4) Lieutenant Henry Terrell Noland (b. December 10, 1825, d. 1895) who married Mary Ann Pace (1828–1889);
5) William Aubrey Noland (b. January 17, 1828, d. 1884) who married Sarah Elizabeth Cheves;
6) Seaborn W. Noland (b. March 27, 1830, d. 1899)
7) Samuel (b. 1834).

Peyton Noland was shown on the 1830 Federal Census as living in Campbell County.

From *The Noland Family Tree* by Sandra Pruett Ruff:

"Peyton Noland, his wife and children moved to Villa Rica in about 1834. He procured a job in a gold mine located in an area now known as Pine Mountain. At age 45, on May 28, 1838, while entering the shaft of the gold mine, Peyton was bitten in the face by a venomous snake. He was taken to his house which was on site of the mining property and died a few moments later.

Fortunately, he and Sarah had become active members of the New Hope Primitive Baptist Church, Villa Rica, Georgia. Unlike many of the other gold miners, their family priorities were as follows: education, work, recreation and morality. Peyton was buried at the New Hope Primitive Baptist Church Cemetery, in Villa Rica, Georgia.

The 1850 Federal Census shows that the Peyton Noland family lived in *Division 11* of Carroll County. Sarah, his widow, age 55, was listed as a miner. Four of Peyton and Sarah's sons are listed as miners: 1) George R.–age 28; 2) Tom–22; 3) Seaborn–20 and 4) Samuel–16. Living next door to this family was E. M. Noland which was probably Sarah and Peyton's son Edwin, also listed as a miner.

Next door to Edwin lived Allison Cheves whose daughter Sarah Elizabeth Cheves (Cheeves) (b. 1839, d. 1904) married Peyton and Sarah Noland's son William Aubrey Noland (b. 1828, d. 1884).

Sarah "Sallie" Mozley Peyton died in 1856 in Villa Rica and was buried at New Hope Primitive Baptist Church Cemetery in Carroll County, near her husband who died eighteen years earlier of a snake bite, at the gold mine.

William Aubrey Noland

William Aubrey Noland

William Aubrey Noland was the son of Peyton and Sarah "Sallie" Mozley Noland of Villa Rica, Georgia. William Aubrey Noland (b. January 17, 1828, Walton County, d. August 29, 1884, Paulding County). His family lived a short time in Campbell County around 1830 and came to Villa Rica in 1834 where his father Peyton was a miner.

On the 1850 census, Sarah and the four boys living at home with her were listed as miners. Her son Edwin, next door, was also a miner.

William married Elizabeth M. Smith on December 18, 1845 in Carroll County. Their first child was Nathan Noland born in 1856 in Villa Rica. Elizabeth Smith Noland died on January 17, 1856.

William married Sarah Elizabeth Cheves (b. June 17, 1839, d. 1904). She was the daughter of Allison Cheves and his first wife Lucy Hitchcock. Sarah Cheves Noland not only took care of the small child, Nathan, whose mother had passed, but she and William Aubrey had thirteen of their own children:

1) Lesbia "Lisby" Kate (b. November 12, 1856, d. 1931);
2) Buddy Aubrey (b. 1858, d. 1897);
3) Seaborn Jackson (b. 1860, d. 1921);
4) Georgia Ann (b. 1862, d. 1934);
5) Marthy "Mattie" (b. 1865, d. 1946);
6) Francis "Fannie" Evelyn (b. 1868, d. 1939);
7) William Allison (b. 1870, d. 1939);
8) Battavia Jane (b. 1872, d. 1915);
9) Edward Peyton "Edwin" (b. 1874, d. 1943);
10) Sarah "Sallie" L. (b. 1877, d. 1880);
11) Ora Emily (b. 1880, d. 1948);
12) Samuel Clemen (b. 1882, d. 1938);
13) Cleveland Dorman b. 1883).

According to the 1870 and 1880 Federal Census Record, this large family lived at Burnt Hickory, Eutah District in Paulding County. The first two children were born in Villa Rica and the rest were born in Paulding County.

William Aubrey Noland died in 1884 and was buried in Dallas, Paulding County.

Seaborn W. Noland

Seaborn W. Noland, (b. March 27, 1830, Georgia, d. October 12, 1899, Villa

Rica) was the son of Peyton and Sarah "Sallie" Noland. He married Mary Elizabeth "Lizzie"Burns (b. 1829, d. 1900) on October 6, 1855 in Carroll County.

Seaborn and Lizzie had six children:
1) William P. (b. 1856);
2) Orah J. (b. 1858);
3) George Franklin (b. 1860, d. 1899);
4) James Edwin (b. October 3, 1865, d. 1907):
5) Sarah A. (b. July 16, 1868, d. 1903);
6) Samuel Burns Noland (b. February 19, 1873, d. 1937).

The 1860 Federal Census, Carroll County, District 2, lists Seaborn Noland as a farmer. During the Civil War, he enlisted as a Private, Company D, 10th Regiment, Georgia Cavalry State Guard.

In 1866 he was listed on the U. S. Appointments of the U. S. Postmaster, appointed on February 3, 1966 and was succeeded in 1868 by William B. Candler.

On the 1870 Carroll County Federal Census, Villa Rica District, Seaborn W. Noland was listed as a Dry Goods Merchant, Retail. The 1880 Carroll County Federal Census for District 642, Villa Rica, lists him as a farmer.

Seaborn died in 1899; his wife, Mary Elizabeth "Lizzie" Burns Noland, died in 1900. Probate records dated December 8, 1900 show that she left 50 acres on the S. E. corner of Land Lot 227, 6th district Carroll County, Villa Rica, to her heirs.

Seaborn W. Noland
Courtesy Villa Rica Masonic Lodge Members

Peyton Noland, Sarah M. Noland, Henry Terrell Noland and his wife, Seaborn W. Noland and his wife, Sallie Noland, and several of their descendants were buried at New Hope Primitive Baptist Church Cemetery, in Villa Rica.

John Thomas Slaughter

John Thomas Slaughter (b. February 19, 1830, Green County, d. February 7, 1890, Carroll County) was the son of Nathaniel Garnett Slaughter (b. 1800, Green County, d. September 16, 1861, Villa Rica). John Slaughter's mother was Angelina Castleberry (b. 1801, Georgia, d. June 23, 1859, Villa Rica). Nathaniel and Angelina Slaughter married on December 17, 1820 in Jasper, Georgia. This family came to Villa Rica in 1844. In 1850 they are shown on the Federal Census Records for *Division 11* Carroll County.

On December 19, 1850, John T. Slaughter married Melvina Eugenia Freeman in Old

Dr. John Slaughter
Courtesy Villa Rica Masonic Lodge Members

Town, Villa Rica. Melvina (b. August 31, 1834, Carroll County).

In 1854 John T. Slaughter was a Junior Warden, Grand Lodge #72 of the Masonic Order in Villa Rica.

He graduated from medical school when he was twenty-one years old and became a prominent and successful physician. He was a member of the state senate in 1876 and 1877 when the legislature called the constitutional convention that made the present constitution of Georgia.

John Thomas Slaughter was one of the first doctors in Old Town Villa Rica. (33°44'54.25"N 84°54'44.96"W) He had a house and a hospital on Old Town Road adjacent to Herrell Road. In 1860, the Federal Census Record shows that John and Melvina lived in District 2 in Villa Rica; John was shown as a Physician and the value of his personal estate was $4,000. Listed are two children: John junior age 8 and Martha Elizabeth age 6.

John's and Malvina's children were: John Thomas, Jr. (b. May 20, 1852, d. October 3, 1903); and Martha Elizabeth (May 4, 1854, d. September 23, 1915).

During the Civil War, John Slaughter enlisted as Private on May 10, 1862. He raised a company in and around Villa Rica which was attached to the 56th regiment of Georgia troops. He was elected Lieutenant Colonel on May 15, 1862, then Lieutenant Colonel. The company and regiment were in the forty-day siege at Vicksburg, Mississippi, when they subsisted on roots, herbs, rats and mule beef. After the surrender at Vicksburg the regiment was again organized and fought under General Johnston to the close of the war. He was wounded at Chickamauga, Georgia on September 20, 1863 and resigned on October 25, 1864.

A newspaper article, dated October 1, 1886, quotes a member of Company I, 56 Georgia Regiment reminisces at a reunion: I, Captain J. M. Cobb was with Colonel J. T. Slaughter of Villa Rica, who stood by his men through thick and thin, in all their hardships and his men by him, both in war and peace. The Colonel with all these companies well remembers the battle of Bakers Creek, Mississippi, and the siege of Vicksburg. At the former place, I had my collar bone broken with a Minnie ball and dear brother killed. Captain G. S. Sharp had a dear son killed in six feet of me. There were 22 men of old Company H killed and wounded at Bakers Creek. At Missionary Ridge the 56th lost many of noble sons, Resaca, Dalton, Kingston, Lost Mountain, Atlanta, Jonesboro, Franklin, Nashville and various other battles these companies went through.

In 1870 this family lived in Covington, Newton County. The Federal Census shows that both their children were in college:

1) John, Junior became a druggist and later a doctor in Villa Rica. He married Sarah Temperance "Sallie" McLarty.

2) Their daughter, Martha Elizabeth married William Beall Candler.

In 1880 John and Melvina returned to Villa Rica; their next door neighbor in Old Town was John Wick of Wick's Tavern.

They moved to New Town Villa Rica after the railroad came through in 1883.

Dr. John Slaughter in 1890; Melvina died August 1,1917 and both were buried at Hillcrest City Cemetery in Villa Rica. Martha Elizabeth and John, Jr. Slaughter were also buried at Hillcrest Cemetery.

Elizabeth Slaughter (Candler) and William Beall Candler

Elizabeth Slaughter, the daughter of Dr. John Slaughter and Melvina Slaughter was born May 4, 1854, in Villa Rica, Georgia. See excerpt above. She married William Beall Candler, born on January 19, 1871. Their children were:

1. Eugenia Candler, who married a Malone.
2. Florence Candler (b. December 7, 1873) who married Oscar Fielder.
3. Elizabeth Candler (b. September 21, 1876) who married James Bruce Upshaw.
4. William Beall Candler, Jr. (b. May 26, 1879) who married Margaret Cobb.

On Sept. 23, 1915, Elizabeth was killed while crossing the railroad while coming back from sewing with her daughter, Florence Fielder. She was looking back and waving to the family when she walked in front of a Southern train going to Atlanta from Birmingham. It was only three blocks to Florence's house and Elizabeth had made the trip many times.

William died April 6, 1928, and both were buried in Hill Crest Cemetery in Villa Rica.

Roland Andrew Tolbert

Roland Andrew Tolbert (b. July 03, 1799, North Carolina, d. July 1, 1896, Villa Rica), the son of Thomas Sanford Tolbert (b. 1780 d. 1860, Carroll County) and Lucy Emmaline Andrews (b. 1773, d. June 19, 1852, Carroll County). In 1819, in North Carolina, he married Elizabeth W. (b. January 30, 1795, North Carolina, d. March 25, 1872, Carroll County).

> From the *Carroll County, Georgia Archives Biographies*:
>
> Roland's educational advantages were meager, as he had to work hard and long and late on the farm. He came to Georgia and settled in Madison County in 1827. In 1832, he came to Villa Rica to work the gold mines.
>
> When he came to Carroll the country and the mines were rough,

whisky was freely drank and free fights of the fists and skull, rough-and-tumble sort, were common. Mr. Tolbert was usually "at home" for all comers, though he sought no conflict. He was a member of the military force which escorted the Indians to their new homes, and draws a pension now for that service. He was the eldest of eight children, and is the only one now living. He is a devout and exemplary member of the Methodist church.

Roland and Elizabeth Tolbert's children were:
1) Clark C. (b. July 11, 1820, North Carolina);
2) William H. (b. 1823, North Carolina);
3) Lucy Minerva (b. Jan 30, 1831,Villa Rica;
4) Roland Harrison Tolbert (b. Feb 28, 1833, Villa Rica);
5) Josiah Thomas (b. February 1836, Villa Rica).

In 1830 this family lived in Madison County, Georgia. By 1840 they lived in District 642, Villa Rica and his occupation was that of miner. In 1850 he was a farmer. In 1880 his Real Estate Value was $1,000 and personal Estate Value was $400. On the 1880 census, Richard W. Slaughter was living in his household and his occupation was that of Mail Carrier.

Roland died in 1896 in Villa Rica; Elizabeth Tolbert, his wife, died in 1872 in Carroll County.

Josiah Thomas Tolbert

Josiah Thomas Tolbert (b. February 1836, Villa Rica, d. 1915, Fulton County), was the son of Roland and Elizabeth Tolbert. On December 19, 1866, Josiah married Elizabeth W. Hodgson (Hodson) daughter of Valentine Mc (illegible) Hodgson and Elizabeth Rice Hodgson.

The Federal Census Records show this family lived in Villa Rica in 1840, 1850, 1870, 1880 and 1900. Josiah Thomas and Elizabeth had six children:
1) Elizzie, (b. 1869);
2) Thomas Wilburn (b. June 29, 1869, Villa Rica, d. 1944);
3) Minnie (b. circa 1882, d. 1920);
4) Elba (b. July 24, 1885, Fulton County, d. September 10, 1909);
5) Montra May (b. before 1900, Carroll County);
6) Abby Estelle Tolbert.(b. before 1900, Carroll County.

From the *Carroll County Georgia Archives Biographies*:

J. Thomas Tolbert was reared on the farm, and work was such an imperative necessity that he attended school but little. In 1862, he enlisted in Company A, Ninth Georgia battalion artillery, Maj. Austin Leyden, with which he served until July, 1863, when he was transferred to Company E, First Georgia cavalry. On one occasion he and five others were out on a scout and suddenly came upon a company of guerrillas, who chased them five miles, shooting at them all the time; but they finally escaped. He was in many hard fights, but never wounded. At the siege of Knoxville, 1864, he was captured by the same men, an interesting coincidence, who chased him when scouting. He was held until after the surrender, sometimes, he alleges, on starvation rations. After his release he went to Cincinnati, where he remained about seventeen months, and then returned to his old home in Carroll County.

. . . After marriage Mr. Tolbert went to farming, supplementing it with trading in stock, prospering beyond his most sanguine expectations He is now one of the most substantial and ranks among the best citizens in Carroll county. Mr. Tolbert's success illustrates the great possibilities of life in Georgia when pluck and perseverance are coupled with energy and fair business judgment. Financially and socially himself and family occupy first class positions. Himself and his wife are members of the Presbyterian church.

Josiah Thomas Tolbert died in 1915; his wife Elizabeth Hodson Tolbert died in 1920.

John Henry Velvin

John Henry Velvin (b. May 21, 1804, North Carolina, d. February 1880, De Roane, Hempstead, Arkansas) was the son of Robert Michael Velvin (b. 1776, d. 1831) and Frances Kilgore (b. 1783, d. 1870). The 1830 Federal Census shows John Velvin living in Walton County. He married Delilah Moore in Walton County, on December 25, 1828. Delilah Moore Velvin (b. 1811, d. 1880, Hempstead, Arkansas).

The 1850 Federal Census shows him living in Carroll County, occupation blacksmith. About 1832, Henry Velvin was a part of an early group that formed a stock company, buying and laying off the lots on which Hixtown and Chevestown were built. John Henry Velvin, W. A. Floyd, and J. T. Tolbert ran both the Hix's Tavern and the Wick's Tavern. The Velvin family were listed in the original membership of the Pleasant Grove Baptist Church constituted in July 1849.

John Henry and Delilah Velvin's children:
1) Sydney Smith Velvin (b. September 29, 1829, Carroll County);
2) Elizabeth (b. 1831, Georgia);
3) Robert Jones Velvin (b. June 1838, Georgia, d. 1912);
4) John Jethro (b. September 25, 1939, Georgia, d. 1912);
5) James Henry (b. 1843, Villa Rica);
6) Mary Frances "Frannie" (b. January 5, 1847, Villa Rica);
7) Thomas B. "Tom" (b. 1849, Georgia).

John Jethro Velvin

John Jethro Velvin (b. September 25, 1839, Georgia, d. February 4, 1912, Villa Rica, Douglas County) was the son of John H. Velvin, and Delilah Velvin.

John Jethro Velvin enlisted on October 1, 1861 as a Private in the Confederate States of America to fight in the Civil War as a member of Co. I, 7th Calvary, Partisan Rangers. Company I was known as the Villa Rica Gold Diggers. John J. Velvin was captured at Vicksburg, Mississippi on July 14, 1863. He lived through the forty-day siege at Vicksburg, Mississippi. He mustered out as full 1st Lieutenant at Greensboro, N. C. on April 26, 1865.

John Velvin married Antoinette "Annette" Jane Green on November 1, 1866. Annette (b. February 10, 1848, Carroll County, d. August 18, 1923, Villa Rica). The Velvin Home, (33°44'13.71"N 84° 55'25.84"W) built in 1892 on Magnolia Street, still exists today.

John and Annette Velvin had three daughters:
1) Rilla A. (b. October 1870, d. 1949, Florida);
2) Jesse Deila (b. July 9, 1872, d. September 15, 1873);
3) Louella (b. December 19, 1873, Villa Rica, d. 1944).

On the 1870 Federal Census Record, his occupation was in grocery/retail; the 1880 Census, shows the hotel on Wilson Street and his occupation was hotel keeper. In 1900 the census shows the hotel on Montgomery Street in Villa Rica. At one time there was a Velvin Street.

The J. J. Velvin Hotel and store, on the corner of Wilson and Montgomery Street, was built in 1884 close to the railroad tracks in the new Villa Rica. He and his wife were in the hotel business for twenty years. The hotel was noted for its excellent food and hospitality. Later known as the Walker Hotel and finally, the Cooke House, it was a source of pride to the community. It survived until 1932.

On July 8, 1892 Judge John Jethro Velvin was part of the Villa Rica delegates to attend the Democratic Convention at the Carrollton Courthouse to endorse the Democratic presidential candidate, Grover Cleveland, for his second term. On July 6, 1888, he was among the delegates to attend the Gubernatorial Convention.

John J. Velvin died in February 4. 1912 and his wife, Annette, died in 1923; both were buried at the Villa Rica Hillcrest Cemetery.

John B. Wick

John B. Wick, who built the second tavern in Hixtown on what is today Highway 61 (33°44'49.07"N 84°54'51"W) also had a general store and attorney's office in Hixtown. The first tavern was built by William Hix, who also had a general supply store for miners who came to mine for gold as early as 1826. By 1832 there were some 300 miners in the area. Later, both the Hix's and Wick's taverns were run by W. A. Floyd, J. T. Tolbert and John Velvin.

John Butler Wick (b. 1798, New York, d. November 1, 1866, Morristown, New Jersey) was the son of Daniel Wick (b. 1714, d. New Jersey) and Hannah Jane

Wick's Tavern
The Times Georgian

Butler (b. 1718, Virginia, d. 1803, New Jersey).

John Wick married Delia Johnson Tuttle on October 16, 1824 in Somerset, New Jersey. Delia (b. October 15, 1793, Morristown, New Jersey, d. August 8, 1868, New Jersey) was the daughter of William Tuttle (b. 1760, d. 1836); Delia's mother was Temperance (b. 1758, d. 1822); both of her parents were from Morristown, New Jersey.

From Abstracts: 7 June 1830, John Poe, Carroll County to John B. Wick, Bibb County. $150. Right to mine minerals and metals, east half of lot #158, 6th district Carroll County. Also: June 14, 1830 John Poe, Carroll County to John B. Wick, Bibb County. $150.00. 15 acres of lot #158, 6th district Carroll County.

John and Delia are listed on the 1850 Federal Census for Carroll County, Georgia *Division 11*. His occupation was an attorney at law, age 52 with a real estate value of $20,000. Delia was also age 52 and listed as housekeeper. They had one daughter, Mary C. age 11, who was born in Georgia. His mother, Hannah, lived with them; she was 84. Hillon H. Bryant age 54, born in New Jersey also lived in this household. In 1850, John B. Wick also had a Mr. Bryant living in his household. He may have been the original carpenter who built the tavern and was housed as a part of his payment.

On the 1860 Federal Census for Carroll County, District 2 Villa Rica, John and Delia were 62. He was again listed as an attorney at law. His real estate value was $7,500 and his personal value was $5,500. Helen B. Bryant age 64 was born in New

Jersey and was listed as a teacher. Their neighbors were John T. Slaughter, J. T. Tolbert and John Velvin. This places the Wick family exactly where Wick's tavern was in Hixtown, later called Old Town Villa Rica.

As a stagecoach stop, the Tavern served miners and travelers until it went out of business sometime after the Civil War and became a home to various families.

During the frontier years of Villa Rica's birth, the Wick's Tavern was a lively place. It was an excellent place on the weekend to have a good fight.

From the *Times-Georgian* July 18, 1999:

> In 1919, Dewren Chastain's father bought the property. In 1932, Dewren and his wife Frances moved into the home. The historical landmark was home to the Chastains for most of the century. "It was fun. Mother always had the prettiest of flowers, it was a manicured place," Chastain remembered. "It had an old basement, a (dirt) cellar." She lived in the house until 1990.
>
> ... In the old Tavern, a ladder was used to get to the second floor where travelers could sleep. ... A partition separated the upper floor of the Tavern for the men and women. Women slept on the side where the fireplace was. Now, steps have replaced the ladder.

From the *Times-Georgian* December 3, 1998: The old Wick's Tavern was moved from its former location on the Dallas Highway on the north end of Villa Rica to its new location on W. Wilson Street.

Wick's Tavern still stands at the time of the printing of this book as the oldest commercial structure in Carroll County. The Tavern was built between 1838 and 1850 in the Dutch or 'German' style of timber framing made of 100% pine. The sills are hand hewn, the remainder of the lumber was sawn on a sash-type saw most likely water powered. I think that the 'sills' refers to the support timbers on the stone foundations. It is a textbook Dutch technique. The timbers are sized as to be hauled by mules and wagons. Though the building has been a house in the past, it was always built as a tavern in mind with a common room upstairs for pallets for bedding; women on one side (next to the fireplace); men on the other. Both Mr. Bryant, the carpenter, and Wick were of Dutch descent which explains the building style as opposed to English which was the other prevalent construction style in the early 1800s.

John Butler Wick and Delia J. Wick were buried at Evergreen Cemetery in Morristown, New Jersey.

9

Early Settlers of the Wesley Chapel Community

Nathaniel Harbin Humphries, a POW of the Civil War, was later the first mayor Villa Rica—in 1884.

William Bozeman Adair

"Bozeman" Adair, Jr. was born in 1771 in Virginia, the son of a Revolutionary Patriot, William Adair, Sr. His mother was Sarah Ann Scott. This family lived in Madison, Georgia in 1820 before coming to Carroll County in 1840. The 1850 Federal Census Records shows Bozeman living in Villa Rica. He married Sarah Ann Harrington circa 1790 in Madison. She was born June 20, 1769 in Georgia.

Bozeman received a good education and became a lawyer, Justice of Peace and Judge of Inferior Court in Jackson County. He served as a State Troop Soldier in 1811 and in the Oconee Indian War of 1787-1790. He was a state representative from Madison in 1819-1826, state representative from Carroll from 1829-1931, and helped organize New Hope Primitive Baptist Church. He and his wife, Sarah were among the first to join this church on January 4, 1829. He was one of the delegates to the Tallapoosa Baptist Association on 22 May 1835.

Bozeman and Sarah Ann Adair had the following children:
1) Judith Adair Williams;
2) William Andrew Adair;
3) Whitmill Harrington Adair;
4) Sarah Sally Adair Bone;
5) Lucy Adair Sanders;
6) John Bluett Adair;
7) James Lee Adair;
8) Permelia Adair Tolbert;
9) Mitchell S. "Michael" Adair.
While living in Villa Rica his wife, Sarah, died on August 6, 1842. Some

Bozeman & Sarah Ann Adair

reports list her buried in an unmarked grave in New Hope Primitive Baptist Church Cemetery. Other information states she was buried in an unmarked grave at Lane Cemetery in Paulding County.

From Abstract land records, Page 283 Carroll County, 15 Jul 1843. BOZEMAN ADAIR, Paulding County to N. JORNIGAN, Carroll County. $1,000.00. Part of land lot 209, 2nd district Carroll County. South from the N. E. corner 105 acres. Attest: Josiah Goggan, Wilson M. Bryant, Benjamin S. Merrell, J. P. 27 Dec 1845.

After his wife's death, Bozeman lived with his son James Lee and his wife Caroline. He and Caroline helped organize the Mt. Zion Baptist Church in Paulding County in December of 1844. He died April 7, 1857 and was buried at Mt. Zion.

David C. Clopton

David Clopton (b. February 22, 1796, New Kent, Virginia) was the son of David and Mary Ann Vanderwall Clopton of Virginia.

David C. Clopton was shown on the 1850 U. S. Federal Census Record living in Paulding County. He was 53; a daughter Martha was 13. His real estate value was $1,800. His was a farmer. On February 20, 1854, David Clopton adopted Martha Jenkins Ellington and changed her name to Martha Jenkins Clopton.

In 1860 he lived in Polk County, Georgia Militia District 1073, Van Wert. David was 64; listed also was David Scarcsey, age 27, born in South Carolina, an overseer who earned $300 per annum. David Clopton's value of real estate was $12,000 and the value of personal estate was $17,300.

David Clopton, 84, appears on the Bienville Parish, Louisana 1880 Federal Census as living with his daughter, Martha, and her husband Fredrice Pentecost. He died in Louisana on February 16, 1888.

At some point David owned the Clopton plantation located on Land Lot #194 in Villa Rica, Carroll County. When the Yankees came through, he hid in the woods This letter, written by David Clopton to Fannie Hardgrove (Hardgrave), daughter of Bright W. Hardgrove—a member of the community of Villa Rica in Carroll County—tells the story. Sherman's troops were in Dark Corner and David Clopton went into hiding. He writes his letter to tell Fannie what has happened since last summer (of 1865) when the Yankees and foragers came through "and left the country almost destitute of anything for the people to live on."

Hart Town Environs

March 21, 1865

Dear Fanny:

Your letter of 12th of last month came to hand a few days back, and as Mr. McClure is with me and will leave in the morning for the low country I will send this by him. If I mail it here it is very uncertain whether you will ever get it. I will not attempt to give you a history of my ups and downs since I saw you; it would take a volume. I will only say I left home Saturday before the Yankees came on Monday. I did expect they would get here on Sunday morning from what I had heard.

They robed [sic] my house, took a part of my meat and corn, and broke up things generally. They found the box containing your bedclothes, etc. and took most of your things, scattered your books all over the yeard [sic], robed Edy of her money and the most of her fine clothes and took many things . . . Your box was under Edy's bed. She thought, and was told that Yankees would not rob . . . Edy sent Mr. Pentecost's trunk to Patience's house and had it hid, but they found it and took out all his clothes.

I camped out in the woods for five or six weeks, thinking the Yankees would be driven back. I then left the country and landed down in Chambers County, Alabama, where I staid [sic] until sometime in September when I thought I would come home and see if I had anything left.

. . . I had been but a short time at home when the Yankees moved up from Stilesborough and for weeks they were camped on this side of the Van Wert and raiding through here every day. They passed my house many times but paid no attention to me. They stripped my house again of everything they wanted and left me almost without anything to keep house on. I have but two old broken knives and forks and would have been without bedclothes to sleep under had not Edy patched up a comfort or two.

The Yankee army has passed twice through here and our army once. The deserters and stragglers of our army have been in here all the summer and all together they have left this country almost destitute of anything for the people to live on.

They have taken five horses from me, about 80 heard (head) of hogs, and everything in the shape of a cow I had on the place and fully half of what little corn that was made. I am now without syrup, without milk, and have only corn and meat enough to last me half the summer.

But I am better off than some of my neighbors. There is poor Kingsbury had every pound of meat, and every bushel of corn, every horse, cow, hog, and chicken taken; the house stripped of everything they could carry off and he and his family left with only the clothes they had on, without one mouthful to eat. And he is not alone.

Dodds and some others here left in the same fix. . . .
   Your friend,
   David Clopton

Carroll Free Press, August 12, 1881:

   Early last spring Mr. Jas. P. Moore of this place, leased the mining interest of the Clopton Gold Mining property near Villa Rica from Mr. Willis Bagwell, and since then has been engaged in trying to find a richer vein of ore in it. After a long search and much hard labor, he has succeeded and it is working a very rich vein. It turns out from one to two pennyweights of gold per 100 pounds of quartz washed out.
   The main lead is four or five feet wide with several lesser ones and gets richer as it is dug deeper; it is only fifteen or twenty feet from the surface as of yet.
   Mr. Moore is working a five stamp quartz mill at present and is marking it pay. We saw some specimen of quartz rock from the mine the other day and could see the gold shining in it with the naked eye. The mine has not been actively worked for seven or eight years, until Mr Moore leased it. We wish him success.

Carroll Free Press, August 19 1881:

   The news from the Clopton Gold Mines on the place of Mr. Willis Bagwell near Villa Rica, at present by Mr. Moore of this place, continues to be good.
   From all accounts, Mr. Moore has struck bonanza. A reliable and trustworthy young man from this place who was up there last Saturday, says he is informed that the mine was yielding about $100. worth of gold per day. We hope Mr. Moore will make a good thing out of it. He worked a long time on faith, but we trust he will be rewarded for his perseverance in the yellow stuff itself.

From a deed dated September 8th 1883 M. N. Webster to Clopton Gold Mining Company:

   . . . A Clopton Gold Mining Company of Louisville, Kentucky incorporated under the laws of Kentucky for the purpose of acquiring holdings and selling lands and mining and milling by water or steam working mineral both gold, copper and Iron for the mineral of the second part. Witness that the said party of the first part W. W. Webster for and in consideration of the sum of thirty eight hundred and seventy three dollars—

thirty two hundred and fifty three dollars of said thirty eight hundred and seventy three dollars—cash to him in hand paid at and before the sealing and delivery of these presents—the receipt of which is hereby acknowledged and the execution and delivery by said party of the second part to said W. W. Webster of its promisory note for six hundred and twenty dollars . . .

Book A , Page 410, Greene County, 13 Sep 1830. ELI S. SHORTER to ALFORD CLOPTON, JOHN WARRAN, JOHN E. MORGAN, WILEY W. MASON, JOHN J. BOSWELL, BENJAMIN FORT and JAMES M. DUNN and LYMAN BURNAPP, Merchants. $1,000.00. Land lot #194, 6th dist. 202 1/2 acres. 1 & 1/2 tenths Alford Clopton, 1/10 John Warran, 1/10 John Morgan, 1/10 Dunn and Barnapp, l/10. Attest: L. Q. C Lamar, Adam G. Saffold J . I . C O . C , 18 Sep 1830.

Book B, Page 99, Carroll County, 3 Sep 1830. DAVID CLOPTON, Muscogee County to HODGE RABUN, Carroll County, PLEASANT HEATH of Jones County, STEPHEN D. CRANE, Jasper County. #375.00. 1/16 land lot #206, 2nd dist. Carroll (now Douglas) County, bought from Allen Lawhorn. Attest: Joseph C Thompson, William Ragland.

Book B, Page 289 Carroll County, 6 Aug 1830. ALLEN LAWHORN to DAVID CLOPTON. $300.00. 1/2 of 5/8 of land lot #206, 2nd dist. Carroll (now Douglas) County. Attest: John Cox, Isaiah Attaway, J.P. 20 Apr 1833.

Book B, Page 322, Paulding County, 15 Sep 1832 JOEL H. DYER, Paulding County to DAVID CLOPTON, Carroll County $33.00. 2/3 land lot #155, 6th district, Carroll, except 10 acres in the N. E. corner. Attest: A. W. McBrayer, Samuel Wilkinson J. P,. 1 Nov 1833.

Book B,Page 289, Muscogee County, 5 Dec 1832. ALFRED IVERSON to DAVID CLOPTON, Carroll County. $1,000.00. 1/8 interest in land lot #193, 6th dist. Carroll County. Attest: Lewis O. Allen, Ellwin E Bessell, J. I. C, 20 Apr 1833.

Book B, Page 396, Carroll County, 18 Jun 1834. WILLIAM WILLIAMSON to DAVID CLOPTON. $5.00 . Land lot #188, 6th dist , Carroll County where Williamson now lives. 202 1/2 acres. Security for a note of $260.00. Attest: Denison .B. Palmer, David Bivins.

Book B, Page 397, Carroll County, 12 Jul 1834. WILLIAM MAJORS to DAVID CLOPTON. Promissory note, $81.25. East half of land lot #119, 6th dist. Carroll County. 101 1/4 acres. Attest S. K. Harrison, Neil Stone, J. P 13 Oct 1834.

Bright Williamson Hargrave

Bright Williamson Hargrave (Hargrove) (b. January 20, 1809, Guilford County, North Carolina) was the son of Frederick Hargrave and Mary Wagg Hargrave.

Both his parents died and he was orphaned at an early age. He grew up with his sister and her husband, but ran away to Georgia at age twelve. His cousin George Prickett deeded him some land and Hargrave soon began adding to it. By 1832 he was in Carroll County as evidenced by a deed he witnessed there.

He married the widowed Mary Ann Emily Schofield Ford in 1839, whose one-year-old daughter Olivia Eliza Ford was from her previous marriage. Together they had twelve children: Frederick, Fannie Franklin Hargrave, Nellie Overtaker Hargrave, Frederick Clopton Hargrave, Hance Stephens Hargrave, Ramath Rice Hargrave, Thornton Burke Hargrave, Hannah H. Hargrave, William Monroe Hargrave, Savannah Hargrave (1), Savannah Hargrave (2), and Flora Hargrave.

Bright Hargrave
At Home in Carrollton

Bright Hargrave was a planter and a stockholder in the gold mines near Villa Rica. By the Civil War, he was one of the wealthiest men in the county.

On the 1850 Federal Census Record his occupation was miner, his value of real estate was $5,000; living with his wife and children was Eliza Wasson, age 55. The 1860 Census shows his occupation as farmer; living with his wife and children was Mrs. Wasson was age 65; the value of real estate was $3,000 and the value of his personal estate was $28,000.

On January 2, 1861, he was elected along with Allen Rowe and Jim Martin to represent Carroll County in Georgia's Secession Convention. All three were opposed to secession; however, Hargrave signed the ordinance for secession and each man supported the Confederacy once the fighting began. Hargrave was killed by Robert Velvin in May 1861, shortly after his return from the convention. It was not clear whether his murder was politically inspired or due to a quarrel.

Hargrave's plantation was left in the care of Ed Holland, but the property was sold for Confederate money and it is unknown what happened to his shares in the gold mine. His widow took the seven remaining children to Atlanta after his death; however, she contracted pneumonia while caring for the six children who were all sick with the measles. She died the next year, circa 1862 while living in Atlanta, Fulton County. The family was broken apart, with the older boys joining the Confederate army and their grandmother, Mrs. Schofield, keeping the younger children. Fannie lived with two guardians: Judge Long in Carrollton, and David Clopton in Van Wert, Georgia. Fannie lost touch with several of her siblings during this time and did not find William until they were both elderly.

Hart Town Environs

Fannie Hargrave Brannan died June 29, 1918 and was buried in Pulaski, Tennessee.

Book C, Page 185, Carroll County, 1 Sep 1836. BRIGHT W. HARGRAVE to WILLIAM MAJORS. $100. Undivided part land lot #206, 2nd dist. Carroll (now Douglas) County. 1/320th part of the land. Attest: William Ragland, James Simpson.

Book C, Page 284, Carroll County, 17 Apr 1836. JOEL H. DYER to BRIGHT W. HARGROVE. $30. 1/64 part land lot #206, 2nd dist. Carroll County. Known as the Pine Mountain Gold Mine. Attest: James Simpson, R. V. C. Ruffin J.P.; 5 Jun 1838.

Book E, Page 98 Carroll County, 1 Aug 1834. JOHN BROWN, Cass County, to B. W. HARGROVE and M. L. PATTON. $166.66. 1/36 land lot #212, 2nd district Carroll [now Douglas] County. Attest: T. Butler, P .S. Bosworth. Charles Hulsey, J. P . 7 Mar 1844.

Book E, Page 99 Monroe County, 16 Jun 1838. MOSES L. PATTON, Texas to B. W. HARGROVE, Monroe County, Ga. $100.00. 1/2 of the 1/36th interest land lot #212, 2nd dist. Carroll [now Douglas] County. Attest: David Clopton, Asbury Kingman, William Ross, J.P. John Hildebrand 7 Mar 1844.

Book E, Page 99 Carroll County, 1 Jul 1843. E. S. Candler, Sheriff, Carroll County to B. W. HARGROVE and DAVID CLOPTON. 1/8 undivided interest land lot #212, 2nd dist. Carroll [now Douglas] County. $38.00. Sold to satisfy writ of fieri facias, Cass County against BROWN and DYER property of JOHN BROWN. Attest: J. C. Williams, Thomas Raburn J. P. 8 March 1844.

Book F, Page 238 Carroll County, 10 Jun 1844. JOHN DEAN, Sheriff to BRIGHT W. HARGROVE and DAVID CLOPTON. $90.00. Land lot #212, 2nd dist. Carroll [now Douglas] County. Sold by virtue of a writ of fifa, Robert B. Smiley vs. JAMES SIMPSON, owner of property and CALVIN HOLLAND, endorser. Attest: N. W . Davis, George W. Hunt, J. P . 10 Jun 1845.

Book F, Page 523 Carroll County, 20 Feb 1851. THOMAS W. GARNER to BRIGHT W. HARGRAVES. Promissory note, $750.00. Security Land lot #147, 2nd dist. Carroll [now Douglas] County, west half of land lot #175, 2nd dist. Carroll [now Douglas] County. Attest: W. E. Slaughter, Joseph C. Williams, J.P. 28 Apr 1851.

Richard Clark Hannah

Richard Hannah (b. July 11, 1833 in North Carolina, d. 1905, Carroll County) was the son of Isaac Hannah (Haney) (born 1790 North Carolina) and Sarah Jane.

On the 1870 and 1880 Federal Census Record, this family lived in Paulding County, but not far from Villa Rica. Isaac, Sarah Jane and children lived less than a mile from Wesley Methodist Church, in what they fondly referred to as "Hannah Swamp."

Richard Hannah, married Celia Elizabeth (Lizzie) in Floyd County, on December 8, 1861. Lizzie was b. August 5, 1840, in Tennessee. Several sons and daughters made their living as most of the courtryfolk, farming.

This family lived in tranquility until the Civil War. Lizzie remained on the farm, plowing and caring for the place while Richard fought with the Confederate States Army. He was in Appomattox, Virginia when Lee surrendered on April 9, 1865; then, began his long and laborious walk home.

Richard and Celia raised their children:
1) Lucinda Jane "Lucy" (b. October 1867);
2) Robert (b. June 1873);
3) Pritchard (b. 1875);
4) Fannice J. "Fannie," (b. 1876) who married an Ivy;
5) Richard Clark "Bud" Hannah Jr. (b. January 1878);
6) Reuben (b. December 1880).

Richard and his family farmed their lands and frequented their church. Isaac Hannah, Richard's father died in 1881; Richard died in 1905; Celia died November 30, 1904; they are buried at the Wesley Chapel Methodist Church Cemetery, just north of Villa Rica.

When Richard died in 1905 in his seventies, the minister wrote in glowing terms of his goodness. His grandchildren have continued in their faith and works to Wesley Chapel, Hugh and Dorsey Hannah having built and presented the Communion Table, end tables and lectern. Today, Richard Rodgers, son of Mrs. Carol Hannah Rodgers, and great-great-grandson of Wesley Chapel's charter member Richard Hannah, attends the church regularly. So the stream flows.

Abel Hill Harrison

Abel Hill Harrison (b. March 31, 1805, Turkey Creek, Buncombe County, North Carolina, d. March 29, 1883, Acworth, Cobb County) was son of Joseph Harrison and Margaret Hill. Abel was in Carroll County, as early as February 1, 1830 when he witnessed a deed. Abe and his brother-in-law, Clayton Williams, were in business together in Carroll County in 1844 where they bought and sold land, D.B.A.—doing business as— A. H. Harrison & Company of Carroll County.

On January 6, 1835 he married Hannah Chambers, daughter of Joseph and Sarah Chambers, in Carroll County.

Abel was enlisted in the Carroll Rangers to fight the Creek Indian War in 1836. He was riding a bay mare, 9 years old and valued at $90.00 according to the army records. He also had a saddle worth $8.00 and a gun worth $25.00. He was at Camp Thomas July 11th, 1836 along with Edward Dyer and Tyre Watson.

On January 28, 1831, Andrew and John Kerr, James and John Hope and Abel Harrison together paid $2,400 for land lot #165, which was adjacent to the intersection at the mining town of Hart Town. In 1842 and 1844 Abel paid taxes on Land Lot #165. On March 13, 1844, Abel H. Harrison paid $1,500 to Nicholas G. Thomas for mining

Hart Town Environs

Able Harrison's Home
Artist Betty A. Norton; Courtesy Roger Smith & Joe Jordan

interest in Land Lot #165, 6th district. On March 8, 1848, Abel H. Harrison paid $1,000 to M. C. Autry for 15 acres of Land lot 165, 6th district Carroll County. He reserved 1/2 mining interest on the southwest corner containing land owned by Dr. N. G. Thomas; on this corner was also a blacksmith shop and a joiners shop.

On August 9, 1837, Abel H. Harrison, Samuel C. Candler and James L. Adair was ordered by the court to review a route for a road from Villa Rica to the county line of Paulding County. Abel Hill Harrison was an early mayor of Villa Rica.

Abel and Hannah appear on the 1840, 1850, 1860 and 1870 U. S. Federal Census as living in Villa Rica. Abel was one of the very earliest merchants in the area. On the 1850 Federal Census, Abel was listed as a Merchant with a real estate value of $1,000. On this census, living in the household, was Able age, 44, Hannah his wife was 33, Sarah Chambers was 7, born in 1843 in Georgia and Mary Hartsfield was 14, born in 1836 in Georgia; Robert Huff, age 22, was a laborer and Jas M. Howell, age 22, was a laborer. It was assumed that Sarah Chamber, age 7 was a relative of his wife Hannah and it was unknown if Mary Hartsfield was his daughter or a neice or an adopted child.

On the 1860 Federal Census, Abel was shown as retired merchant and his real estate value was 500 and personal value was $20,500. His mother-in-law, Sarah Chambers, age 78, was living with him and his wife Hannah.

On the 1870 Federal Census his personal estate value and real estate value was $200 each. Living in the household in 1870 was Ann Boyce, age 25, born in Virginia.

On the 1880 Federal Census, Able was 75 and Hannah was 62; they lived at Acworth, Cobb County. Abel and Hannah both died in Acworth, he in 1883, and she on October 3, 1882. Both were buried at Liberty Hill Cemetery, near Acworth.

Nathaniel Harbin Humphries

Nathaniel Harbin Humphries (b. February 28, 1823, Pendleton, Anderson County, South Carolina, d. May 13, 1909, Villa Rica) was the son of William Saddler Humphries (b. 1769, d. 1855) and Sarah Harbin (b. 1780, d. August 1866). The Nathaniel Humphries family lived in District 10 of Campbell County in 1850, where he was a shoemaker. In 1852, he married Edna Emaline Holley in Decatur. Edna (b. February 26, 1831, d. January 21, 1891).

The Humphries' children were:

1) Sarah Alice (b. Oct 29, 1853, d. June 26, 1911);
2) John Wiley Humphries (b. August 20, 1855, d. July 14, 1916);
3) James William Humphries (b. April 14, 1857, d. July 18, 1933).

Nathaniel Humphries served as a 2nd Lieutenant during the Civil War, in Company D 10th Georgia Regiment, Georgia State Guards. While he was working at New Manchester Manufacturing Company in Campbell County (later Douglas County), the mill was captured and burned and all workers taken as prisoners.

Nathaniel was held prisoner in Jeffersonville, Indiana for eleven months. After the Civil War ended, he made his way back to Georgia.

In 1870, Nathaniel and Edna Emaline lived in Fulton County; he was a shoemaker; in 1880 they lived in Smyrna, Cobb County where he was a farmer. He moved to Villa Rica in 1883. In 1884, Nathaniel was elected the first mayor of Villa Rica. He was a long-time member of the Villa Rica Presbyterian Church. By 1900, he worked as a shoe inspector.

Nathaniel Humphries died in 1909 and was buried at Hillcrest City Cemetery.

Needham Jornigan

Needham Jornigan moved to Carroll County and bought land in District 6 and District 2 circa 1841.

Needham (b. May 25, 1803, Grainger County, Tennessee, d. September 17, 1845, Carroll County) was the son of Noah Jarnagin (b. 1768, d. 1849) and Mary Ann Russell (b. 1765, d. 1857) .

Needham married Margaret Nuney in Jefferson, Tennessee on February 25, 1828. In 1840, they lived in District 642 Carroll County. By 1850, they lived in Bradyville, Cannon County, Tennessee.

No date was found for Margaret Nuney Jornigan's passing, but Needham married for the second time to Sarah Niven on November 9, 1842 in Cannon, Tennessee. No children were listed for Needham nor for either his first or second wife.

He died in 1845 and was buried at New Hope Primitive Baptist Church Cemetery.

Page 282, Book E, August 18, 1841. John Hill of Augusta City by attorney in fact for Fleming Jourdin and David Reese to Needham Jarnagin of Carroll County. Sum of $900.00. Land lot #224, 6th district Carroll County. Know as the Hill Lot or Gold mine. Attest: J. W. Barney, Cas. Jourdin, J.I.C. November 10, 1845.

Page 282, Book E, Jasper County, 18 Aug 1841. J. E. A. BRODDAS, Jasper County to NEEDHAM JORNAGIN. $125.00. 1/6 interest lot #224, 6th district Carroll County, known as the Hill Goldmine, all his rights and only reserving right to any gold veins. Attest: William Goolsby, Chas. Jordan, J.I.C. 10 Nov 1845.

Page 280, Book E, Carroll County, 9 May 1843. JESSEE WOOTEN, JONATHAN

W. DAVIS and JOHN ROGERS to N. JORNAGAN. $600.00. Mining interest land lot #210, 2nd district Carroll [now Douglas] County. A certain creek being the line run between Robert Huff and Chambers. Attest: Wilson McBrayor, F. M. Little, Joseph C Williams, J.P. 17 Nov 1845.

Page 283, Book E, Carroll County, 25 Jul 1843. JAMES ROBERTS to NEEDHAM JARNAGIN. $100.00. Part of land lot #210, 2nd district Carroll [now Douglas] County. 1/2 acre. Attest: A. C. Williams, R. V. C. Ruffin, J.P. 11 Nov 1845.

Book E, page 465, 10 June 1844, Carroll County, EDMUND W. HOLLAND, agent DAVID CLOPTON, DAVID BROADDUS, BENJAMIN CHAPMAN, EDMUND W. HOLLAND, JOSEPH CHAMBERS, JESSE H. CHAMBERS and CLAYTON WILLIAMS to NEEDHAM JARNIGAN. $91.68. 11/12 of town lots #8, #10, #14, #16, Villa Rica, land lot #193, 6th district Carroll County. Attest: A.C. Williams, R. V. C. Ruffin, J.P. 8 Feb 1847.

10

Early Settlers of Hill's Crossing and Simsville

In 1867, twenty-nine families from Carroll County traveled to Honduras and formed an American colony to escape the Reconstruction period in the United States.

Hill's Crossing

Early settlers of Land Lot #s 168, 169, 170, 183, 184 and 185 came through Hill's Crossing to access Simsville. This crossing was just west of the Little Tallapoosa River and the fork going northwest to what was Ringer's Crossroads, later called Temple Road. Hill's Crossing was near Hill Creek.

Those who bought, sold and lived on these Land Lots were Nelson Almon, William Brooks, Isaac Cobb, William Cobb, Sr., Ethan Davis, Felix Davis, David Hiden, Jackson Lafayette Hill, A. Hogan, James McElrath, Benjamin McKinney, W. W. Merrell, Willis Raburn, William Smith, Simon Waddell, Alford Waddell, William West, and Robertson Wood. (33°44'12.53"N 84°59'19.21"W)

Reverend William James Brooks III & Family

William Brooks (b. February 5, 1812, Montgomery, North Carolina, d. July 15, 1887, Carroll County) was the son of William James Brooks II (b. 1779, d. 1846) and Mary "Polly" Burleson (b. 1780. d 1852). William married Catherine Matilda Clontz on November 21, 1833 in Mecklenburg, North Carolina. Catherine (b. November 7, 1837, d. September 20, 1897, Carroll County). He settled with his family in the Hill's Crossing area, District 6 Carroll County, before 1860.

Reverend Brooks preached at Concord Methodist Church and Asbury Chapel Methodist Church and at Simsville, before Temple was settled.

Their children were:
1) Mary Isabelle, a twin (b. 1834, d. 1901);
2) Sarah, a twin (b. 1834, d. 1916);

3) Catherine (b. 1837, d. 1901);

4) Janie E. (b. March 13, 1839, d. December 7, 1923 who married William Thomas Wynn in 1889;

5) Private John Wesley Brooks (b. 1841, d. 1911);

6) Private William Jacob Brooks (b. 1843, d. 1883);

7) Lugeri Frances (b. 1847, d. 1865);

8) Thomas Sanford (b. 1850, d. 1876);

9) Doctor James Fletcher (b. April 1853, d. July 31, 1893).

On the 1860 Federal Census Record, the family was listed in Carroll County; William's value of real estate was $2,000 and value of personal estate was $1,000. In 1870 they lived in the Villa Rica district; his value of real estate was $1,000 and value of personal estate was $1,000. In 1880 they were in Militia District 649—Temple.

In Reverend Brooks will, he divided his holdings and Land Lots #203 and #184 among his wife and children. He was buried at Asbury Cemetery with Masonic honors. Catherine Brooks was buried at Asbury Cemetery also.

Isaac Eugene Cobb

Isaac E. Cobb (b. August 12, 1805, Abbeville, South Carolina, d. August 5, 1852, Temple) was the son of James H. Cobb (b. 1770, South Carolina, d. 1850, Forsyth County). His mother was Elizabeth Mitchell (b. 1770, South Carolina, d. 1819 Forsyth County).

On the 1830 Federal Census, Isaac Cobb was in Franklin County, Georgia Captain Smith's 17th District Land lot #134. He married Francis Carter Chandler on March 22, 1829. She was born in Franklin County in 1810 to Joseph Chandler and Sarah Farmer Chandler.

Isaac and Francis Cobb's children:

1) William Washington Cobb (b. April 21, 1830, Franklin County, d. August 3, 1864, LaGrange) married Sarah Jane Hart, daughter of Samuel Hart. For more on William and Jane Hart Cobb, see the next excerpt.

2) John Marion Cobb (b. February 8, 1833, d. 1905, Villa Rica). He was a Captain in Company I, 56 Georgia Regiment; he was severely wounded at the battle at Jonesboro (Georgia) in July 1864 and never entirely recovered. John Cobb married Adaline Embry. He was a Justice of the Peace for 30 years after the war.

3) Martha S. Cobb (b. July 2, 1835, d. 1858) married Lawrence Baskin of Hickory Level. She died in 1858 leaving two daughters, Alice Turner and Fannie Chambers of Carrollton.

4) James H. Cobb (b. July 6, 1837, d. 1907) married Lizzie Walker. He served as Private, Co. E, 1st Georgia Calvary Confederate States Army.

5) Mary Ann Cobb (b. November 4, 1839, d. 1922) married Reverend C. M. Baskin of Hickory Level.

6) Thomas B. Cobb (b. 1841, Carroll County). He served in Company F, 7th Georgia Regiment, Infantry, Confederate States Army and died in 1864 in the Con-

federate Army. He was buried at Oakland Cemetery in Atlanta.

7) George H. Cobb (b. 1844, Carroll County, d. 1866). He served in Company F, 7th Georgia Regiment. After the war, he settled in Texas. He never married.

8) Joseph Lafayette Cobb (b. April 27, 1847, Carroll County, d. 1917). He served in the Confederate States Army for two years. He married Augusta Grow and they had two sons: Hugh B. and Joseph Cobb. Joseph was Pvt. Joe Cobb the author of the history book, *Carroll County and Her People,* published in 1906.

William & Jane Hart Cobb
Courtesy Mrs. Henry Cobb

In 1840 this family was shown in District #714 in Carrollton. In 1842 and in 1844, Isaac Cobb payed taxes on the Georgia Property Tax Digest for Land Lots #169, #170, #184 and #151 all in the 6th district of Carroll County.

Isaac Cobb was the sheriff of Carroll County for several years. He later represented Carroll County four times in the Legislature, three times in succession. He moved from Carrollton to Temple where he bought Buckhorn Tavern, a waystation for stagecoach travelers. (33°44'13.41"N 85°00'16.97"W) He served as a postmaster there at Buck Horn, Georgia in February 1849. His son, William was the postmaster in October 16, 1852. Joseph L. Hart, the oldest son of Samuel Hart, was the postmaster as of September 16, 1856. Thereafter the post office was discontinued after 1857.

In 1850 Isaac lived in Carroll County with a real estate value of $6,000.

After the death of his wife, Francis Chandler, on November 7, 1849, Isaac E. Cobb married Mary Chandler on January 26, 1851 in Carroll County. Mary was born in 1805 and died in 1863.

Isaac E. Cobb died in 1852 at age 49 and was buried at the Old Bethel Primitive Baptist Church at the site of Old Simsville. His tombstone reads: He died as he had lived, a philanthropist, an honest man and a Christian. Here sleeps his remains. Peace to his ashes.

William Washington Cobb

William Washington Cobb was the oldest son of Isaac and Sarah Cobb's eight children. Circa 1856, William Washington Cobb purchased land and a cabin a mile west of the headwaters of the Little Tallapoosa River from Robertson Wood who had settled there in 1840. The road beside the house and through the farm was originally the Atlanta-Birmingham Road, later named the Villa Rica—Temple Road and today is Old Villa Rica Road.

William Cobb married Sarah "Jane" Hart, daughter of Samuel Hart. She was

Isaac, Almeda and Lucy Cobb
Courtesy Mrs. Henry Cobb

(L-R) **Ossie, Jr., Frank, Lewis and Henry Cobb**
Courtesy Hart Cobb

born November 3, 1830. William and Sarah married on January 17, 1856.

William Cobb farmed ninety acres of his total two-hundred seventy acres in cultivation and had forty-five heads of livestock. They had children:

1) Isaac Osceola "Ossie" (b. December 14, 1856, d. May 9, 1907);
2) An infant who was born and died in 1858;
3) Eldorado H. "Bud" (b. 1859, d. 1935);
4) John T. Cobb (b. 1861, d. 1884).

This land and log cabin was located on the line of Land Lots #185 and #168 on the Temple Road—the one going to Buckhorn Tavern—just a mile or so east of the Buckhorn Tavern. As the stagecoach passed their log cabin, a horn was blown as many times as there were the number of passengers on board so the meal could be prepared and the table set to accommodate them.

A few years later, William Cobb added three large rooms and two more chimneys to the original house. These new rooms were built from *planed* lumber, with ten foot ceilings and six foot windows.

After the Civil War broke out, William enlisted on May 8, 1862 with Company E of the 1st Georgia Cavalry. In 1864 at the Chattahoochee River near Atlanta, he contracted chronic dysentery. He was taken to a LaGrange hospital where he died on August 2, 1864. He was first buried in LaGrange, but J. L. Cobb who was in the same unit, had his body disinterred in July 1865 and reburied in Carroll County at Pleasant Grove Baptist Church Cemetery.

Sarah Jane was alone in the big house and lived on the farm trying to raise her three boys. After the war, she taught school at Pleasant Grove School and walked the three miles with her boys every school day. In 1884, her youngest son, John, died of typhoid fever.

In 1883, when the Georgia Pacific Railroad came through, parts of several land lots were bought from the Cobb family for the railroad right-of-way and crossing. The crossing was known as Cobb's Crossing for several generations.

Hart Town Environs

33°44'14.77"N 84°59'19.35"W. The next crossing was Hill's Crossing. Jane Cobb lived out her years in the "Cobb House" and died on March 2, 1909, one of the oldest members at Pleasant Grove Church. She was buried along side her husband there.

Isaac Osceola Cobb, her oldest son, inherited the home; he married Esther Almeda Connell (b. 1868, d. 1947). They raised five children:

1) Lucy Cobb (Robinson) (b. August 11, 1891, d. 1972);
2) Lewis Connell Cobb (b. May 23, 1902);
3) William Frank (b. December 16, 1903, d. 1979);
4) Henry Hart Cobb (b. March 26, 1906, d. 1986);
5) Isaac Osceola "Ossie", Jr. (b. 1907, d. 1949).

Isaac Osceola Cobb, Sr. continued to farm the land, but worked at a hardware store in Temple.

About 1903, he added an east and west porch, two rooms and a front hallway, ornate trim, and balustrades and two more chimneys, making it look like a true Victorian home. The Cobb house remained in the family until 1945 when the Kittle family bought it and 204 acres. This rambling home was known as the Cobb—Kittle house for several generations. (33°44'18.73"N 84°59'16.45"W)

Cobb–Kittle House
Courtesy Buford Kittle

Alexander & Mary Hart Colclough

Mary Hart, the sister of Samuel Hart, of Hart Town, (b. 1800, Wilkes, Georgia, d. August 29, 1869, Bowden). On December 28, 1831, she married Alexander Colclough in Taliaferro County; Alexander (b. 1802, North Carolina, d. 1888, Alabama). Alexander's father was William Colclough. They had three children:

1) Eli H. (b. 1833; d. 1907);
2) Susan Rebecca Colclough (Morris) (b. 1835, d. 1908);
3) William A. b. (1837, d. 1873).

Susan, daughter of Mary Hart and Alexander Colclough

In 1830 they were in North Carolina; between 1840 and 1850 the family left Taliaferro County to move to Carroll County to settle near Hart Town, near her brother, Samuel. In 1850, they lived in *Division 11* which covers all of Carroll County. The value of their real estate was $2,400. Entry 414 page 63 places them in Hill's Crossing as they had neighbors, Isaac Cobb entry 418 page 64, on Land Lot# 169, and Buckhorn Tavern (near present day Temple, Georgia). In 1860, they were in *District 11,* Laurel Hill, in Carroll County and in 1870 in the Bowdon Community in Carroll County.

Mary Hart Colclough, died in 1869; she was buried at the First United Methodist Church Cemetery, Bowdon, near her husband, Alexander, and son, William.

An early document, lists the petitioners who drew a land lottery because of service in the War of 1812. The list of signatures includes both William Hart and William Coolbaugh [sic], 2nd. See Chapter 5.

William Hart appeared on the 1830 census of Carroll County. Alexander Colcough and Mary Hart Colcough lived near Hart Town in 1850, at Hills' Crossing. This poses an interesting historical question. Is the William Hart, of Hart Town, the one who signed this petition of 1812 soldiers? Is this William Coolbaugh—Mary Hart Colcough's father-in-law?

Jackson Lafayette Hill

Jackson Lafayette "Jack" Hill (b. August 26, 1828, Harris County, Georgia) was the son of Isaac Abner Hill III (b. 1797, Harris County, d. 1833, Harris County), and Isabelle Cox Hill (b. 1801, Warren County, Georgia, d. October 1809, Bremen).

Jack married Isabella Baskin McCain on October 18, 1847 in Troup County. She was born in 1828. In 1850, they lived in Troup. In 1860, they lived in Carroll, near Temple, on the south 2/3rds of Land Lot 168, known as Hill Place, at Hill Creek. His value of real estate was $1,080 and his value of personal property was $3,250.

Jackson Lafayette and Isabella's children:
1) Isaac Sion (b. October 19, 1848, Troup County, died 1908);
2) Margaret Jane (b. February 8, 1850, d. 1927);
3) James Alexander (b. July 17, 1853, Carroll County, d. July 31, 1921);
4) William H. (b. 1856, Carroll County);
5) Ellen Pemelia (b. March 08, 1858, d. 1941);
6) Benjamin Newton (b. October 19, 1859);
7) Isabella Virginia (b. November 4, 1862, d. 1920).

Jackson Lafayette Hill enlisted August 1, 1862 in the Confederate States Army,

Company I, 19th Georgia Regiment as a Private. He was admitted to the Institute Hospital at Richmond, Virginia on December 16, 1862 and died there on December 28, 1862 from wounds he received in the battle in Richmond. He was buried in grave No. 32 in Hollywood Cemetery in Richmond.

When her husband left to fight in the Civil War, Isabella had five children including, the youngest, a two-year-old. When he was killed in December 1862, she had a one month old, Isabella Virginia, born in November 1862.

On the 1880 Federal Census Record, the household of Isabella Hill, 51, was shown on the next entry to the household of Sarah J(ane) Hart Cobb, also a Civil War widow. Listed with Isabella are her five youngest children: James A. age 26; William H. age 24; Ellen P. age 21; Benjamin M. age 20 and Isabella H. age 18 and Franklin G. Goldin, a farm laborer.

Private Jackson Hill

In Bethel Baptist Church Cemetery near Temple in Carroll County, Jackson Lafayette Hill has a C.S.A. marker between the graves of his wife, Isabella Baskin McCain Hill (b. August 26, 1828, d. March 6, 1898) and his youngest son, Benjamin Hill (b. October 10, 1859, d. October 26, 1902).

William Smith West

William Smith West (b. September 1, 1826, Laurens County, South Carolina, d. January 10, 1897, Temple) was the son of William Wister West and Winnefred Tankersley. This family was shown on the 1840 Census as living in District 649 in Carroll County; William Smith West was fourteen. In 1850 he was 24 years old and living in *Division 11*, Carroll County.

On March 23, 1856, William Smith West married Mahala Jane Adams, the daughter of Absolom Adams and Mary Elizabeth Reid, in Carroll County. Mahala (b. September 17, 1834, d. October 7, 1919, Temple). In 1860 their residence was District Carroll County, Post Office—Villa Rica; in 1870 Carroll County; 1880 District 649 Carroll County.

William and Mahala had 8 children:
1) Robert William West (b. September 1858, d. 1937);
2) Elizabeth W. West (b. 1860, d. 1864);
3) Gilbert Taylor West (b. 1864, d. 1907);
4) Thomas Smith West (b. 1867, d. 1952);
5) Allen Absalom West (b. 1871, d. 1952);
6) Talulah Jane West (b. 1873, d. 1950);
7) Martha Ella West (b. 1875, d. 1875);
8) Antha Willie West (b. 1879, d. 1900).

William Smith West **Mahala Adams West**

William Smith West enlisted in 1864 to serve in the Confederate States Army; he joined Company B, Benson's Mounted State Troops Calvary. He served until the surrender, where he was home on sick furlough.

William West was buried at Concord United Methodist Church Cemetery. Mahala Jane West was buried at Concord also. William purchased land in and around Hill's Crossing, near Simsville.

Book C, Lot #169, Page 65, Washington County, Georgia. March 5, 1836. Robert Whitfield of Washington County to William West of Carroll County. Sum of $500.00 for land lot #169, in the 6th district of Carroll County. Containing 202 1/2 acres. Attest: James Majors. Clayton Williams.

Book D, Lot #169, Page 349, District 6, Carroll County, Georgia, Carroll County, March 8, 1842. William West to Isaac E. Cobb. Sum of $400.00 for land lot #169, in the 6th district of Carroll County. Land lot #170, in the 6th district of Carroll County, except 9 acres owned by David Hiden. Land lot #184, in the 6th district of Carroll County. Land lot #151 in the 6th district of Carroll County, land lot containing 15 acres. Attest: William W. Merrell, B. S. Merrell, J.P.; November 16, 1842.

Simsville

Just west, about three miles from Hart Town was the thriving settlement of Simsville (33°43'24.01"N 85°00'07.42"W). Before the railroad, it was accessible by going west down the Atlanta-Birmingham Road (later called Old Villa Rica—Temple Road) and then over to what is now Bar J Road by crossing at Cobb's Crossing then Hill's Crossing.

Early family histories and abstract deeds show there was a small town that began with settlers who came as early as 1829 to the Land Lots #s 137, 138, 151, 152, and 153. Among these early settlers and their ancestors were Absolom Adams, James H. Allen; Nelson Allum; George Awtry; Rev. James F. Williams, John and Elisha Brooks; Wilson Cartwright, James Chance; John M. Cobb; Gilbert Cole; Henry Coleman; William Allen Coleman; William N. Davis; Able Emery;

Nathaniel J. Grace; Andrew, Anderson, and Alexander Green & William Mercer Green; David and Samuel Grey; J. P. Griffin; H. M. Mastenn; Hendon, David & George Hiden; George Holcomb; Benjamin J. McCain; Elijah McPherson; William McGee; William Morgan; Rev. John & Stephen Riggs; Dr. R. L. Rowe; Rev. Sterling Tucker "Uncle Tuck" Sims; John M. Steel; James D. Stone; Alford, Simon & Nancy Waddell; and John Wright.

The History of Temple, Georgia, A West Georgia Town of Carroll County, includes an early history of Simsville:

> ... Simsville had a population of 200 and was a flourishing community for a number of years before the railroad was built through Ringer's Cross Roads (later Temple). A post office was established in Simsville on July 20, 1876, with George W. Autry as the first postmaster. B. J. McCain also served as postmaster there. The post office which received mail once a week was discontinued in 1883.
>
> The two doctors were James F. Brooks and Richard L. Rowe. Dr. Rowe was one of the county's two representatives to the State Constitutional Convention of 1877.
>
> The main crops grown in Simsville were cotton and corn, and at one time there were four cotton gins. These cotton gins were operated by J. P. Griffin, J. M. Street, H. McPherson, and the Hill Brothers. Sawmills and grist mills were run by James Chance and J. P. Griffin. Williams' Mill was also located there. A. L. Waddell operated a flour mill.
>
> The Justices Court Ground of the old Sixth District was located at Simsville at Sharp and Cheney's store. An old man and his wife were always there in a covered, one-steer wagon with ginger cakes, 'simmon beer,' and apple cider to sell. The cakes sold for a 'thrip' as did cider and beer per cup. A 'Thrip' was a small, silver five-cent piece.
>
> The nearest railroad was twelve miles southward at Carrollton. From that point, the farmers shipped their cotton to market. They also traded with the merchants there whose wares were brought from Atlanta by wagon train.

From Pvt. Joe Cobb's, *Carroll County and Her People* published in 1906:

> Beyond the creek, on the hill, the first occupant was Mr. Hendon, a primitive Baptist preacher, more than sixty years ago (approximately 1846). Then comes the Green place, high above and near the river. Uncle "Tuck" Sims afterwards owned the place and lived there many years. The Waddell place was the home of the father of Mr. 'Sims' Waddell, who still lives and is now an old man himself. It was first settled by Geo. Hyden. Old Bethel, Primitive Baptist church is next. It was built at a time "whereof the memory of man runneth not to the contrary." It was made of large logs and covered with boards from the forest.
>
> It had no steeple pointing high towards the heavens; no bell to toll

the knell of parting day, or call yeomanry [sic] to prayer and praise. But at stated times the rustic farmers would gather in the house, the good old elder would ride up, tie his horse to a sapling in the grove, take his saddle bags on his arms, walk up to the church, shake hands with all his brethern, go into the rudely constructed pulpit, read, sing and preach the gospel in its simplicity and honesty as he understood it. That custom even pertains to this day. This sect has always been regarded as honest and sincere, and their love for one another very strong indeed.

Near the old church is a very ancient graveyard, perhaps a hundred years old (1806). Some time ago in the evening twilight, the writer stood in the quiet "city of the dead" between the graves of his own departed parents, (Isaac and Francis Cobb) who have rested there for more than half a century, and with uncovered head and serious thoughts, the beautiful lines from Grey's Elegy came into the mind.

Shole's Georgia State Gazelle in 1879-80 shows Simsville, Carroll County, Georgia located on the Little Tallapoosa River with a population of 108. It had a furniture factory, a cotton gin operated by steam, a common school and three nearby churches: a Primitive, a Missionary Baptist and a Methodist. The town had a weekly stage communication with Villa Rica. Furniture and cotton were the principal exports. Carrollton, the County Seat, was twelve miles away with the nearest shipping station to Atlanta.

C. W. Baskin was listed as the Methodist Minister. Reverend William Brooks was also a Methodist Minister. Reverend Sterling Tucker Sims was the Primitive Baptist Minister at Bethel Baptist. Reverend George Holcomb was also a Baptist Church Minister. James H. Allen, Stephen Riggs and James D. Stone were the carpenters in Simsville. John M. Cobb was the Justice of the Peace; Nathaniel J. Grace was a blacksmith; and H. M. Mastenn was a furniture manufacturer. R. L. Rowe was the physician. The mail came weekly by horseback, brought by Benjamin McCain who also ran a general store.

Alfred Waddell's store was the hub of activity. The Post Office was established there in 1876, where mail was delivered once a week and was the site of the 4th of July celebration in 1876.

Today any evidence of the early town of Simsville has disappeared. There only remains an old cemetery of 75–100 graves; many of these are unmarked. These are obviously the graves of the residents of the once thriving town of Simsville. The old church structure is gone and a new Bethel Baptist Church was built later on Highway 113.

Absalom Drury Adams

Absalom Drury Adams (b. February 15, 1810, Monroe County, Tennessee, d. August 23, 1875, Temple) was the son of William F. Adams. Jr, (b. 1777, d. 1856, Temple). His mother was Sarah Blakenship Adams (b. 1779, d. September 30, 1856, Coweta County).

Absalom Adams came to Georgia and bought Land Lots #s 117, 115, 86 and 53 about 1842. Absalom Drury Adams married Mary Elizabeth Reid in Tennessee circa 1828, which would make her about 14. Mary Elizabeth (b. circa 1814, d. 1885).

Mary and Absalom were shown with their family on the 1830, 1840, 1850, 1860, 1870 and 1880 Federal Census for the Villa Rica area #649 and in 1850 for *Division 11* which was all of Carroll County.

They had thirteen children, all born near Temple:

1) Alley died in 1851;
2) Edmund Hunt Adams (b. October 18, 1828, d. 1899);
3) William B. Adams (b. Oct 7, 1830, d. 1899);

Absolom Adams

4) William Jasper Adams (b. February 16, 1832, d. March 16, 1862). He died while serving in the Confederate Army;
5) Machaley (Mahaley) (b. September 17, 1834, d. 1919);
6) Edith C. "Edy" (b. January 19, 1837, d. 1898);
7) Phoebe Elizabeth (September 18, 1839, d. 1885);
8) Gilbert Marion Adams (b. 1842, d. June 26, 1862, Hanover, Virginia). He died while serving in the Confederate Army, see below;
9) Zachariah Taylor Adams (b. October 3, 1845, d. 1916);
10) Sarah Ann (b. 1846, d. 1931);
11) Margaret D. H. Adams (b. August 20, 1854; d. 1890);
12) Jonah Adams (b. 1855);
13) Lydia Adams (b. 1860).

Two of their son died fighting with the Confederate Army. Gilbert Marion Adams enlisted as Private on June 11, 1861 with Company F, 19th Regiment Georgia Volunteer Infantry Carroll County Guards. He was killed at Mechanicsville, Hanover, Virginia on June 26, 1862. William Jasper Adams died in March 16, 1862.

Abstract Book D has an entry that gives enlightment into their sibling family life:

Page 347 Carroll County, April 23, 1842. William Adams to Mary Ann Williams' heirs and Phebe Adams. Good will and affectionate feeling, and to make them equal with the rest of his children. Mary Ann's heirs, sorrel mare, 5 years old, colt one year old, 2 cows and calves, 3 year old heifer and their increase. Phebe, 3 cows and calves and their increase, 18 gallon kittle. Attest: Henry S. Chance, Wilson Cartwright, J.P.; October 23, 1842.

Absalom Adams was buried at Old Bethel Primitive Baptist Church Cemetery.

Elizabeth Adams died in 1885. No record of where she was buried was found. There are many unmarked graves at Old Bethel Primitive Baptist Church Cemetery.

Page 120 Carroll County, April 17, 1840. Peter E. Duncan to Absalom Adams. $300. Land lot #86, 6th district Carroll County. 50 acres. Lot granted to Short's orphans. Attest: G. H. West, Henry S. Chance J.P.; 6 Nov 1840.

Page 249, Carroll County, 3 Apr 1841. William Adams to Absalom Adams. $150. Northeast corner land lot #53, 6th district Carroll County. Attest: Clayton Williams, James B. Tamme, J.P.; 22 Dec 1841.

Henry Allen Coleman

Henry Allen Coleman (b. January 28, 1814, d. October 27, 1890, Temple). His parents were George Coleman (b. 1780, d. 1819) and Nancy Bufford Coleman (b. 1782, South Carolina, d. 1866, Carroll County). In 1820, the family lived in Putnam County; in 1840 and 1850, they lived in Cobb County. They came to District 6 Villa Rica and lived near Temple in 1860. Here, Henry's value of real estate value was $1,775 and his value of personal estate was $700. In 1870, the census shows they were in the Carrollton area; in 1880, they were listed in District 649.

Henry married Sarah Ann Barnes circa 1833 in Georgia. Sarah Ann (b. August 27, 1807, Lincoln County, d. October 4,1880, Carroll County).

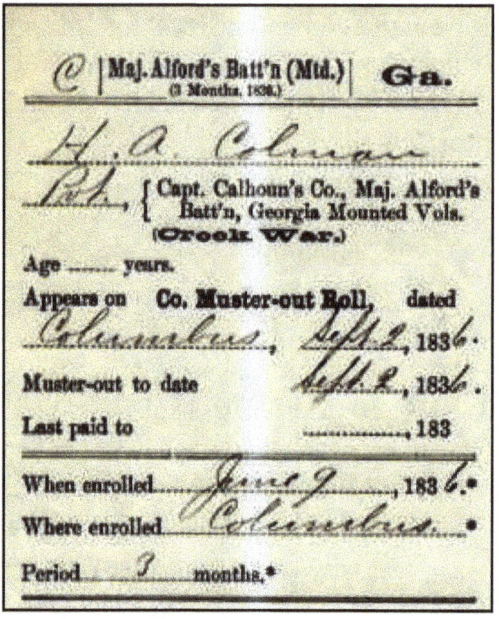

Muster Roll 1836 Creek Indian War
Fold 3 Military Program

On June 9,1836, Henry went to Columbus, and enlisted as Private under Captain Calhoun's Company, Major Alford's Battalion, Georgia Mounted Volunteers to fight in the Creek Indian War of 1836.

Henry and Sarah Ann Coleman's children:
1) James P. Coleman (1833-1915);
2) Nancy Catherine (born 1834);
3) Sarah Jane Coleman (1836-1894;
4) William Allen Coleman (1838-1917;
5) John Henry Coleman, Sr. (1841-1932;
6) Rebecca Catherine (1843-1911);
7) Elizabeth Ann (1844-1924);
8) Mary F. (1846-1880);
9) Martha L. (1848-1919);
10) Eliza M. Coleman (1855-1906).

Henry's mother Nancy Bufford Coleman died in 1866 and was buried at the

Bethel Primitive Baptist Church Cemetery near Temple, Georgia.

Henry's father-in-law and mother-in-law, who were Sarah Ann's parents, were James Barnes (b. 1788, d. 1846, Cobb County) and Sarah McKenzie (b. August 24, 1807, Lincoln County, d. January 8, 1876, Carroll County.) In her later years Sarah McKenzie Barnes lived in Carroll County; she was also buried at Bethel Primitive Baptist Church Cemetery.

William Allen Coleman

William Coleman (b. 1838, Cobb County) was the second son and fourth child of Henry Allen Coleman and Sarah Ann Barnes Coleman, above. William Allen Coleman married Cynthia F. Riggs, daughter of Reverend John Riggs and Jane Florence. Cynthia (b. 1837, Butts County).

William Cynthia had two sons, John W. Coleman born in 1859 and William Forrest Coleman born in 1864. The family farm was in Carrollton. W. A. Coleman served with the 1st Georgia Cavalry, C.S.A. from 1861–1865 under Nathan Bedford Forrest and Joe Wheeler.

After the Southern War for Independence, he took his family to Honduras, Central America, to escape Reconstruction. Preparations for the family's move to Honduras were made in Carrollton and in New Orleans, Louisiana in 1866-67. The family finally settled in San Pedro Sula, Honduras in 1867 along with about twenty-nine other Southern families forming an American colony in San Pedro Sula and nearby villages. With the exception of the Coleman family, most of these families returned to the United States by 1869 due to the hardships they encountered. John Henry Coleman also returned alone to Carrollton in the year 1894.

Cynthia Riggs Coleman & William Forrest Coleman

Cynthia F. Riggs Coleman had a third child while in Honduras but returned home for a better climate to restore her health. In route, her child, who was about seven months old, died and was buried in Balize, British Honduras. Cynthia was very sick and died while traveling by train between New Orleans and Montgomery; her remains were coffined in Montgomery.

The travel group who accompanied her from Honduras to Carroll County, included Cynthia's brother-in-law, John Coleman who had gone to Honduras to retrieve her. Her youngest son, William Forrest Coleman, age twelve, was also with the group. Her body was brought to Carrollton and buried at Bethel Primitive Baptist Church

Cemetery, near Temple, where her parents and parents-in-law were buried.

An account of Cynthia Coleman's death appeared in an obituary from the *Carroll County Times*, February 9, 1877:

Her remains were escorted by her youngest son, William Forrest Coleman, who was only 12 years old at the time. The father, William Coleman had given money to his brother, John Coleman, for a proper funeral for his wife, in case Cynthia succumbed to bad health and arduous journey. Twelve-year-old William Forrest, distraught from losing a sibling and now of burying his mother left the graveside abruptly. He refused a ride offered by his kinfolk and walked back to Carrollton where he arranged for transport back to the port of New Orleans, and then on to Honduras.

William Allen Coleman, the father, remained in Honduras with his oldest son to finish planting on their planation there. Also W. A. Coleman had been commissioned to build a mill and had remained in Honduras with his oldest son in order to complete this contract.

W. A. Coleman continued to live in Honduras for 25 years. Later he returned to Carrollton, built a fine house there and became the mayor. He married a 2nd time to Clara Kolbe of Cobb County and a 3rd time to Mollie Bailey of Carroll County.

When W. A. Coleman returned to Carroll County, he left his Honduras Plantation in the care of his youngest son, William Forrest Coleman for his oldest son, John W. Coleman had died. William Forrest Coleman, who was educated at Mercer University, continued to live in Honduras where he married and raised a family.

William Mercer Green

William Mercer Green (b. 1786, Burke, North Carolina, d. March 24, 1847 Carroll County); he came to Carroll County circa 1830 from Haywood, North Carolina. William and his wife Nancy Porter (b. 1794, d. March 6, 1847) were the parents of twelve children;
1) Robert born 1812;
2) Ambrose born 1813;
3) Rebecca (b. 1816) married Jacob Candler (b. 1820, d. 1862); they lived at Hickory Level;
4) Alexander Porter b. 1818;
5) Mary Elizabeth Green Hulsey (b. 1820, North Carolina, d. 1880); buried at Old Bethel Primitive Baptist Church Cemetery;
6) Nancy was born in 1822;
7) Robert born 1825;
8) Thomas born 1826;
9) William born 1829;
10) John Young born 1831;
11) Martha (b. 1832, d. 1903); was buried at Old Bethel Cemetery;

12) Martin La Layette Green (b. August 31, 1838, Carroll County, d. July 1914, Paulding County); was buried at Mt. Zion.

Two of the sons, Ambrose and Alexander, and brother, Anderson, came with Alexander Porter Green to Villa Rica. They either bought the 202 1/2 acres or half acreages, 101 1/4 acres, of land lots: #s 90, 114, 123, 136, 137, 138, 151, 152, and 158 all in the 6th district of Carroll County. William Mercer and his sons, and Anderson bought these Land Lots, all of which were south or southwest of Hart Town toward the Hickory Level and the Simsville area, from 1830 to 1852.

Deed Book B, Page 474 Carroll County, 9 Jun 1834. MARK E. MOORE, Shelby County, Ala. to WILLIAM GREEN. $63.00. Part of lot #136, 6th district Carroll County, beginning in the N. W. Corner. Attest: Anderson Green, John Justice.

Deed Book A, B, Page 366 Carroll County, 20 Jul 1830. JOHN BROOKS, Paulding County to WILLIAM GREEN. $1200.00. Land lot #137, 6th district Carroll County. Attest: William S. Hawthorn, Wm. M. Porter, Neil Hibbler, Phillip Riley, Carrington Stone, J . P . 20 May 1834.

Deed Book A, B, Page 366 Carroll County, 5 Dec 1833. ALEXANDER HOGAN to ANDERSON GREEN. $800.00. North half of land lot. #138, 6th district Carroll County. 101 1/4 acres. Attest: Neil Stone, J.P. 19 May 1834.

Deed Book B, Page 370 Carroll County. 20 Jul 1833. JOHN BROOKS, Paulding County to ANDERSON GREEN. $600.00. 1/2 land lot #151, 6th district Carroll County. Attest: Wm. M. Porter, Wm. Green, Neil Stone J.P. 13 Jun 1834.

Deed Book Page 438 Carroll County, 7 Feb 1835. WILLIAM GREEN to DAVID HIDEN. $172.50. Part of land lot #152, 6th district Carroll County. 101 1/4 acres. Attest: Thos. Chandler, Neil Stone, J.P., 25 Apr 1835.

William Mercer Green died March 24, 1847 and his wife Nancy Porter Green also died in 1847. Both were buried at the Old Bethel Primitive Baptist Church Cemetery, near Temple.

Benjamin Jasper McCain

Benjamin Jasper McCain (b. December 8, 1842, Troupe County, d. February 20, 1918, Leesburg, Lake County, Florida) was the son of William Baskin McCain (b. 1794, South Carolina, d. 1865, Georgia) and Margaret Nisbet McCain (b. 1802, Union, North Carolina, d. 1865, Temple). Benjamin's grandfather, Hugh McCain came from North Carolina and was a soldier in the Revolutionary War.

Benjamin's parents came to Georgia and settled in Troup County in 1840, where his father cleared a farm and built two mills, a saw mill, and became a merchant. Benjamin grew up on the farm in Troup County. His early education was obtained at a country school. In 1860, he lived in District 649 Carroll County.

Benjamin J. McCain enlisted on May 1864 with the Confederate States Army in a state-organized militia at Andersonville, Georgia, Company F, 1st Georgia Infantry. At the close of the war, he served as Corporal. He fought in two battles at Coosahatchie. He served as a guard at Ft. Sumter. After the surrender, he stacked arms at

Albany, Georgia.

After the war he returned to farm, but in 1868, he attended school in Carrollton. The next year he worked on the farm, and the next year, he attended a private school for four months. In 1871, he finished his preparatory commercial education by attending Moore's Business University in Atlanta.

In August 1872, he engaged as a clerk with J. C. Carter, with whom he remained four years. After that he entered into partnership with Gus Smythe, but at the end of fifteen months, he sold out to his partner and formed partnership with L. P. Barnes. Twelve months after he retired from this business, and with George and John McGahee and I. Y. Sawtell, organized the Atlanta Wild Land company. He remained in this company ten months, and then, in the fall of 1878, located in Simsville, and engaged in a successful general merchandise business. He also served as Postmaster while in Simsville.

On August 5, 1875, he married Tallulah Victoria Cook in Atlanta, Fulton County. Tallulah (b. August 16, 1853, d. 1951) was the daughter of Major D. A. Cook and Nancy W. Collier, of Atlanta.

Benjamin and Tallulah McCain had three children:
1) Samuel E. (b. 1877, d. 1878);
2) William Benjamin (b. September 1883, d. 1924);
3) Ida Tallulah "Lou" McCain (b. November 1887).

Benjamin McCain was a master Mason, and his family became members of the Methodist church. Benjamin exerted a well-earned influence in the community and county.

In 1882, he left Simsville and permanently settled in Temple, where he built a large and profitable trade and was a leading business man and citizen. He was a trustee at the Temple United Methodist Church.

In 1880, the family lived in District 649 where he was a grocer; in 1900 they lived in Fulton County and in 1910, they lived in Clemont, Lake County, Florida. He was 66; Tallulah was 56 and Will was 27.

Benjamin died in Leesburg, Lake County, Florida and was buried at Bethel Baptist Church near Temple.

Elijah Daniel McPherson

Elijah Daniel McPherson (b. July 13, 1789, Hawkins, Tennessee, d. December 9, 1875, Carroll County) was the son of Daniel McPherson (b. October 22, 1755, d. January 7, 1841, Rockford, Tennessee) who served as a Revolutionary soldier. Elijah's mother was Susannah Kincheloe (b. September 22, 1755, Virginia, d. July 12, 1850, Rockford, Tennessee).

Elijah Daniel McPherson fought in the War of 1812 with the Tennessee Militia in Captain White's Company, Cocke's Division. During this time, he helped survey the site of the city of Chicago. Elijah McPherson's pension application reveals that he enlisted at age 22; he was 5'9" tall, had fair complexion, sandy hair and blue eyes.

As a young man, Elijah McPherson worked on international sailing ships for several years. This enabled him to obtain a knowledge of other languages, including French, Spanish, and Portugese. He was an educated man as a result of his studies, travels, and experiences. Elijah McPherson played many stringed musical instruments, including the violin.

Elijah was married in Rhea, Tennessee on October 9, 1826 to Sarah Ann Small (b. May 22, 1809, Ireland, d. April 23, 1879, Carroll County). Her parents and their three children emigrated to this country and shortly thereafter, her parents both died. Sarah was subsequently taken into the home of James M. Carroll and Hannah McPherson Carroll, who were the brother-in-law and sister of Sarah's future husband. Sarah married Elijah Daniel McPherson at the age of 17 and a few years later, they moved to Carroll County.

The family lived in Carroll County during the years: 1830 District 6 (see abstract below); 1840 District 813; 1850 *Division 11*; 1860 Carrollton; and 1870 Carrollton.

John and Sarah Ann McPherson had twelve children:
1) William Barton (b. 1828, d. 1892);
2) Emily (b. 1829, d. 1884);
3) Amanda (b. 1830, d. 1830); she died as an infant;
4) William Nelson (b. 1832, d. 1862);
5) Louisa (b. 1834, d. 1914);
6) Mary Ann (b. 1836, d. 1885);
7) Charles Lafayette (b. 1838, d. 1839);
8) Elijah Houston (b. 1841, d. April 01, 1921);
9) Charles Lewis (b. 1844, d. 1909);
10) Henry Livingston (b. 1846, d. 1889);
11) Delphia (b. 1848, d. 1896);
12) John "Jack" Howell McPherson (b. 1850, d. 1885).

Two of Elijah and Sarah Ann's sons served in the Confederate States Army. Charles Lewis McPherson served in the 7th Georgia Regiment; and Elijah Houston McPherson served Company F, 19th Regiment Georgia Volunteer Infantry Carroll Guards. He enlisted as Private on June 11, 1861. He surrendered at Greensboro, North Carolina on April 26, 1865.

Their large farm, Buck Creek Plantation, included water powered mills for gain and lumber. His sawmill was among the first in Carroll County, operating in 1840.

Elijah McPherson was buried at the Old Concord Primitive Baptist Church Cemetery on Spence Road, 5 miles north of Carrollton. Sarah Ann McPherson died in 1897 and was buried there also.

Book D, Page 285, Carroll County, August 27, 1840. William R. Burnes to Elijah McPherson. Sum of $1,000. for land lot #153, in the 6th district located in Carroll County. Land lot containing 202 1/2 acres. Attest John Farmer, Henry S. Chance, J.P.; March 17, 1842.

John Riggs

John Riggs (b. May 22, 1812, North Carolina, d. December 30, 1861, Temple). He was buried at Bethel Primitive Baptist Church Cemetery. On May 22, 1814 in Lincoln, Georgia, he married Jane Florence (b. 1841, d. May 5, 1869, Carroll County). She was the daughter of Thomas Florence and Lucy Blaylock of Lincolnton, Georgia.

John and Jane Riggs' children were:
1) Sarah M. Riggs (b. 1833) who married Thomas Cartwright;
2) Josephine B. Riggs (b. Dec 24, d. 1835) who married William B. Adams;
3) Cynthia Florence Riggs (b. Mar 27, 1837) who married. William Coleman;
4) James Madison Riggs (b. 1839) who married Susan Florida Crockett;
5) Alice W. Riggs (b. 1843) who married William J. Sims;
6) Stephen Alexander Hamilton Riggs (b. September 3, 1846) who married Mary Jane McCain;
7) John Q. Riggs (b. April 22, 1848) who married (1st) Anna V. Crockett, (2d) Lizzie D.
8) Emma B. Riggs (b. Jan 31, 1850) who married Zachariah T. Kinney.

When John Riggs was 16, he moved to Georgia and became a Baptist minister. In 1850 John Riggs was living in Butts County with real estate value of $500.00. He helped take this census as his signature appears at the heading of the census record. He resided in Butts County, where he was recorded as a member of the Grand Jury in 1845. In 1857, he was recorded on the Carroll County, Tax rolls for the sixth district. On June 26, 1854, John, Jane and Sarah Riggs were shown as charter members of the "Old" Bethel Primitive Baptist Church in Carroll County, Georgia.

According to the Georgia Tax Digest, 6th District, in 1857 and 1858, he owned 405 acres including Land lots #s 147 and 124, 6th District: land value $1,620, cash $90, other property, $325, total $2,035. He and many members of the Riggs family were buried at the Bethel Primitive Baptist Church Cemetery, near Temple.

Reverend Sterling Tucker "Uncle Tuck" Sims

Sterling Tucker Sims (b. November 18, 1818, Laurens County, South Carolina, d. October 27, 1906, Carroll County) was the son of John Hiram Newton Sims (b. 1785, South Carolina, d. 1847, Chambers County, Alabama) and Mary Luncinda Abercrombie (b. 1789, South Carolina, d. August 1856, Chambers County, Alabama).

Tucker married Emily Bradberry on May 17, 1842 in Henry County, Georgia. Emily (b. 1821, Madison County, d. 1878). Tucker and Emily moved to Carroll County before 1850 as they were listed on the 1850 Federal Census Record for *Division 11* for Carroll County.

In 1860, the Tucker Sims' family lived in District 6, Carroll County; Tucker's occupation was Reverend; value of real estate $900; value personal estate $720. On the 1870 Census, he was listed in District 649; his occupation—minister; his value of real estate was $1,500 and value of personal estate was $600. On the 1880 Census he was listed in District 649; his occupation was Minister of the Gospel. On the 1900 Census, he was listed as a farmer and lived in District 642.

Tucker and Emily Sims had eight children:

1) William Jasper (b. January 29, 1843, d. August 7, 1924) married Alice Florence Riggs;

2) Lorinda "Lavada" (b. 1844, d. after 1860);

3) James Newton Sims (b. January 22, 1847, d. May 30, 1934) married Mary Elizabeth Davis;

4) Hiram Thomas Sims (b. March 24, 1849, d. October 6, 1894);

5) Millard Fillmore Sims (b. 1853, d. November 23, 1928) married Mary Elizabeth Dickens;

Rev. Tucker & Emily Sims & Children
Courtesy Don Levans

6) Robert Toombs Sims (b. January 5, 1855, Carroll County, d. October 11, 1939);

7) John Sterling Sims (b. December 10, 1857, d. December 10, 1930, Carroll County) married Mary Virginia Reese;

8) Mary Sims (b. September 19, 1860, d. June 7, 1943) married William Jasper Newman.

On the Georgia Property Tax Digest for 1885-1887 for District 6, Temple, it was shown that Sterling Tucker Sims paid taxes on Land Lots #s 30, 60, 70, 74, 75, 134, 135 and 136 which all total the land had an agriculture value of $2,200.

Emily, Tucker's wife and mother of his eight children, died in 1878. Tucker married on July 9, 1879 in Carroll County to Sophronia Elizabeth Turner. On July 1881, they had a son, Sterling Tucker Sims, Junior. Sterling, Junior married Mahale Avarilla Hutcheson. He died on June 14, 1943.

Reverend Sterling Tucker, Sr. died at age 87 and was buried at the Bethel Baptist Church Cemetery near Temple. His second wife Sophronia died in 1929 and was buried at Pleasant Grove Baptist Church Cemetery.

Book F, page 353, Carroll County, 10 Mar 1849. GILBERT COLE to ELISHA BROOKS, WILLIAM. N. DAVIS and ISAAC E. COBB, trustees of PRIMITIVE BAPTIST CHURCH at BETHEL MEETING HOUSE. $9.00. Part of Land lot #152, 6th district Carroll County. 3 acres. Attest: Anderson Green, G. M. Hiden, Henry S. Chance, J. P. 25 Dec 1849.

Book G, page 547, Carroll County, 28 Nov 1853. GILBERT COLE to ALFRED WADDELL, Meriwether County. $950.00. South half land lot #152, 6th district Carroll County. Except 3 acres where BETHEL MEETING HOUSE now stands. Attest: L. C. McAlmon, John T. Meador, J. I. C. 11 Oct 1854.

**Two of Rev. Sims' Sons
(L-R) An Older Son and
John Sterling Sims**
Courtesy Don Levans

11

Families of the Hart Plantation

Samuel Hart had 545 acres, three gold mines, fourteen children and 32 workers on the plantation.

Occupants of the Hart House

John Long circa 1826–1827; Samuel & Martha Hart & family circa 1843–1881; Abraham & Mary Leathers family 1881–1919; William & Lilla Brooks family 1919–1958; Guy & Addie Hixon family 1958–1985; John & Anna Johnston family 1985–2002.

James Young Long

James Young Long was born January 7, 1781 in Augusta County, Virginia, the son of John Long (1737–1826) and Jane Young Long (1740–1826) of Grainger, Tennessee. He married Jane Walker on March 3, 1803 in Hawkins County, Virginia. James sold several parcels of land in Hawkins County, Tennessee in 1819, 1820 and 1823 before moving to Georgia. James and Jane moved in 1826 to the Little Tallapoosa River in Carroll County, Georgia, where he was killed in 1828.

He left one child, Nancy Davis Long. No death date was found for Jane Walker Long.

Nancy Davis Long & John Long

Nancy, daughter of James and Jane Walker Long (b. March 12, 1806, Hawkins County, Tennessee, d. February 22, 1880, Carrollton), married her cousin, John Long, the son of Robert Long. John Long was born in Marshall's Ferry, Tennessee and lived at the ancestral home, until about 1826, when he and his family moved to the area that was later known as Hart Town. "This was an area which was opened circa 1825, formerly the property of the Creek Indians. John Long was amoung [sic] the first white settlers to the area." His tombstone was inscribed, 'John Long born in Tennessee in 1797. He moved to Carroll County 1826 one of the first settlers. He died October 17, 1870.'"

According to the *History of Villa Rica:* Samuel Hart rented the property to John Long of Tennessee in 1826 and Mr. Long moved his family into the house. The following year, 1827, Benjamin McFarland Long was born here. He was the first white child born in the county after it was constituted.

Living there until after his first son was born in 1827, the family then moved to Carrollton and bought a hotel from Jiles Boggess.

John Long began a long and successful career: he served in the Georgia House of Representatives in the Session of 1868. He served in the Georgia legislature, 1888–1889, and was Clerk of the Supreme Court at Carrollton for thirty-two years, and was afterwards a Judge. He was one of the Justices of the first Inferior Court established in Carroll County. Nancy and John Long's children: 1) Benjamin McFarland Long, (b. November 5, 1827, d. June 17, 1903).

John Long
At Home in Carrollton

2) John Orville Long (b. November 8, 1829). In a patriotic fervor he joined the army and served in the Mexican War, when a mere lad. He was taken prisoner by the Mexicans and six months after he returned home, in spite of the loving care he received from his mother, he died from abuses he suffered in prison. He had told his mother, while he had been trying to recover, that many times while in prison he would have almost given his life for the crumbs that fell from her table. He was a gallant youth. He died August 28, 1848, before he was nineteen years old.

3) Isabella Jane Long (b. August 30, 1832, d. 1906), married David R. Hay.

4) Looney James Long (b. October 21, 1835, d. December 6, 1839). At four years of age, he died in a tragic manner. His father was hauling logs and the little boy was riding on the logs. His father turned to speak to a passing neighbor and the child fell off the wagon and was crushed by the wheel.

5) Louisa Susan Long (b. November 11, 1838, d. March 3, 1848).

6) William Leeper Long (b. December 10, 1840, d. April 29, 1865). He served bravely through the War. After Appomattox he was returning home with numbers of other Confederate soldiers who were riding in freight cars, some inside and some on top of the cars. In the night on going up a long grade, the train broke in two. Their part of the train ran down the grade at a terrific speed. Seeing the lights of the station

below, and thinking the lights were from another locomotive and fearing an immediate collision, they jumped from the top of the car. He, falling on a pile of rocks, was hurt so badly that he died from the injury.

The family Bible of John and Nancy D. Long, includes the simple notation: "William Leeper Long died 29th April, 1865 by jumping off the cars. Aged 24 years, four months and nineteen days."

7) Caroline Eliza Grantland Long (b. June 29, 1845, d. 1933).

John Long was married twice. He married first—Charity Taylor May of Blount County, Tennessee, circa 1819. They had one child: Calvin Long (b. August 20, 1818, d. February 23, 1920).

Reiterating: From *The History of Villa Rica*, published in 1976, page 80:

> Gold was discovered around what was later to become Villa Rica in 1824, and several whites moved into the section. One of these was Samuel Hart. He chose a claim and built a nice two-story dwelling facing the Jacksonville Road.
>
> Samuel Hart rented the property to John Long of Tennessee in 1826 and Mr. Long moved his family into the house.

Long moved to Carrollton. Many historians have placed the Hart family at the intersection of Hart Town as early as 1824, but records indicate otherwise.

Benjamin McFarland Long and Amanda Wooten Long
At Home in Carrollton

Captain Samuel Hart, Sr.

Extensive research of Federal Census Records, Military Records, newspaper articles and private and public genealogies, reveal the following details:

Samuel "Lemuel" Hart, Sr. (b. 1755 in Orange County, North Carolina, d. July 1808, Hancock County) descended from early American pioneers: his grandfather, Thomas Hart, Jr. (b. 1679, England, d. circa 1755, Hanover, Virginia); his grandmother was Susannah Rice of Hanover, Virginia and later Orange County, North Carolina.

Samuel Sr. served as a Lieutenant in the 9th Regiment in North Carolina during the Revolutionary War. He received land grants because of his service in the Revolutionary War, drawing land in both Hancock and Talbot Counties. Samuel Sr. was buried in the Hart Family Cemetery Crawfordville, Georgia in Taliaferro County. (33°77'54.00"N 82°55'23.20"W).

Painting, Susanna Borin Hart

Samuel Sr. married Susanna Borin (b. 1758, Caswell County, North Carolina, d. April 1, 1837, Taliaferro County) who was the daughter of Joseph Borin(g) and Susannah Teague. Samuel Sr. and Susannah Borin Hart had Samuel Hart, Jr. and ten other children, all listed later in this chapter. She was also buried in the Hart Family Cemetery, at Crawfordville which has about twelve unmarked graves. It has one engraved headstone, that of Samuel Hart, Sr which was placed in 1939 by the Daughters of the American Revolution.

Famous ancestors - Samuel Hart, Sr.'s mother was Nancy Hart and *her* cousin was Daniel Boone.

Nancy Hart's Cabin
Elberton, Georgia

Nancy Hart, patriot and heroine

Samuel Hart Sr.'s father, Benjamin Hart, (b. October 1, 1732, Hanover County, Virginia, d. January 2, 1802, Brunswick, Glynn County, Georgia); Samuel, Sr.'s mother was Nancy Ann Morgan (b. March 17, 1735, Orange County, North Carolina, d. 1830 in Henderson, Kentucky). She was the daughter of Thomas Morgan (b. 1692, Berks County, Pennsylvania, d. 1778, Savannah, Chatham, Georgia) and Rebecca Alexander (b. 1717, d. 1778). Benjamin and Nancy Ann Morgan Hart married in 1760 in Chapel Hill Durham, North Carolina.

The famed Nancy Hart fought Tories in the Revolutionary War at the Battle of Kettle Creek;

she killed Tories that invaded her home in Elbert County. Hart County is named for her, the only county in Georgia that is named for a woman; the county seat of Hartwell is named for her and her cabin in Elberton, Elbert County, is part of the Nancy Hart State Park where tribute is paid to her and her acts of heroism.

Daniel Boone, early American pioneer and explorer

Daniel Boone (b. October 22, 1734, Berks County, Pennsylvania, d. November 02, 1820, St. Charles County, Missouri) was the son of Squire Boone (b. 1696 Devonshire, England, d. 1765 Rowan, North Carolina) and Sarah Morgan (b. 1700, Exeter, Berks, Pennsylvania, d. 1777, Rowan, North Carolina). His mother, Sarah Morgan, was Nancy Morgan Hart's aunt, the sister of her father, Thomas Morgan (b. 1692, Bucks County, Pennsylvania, d. 1778, Savannah, Chatham, Georgia) see above under Nancy Hart.

Portrait of Daniel Boone
by Chester Harding

Daniel Boone married Rebecca Bryant on September 14, 1756. Rebecca (b. February 7, 1739, Winchester, Frederick County, Virginia, d. March 18, 1813, Marthasville, Warren County, Missouri) was the daughter of Joseph and Alice Bryant. Daniel and Rebecca Bryant Boone had ten children. Daniel Boone was an American pioneer, explorer, woodsman and frontiersman whose frontier exploits made him one of the first folk heros in the United States.

Samuel S. Hart, Jr.

Samuel S. Hart, Jr. (b. July 2, 1798, Hancock County, d. August 8, 1879, Carroll County) was the son of Samuel Hart, Sr. (above). In 1812 Samuel Hart Jr, was living in Hancock County. He served with the Georgia Cavalry and Mounted Riflemen and was an Indian Scout from November 9 to November 22, 1814 stationed at Fort Mitchell. He was about 16 at the time. He was listed as Captain of the Georgia Militia District 608 Hancock County in 1819, 1827 and 1828. In 1821 he drew land in Monroe County and his mother, Susannah Boring Hart, drew land in Henry County. The land was returned for taxes until 1830.

On October 2, 1826, Samuel married Martha Susan Veazey in Hancock County. Martha (b. September 16, 1806, Powelton, Hancock County, d. September 2, 1860, Hart Town). Her parents were John Veazey, Sr. and Sarah Jane Raburn who, according to the census record, lived in Taliaferro County in 1830. John and Jane Raburn Veazey were devout Baptists when the Georgia Baptists were first organizing. They were connected

Martha & Samuel Hart

with the Baptist movement in Powelton, Georgia, site of the first Georgia Baptist Convention in 1822.

Samuel Hart, Jr. is referred to in some genealogy as a resident of Indian Country who settled in the Carroll County. In 1836, he served as an Indian Scout; then, as Private in the Creek Indian War in the Alabama-Georgia area in Captain Mims' Company in Beall's Georgia Mounted Rifleman Volunteers.

After he served in the Creek Indian War, Samuel, Martha and their family moved to Talbot County where he voted in the militia election and owned land known as the "Hottley's Grocery Lot."

After his father died, Samuel was the executor of his mother's estate in Hancock County; she died on April 1, 1837. Samuel Hart was shown as the head of family on the 1840 United States Federal Census for Talbot County. In 1843 he sold his mother's land and moved to Carroll County.

In 1850, 1860 and 1870, he and his family lived in Carroll County. The Hart house at Hart Town, a two story plantation house facing the Atlanta-Jacksonville Highway where it crosses Old Van Wert Road, was probably built by his brother William who appears on the 1830 Georgia Federal Census for the Carroll County.

From about 1850, the family resided in this two story house until Samuel's death in 1879. Here in Hart Town, also known as the gold village, Samuel ran three gold mines: one directly across the road from his house, one a few hundred feet to the west, and one about 500 yards northwest.

The 1873 Georgia Property Tax Digest shows Samuel owning a total of 545 acres including Land lots #s 165, & 189, each 202 1/2 acres and 100 acres of Land lots #s 167 & 188 and 40 acres of Land lot 166. In 1860, he had 32 workers living on the plantation, working the farm and the three gold mines. Their families were housed in cabins to the northeast of his home. On the 1860 Federal Census, his real estate value was $3,500 and value of personal estate was $17,600.

Samuel and Martha Hart were the pillars of the community and founding members of the Pleasant Grove Baptist Church. They had fourteen children. The joy of their children were many times overtaken by sorrow: their ninth child, Samuel Hart III, died at eight months old; their daughter Louisiana died at age eleven; they lost sons John Thomas, William and Francis Eugenius Hart in the Civil War. Three of their son-in-laws were also killed in the war: George Washington Parker who married their daughter, Mary Elizabeth; William Washington Cobb who married their daughter Sarah Jane; and Lindsey Dobbs who married their daughter Susan. Samuel Hart himself served as Private in Company D, 5th Battalion Georgia Infantry State Guards, at age sixty-three.

Fourteen Children:
   1) Private Joseph Lemuel Hart was Samuel, Jr. and Martha Hart's oldest son (b. November 6, 1827, Taliaferro County, Georgia, d. November 5, 1909, Chandler, Henderson County, Texas). He was the first postmaster at Buck Horn, Georgia in 1856 –1857. The post office was in Buckhorn Tavern, a stagecoach waystation.

   He served as a private in Co. I, 56 Regiment, Georgia Infantry, C.S.A., enlisting on May 10, 1962. He was captured at Nashville, Tennessee on December 16, 1864 and imprisoned at Military Prison at Louisville, Kentucky and Camp Chase, Ohio where he was released on June 12, 1865.

   Joseph Lemuel Hart married Catherine Elizabeth Parker (b. December 3, 1836, d. aft 1900) on December 19, 1854 in Taliaferro County. Joseph and Catherine had seven children:
   1) Eudorah T. (b. October 20, 1855, Carroll County, d. March 20, 1881, Texas);
   2) William S. (b. circa 1857, Carroll County, d. after 1860);
   3) Cynthia S. (b. 1861, Temple, d. 1938, Texas);
   4) Joseph J. (b. circa 1864, Carroll County);
   5 Francis Maxion [sic] (b. 1867, Carroll County, d. 1950, Texas);
   6 Nancy) b. 1869, Carroll County);
   7) George Barnes Hart (b. 1874, Carroll County, d. 1953, Henderson Texas).

   Joseph and his family left Carroll County and moved to Texas where they were shown on the 1880 and 1900 Federal Census Record for Henderson County, Texas. Joseph Lemuel Hart was buried in Chandler, Henderson County, Texas in the Concord Cemetery.

   2) Harriet Ann Hart (b. January 16, 1829, Taliaferro County d. February 19, 1885). She was buried at Pleasant Grove Baptist Church Cemetery. She never married.

   3) Sarah Jane Hart (b. November 3, 1830, Taliaferro County). She married William Washington Cobb on January 17, 1856; William W. Cobb (b. April 21, 1830) was the son of Isaac and Francis Cobb of Carroll County.

   Sarah and William Cobb lived in a log cabin where Land Lot#s 185 and 168 come together, about a mile east of Buckhorn Tavern, which his parents ran. Sarah and William Cobb had three boys: Isaac Osceola "Ossie" Cobb who was born in 1856 in Carroll County and died in 1907 in Carroll County; an infant son born and died in 1858; Eldorado Hart "Bud" Cobb who was born in 1859 in Carroll County and died in 1935 in Carroll County; and John G. Cobb who was born in 1861 in Carroll County and died in 1883.

William W. Cobb served as Private in Co. E. 1st Georgia Regiment, Cavalry, Confederate States Army. On August 3, 1864, he died of disease in a LaGrange Georgia Confederate hospital. His body was sent home to be buried at the Pleasant Grove Baptist Church Cemetery.

After the Civil War, Jane and her three boys walked each school day the three miles to the Pleasant Grove School on land lot #155 where she was a teacher. John, her youngest, died of typhoid in 1884. She attended Pleasant Grove Baptist Church until her death in March 2, 1909; she was also buried at Pleasant Grove Baptist Church Cemetery.

4) John Thomas Hart (b. July 23, 1832, Taliaferro County) married Lundah Bailey on January 16, 1855 in Coweta County. Lundah (b. January 1838, d. March 16, 1916, Texas) was the daughter of Ezekiel Bailey and Mary Steed.

John was a teacher and a farmer. Their children were:
1) Charles A. Hart;
2) Cicero Oscar "Cain";
3) George Olin Hart.

John Thomas Hart and his family appear on the 1860 census for Carroll County. Sometime shortly after, they moved to Texas. He enlisted on May 6, 1862 with Company H. 18th Texas infantry in Upshur County, Texas. He died October 13, 1862 from pneumonia after the amputation of an arm at Camp Nelson, Old Austin, Arkansas. He was buried in an unmarked grave at the Camp Nelson Confederate Cemetery in Cabot, Lonoke County, Arkansas.

Lundah married James Adams Redus, (Reedus) either in Georgia or Texas on August 17, 1869. They later lived in Pittsburg, Texas.

5) Susan Hart (b. August 17, 1834, Talbot County, d. January 21, 1908, Carroll County) married Lindsey Dobbs (b. 1831–d. 1862) on February 28, 1856 in Carroll County. He served in Co. E, 1st Ga Regiment, Calvary; he was killed in the Civil War.

Their children were:
1) Willard Dobbs (b. 1857, Carroll County d. 1931, Carroll County);
2) Mary "Mollie" Dobbs (b. 1859, Carroll County);
3) Martha Dobbs (b. 1860, Carroll County, d. 1932, DeKalb County);
4) Fannie E. Dobbs (b. 1862, Carroll County, d. 1941, Fulton County).

Susan Hart Dobbs was buried at Pleasant Grove Baptist Church Cemetery.

6) Mary Elizabeth Hart (b. December. 2, 1836, Taliaferro County, d. February 28, 1904, Haskell County, Texas) married George Washington Parker on July 10, 1860 in Carroll County. He died in the Civil War. They had two children:
1) Atlanta H. Parker Carson
2) George William "Willie" Parker, Jr.

7) William R. Hart (b. December 20, 1838, Taliaferro County) enlisted with the Confederate States Army in Co. I, 19 Georgia Regiment, Villa Rica Gold Diggers on June 22, 1861. He was killed in the Seven Days Battle in Virginia on June 15, 1862. He was buried in Virginia.

8) Martha Ann Hart (b. December 19, 1841,Talbot County, d. August 14, 1909) married on September 1, 1859 to Robert Wood Mason (b. December 3, 1832, d. November 25, 1889).

They had five children:
1) Lucian Mason;
2) Henry H. Mason;
3) Homer Mason;
4) Adell Alfred Mason;
5) Robert Ridley Mason.

Martha Ann Hart Mason was buried at the Old Enon First Baptist Church Cemetery at Cliftondale in Fulton County.

9) Samuel Hart III (b. February 19, 1843, d. October 7, 1843) only lived eight months. His birth and death was recorded in the family Bible, but his tombstone is yet to be identified.

There is a baby's grave and tombstone adjacent to Samuel's, almost touching, at Pleasant Grove Baptist Church Cemetery in Villa Rica. But the markings have deteriorated so as to not be visible any longer. If this is his tombstone, he was buried in 1843, the church was founded in 1849 and Samuel died in 1879, 36 years after his infant son. So, the baby's tombstone being one of the first placed, may explain why it is at a right angle to his father's.

10) Private Francis Eugene Hart (b. August 17, 1844, Carroll County) enlisted with his brother, William R. Hart, in Co. I, 19th Georgia Regiment, Georgia Volunteer Infantry, "Villa Rica Gold Diggers," on June 22, 1861. He died of typhoid fever on May 23, 1862 at the home of Mr. Houtchins at Farmville, Cumberland, Virginia and was buried at Hollywood Cemetery at Richmond, Virginia. His tombstone stands at Pleasant Grove Baptist Church Cemetery in Carroll County.

Pvt. Francis Eugene Hart
Courtesy Lee Joyner Monroe

11) James Madison "Doll" Hart (b. July 3, 1846, Carroll County, July 9, 1927, Paulding County). The nickname, "Doll" originated when he was born. The family gathered around after he was born and one of his sisters remarked that he "looked like a doll." This name stuck through-

Martha Vella Wright Hart
Courtesy Jack Hart

out his life, even as a soldier in the Civil War, he was called Doll Hart.

He enlisted on September 9, 1862 and served as Private in Co. I, 56th Georgia Infantry Regiment, Confederate States Army; then, with the Villa Rica Gold Diggers. He fought in the Battle of Atlanta and was injured at the Battle of Decatur resulting in his walking with a limp the remainder of his life. Doll Hart was denied a pension because he did not rejoin his unit after going home to secure a mount when he was shot. When he arrived home to get his sister's horse, it had already been taken by the troops. He mustered out on April 26, 1865 at Greensboro, North Carolina.

On December 24, 1874, he married Martha Velma "Vella" Wright (b. January 7, 1853, d. April 11, 1922). They moved to Texas circa 1881 then back to Carroll County. They purchased Land lots #s 707, 732 and 781 in Paulding County for $1,500. They lived in a log cabin then built a larger house which still stands on Hart Road in Paulding County. James Madison Hart and Martha Velma Hart were the parents of ten children:

    1) Ella (b. December 28, 1875, Carroll County) married Gilliam Andrew Scoggins.
    2) Effie Teressia (b. January 11, 1877, Carroll County) married Jasper Aaron Brown.
    3) William A. "Billy" (b. October 30, 1878, Carroll County) married Clara Mae Babb.
    4) Enoch Tyre (b. May 30, 1880, Carroll County) married Mary Ella Boggs.
    5) Elizabeth (b. March 10, 1885, Paulding County) married Lunas Martin Teal.
    6) Charles (b. October 10, 1886, Paulding County) married Susie Teal.
    7) Bertha (September 21, 1888, Paulding County) married John Benjamin McClung.
    8) Bessie (December 7, 1890, Paulding County) married Charles Grady Cooper.
    9) Samuel "Ossie," a twin, (b. June 7, 1892, Paulding County) married Leona Hodge; his second wife was Nell Mullins.
    10) James "Arthur," a twin, (b. June 7, 1892, Paulding County) married Cora Belle Parsons.

James "Doll" and Vella Hart were buried at Mt. Zion Baptist Church Cemetery.

12) Louisiana Hazeltine Hart (b. March 17, 1848, Carroll County, d. December 19, 1859); she died, age eleven & was buried at Pleasant Grove Baptist Church Cemetery.

13) Charles Stillwell Hart (b. March 6, 1850, Carroll County, d. March 20, 1929, Carroll County) married Mary Antionette "Nettie" Chambers on November 22, 1872. Nettie (b. May 1, 1853, d. December 26, 1891) was the daughter of Josiah and Mary Jane Andrews Chambers. When she died in 1891 she left their eleven children

Front row L-R: Samuel Hart, Charles S. Hart, Rufus Hart, Ethel Hart; *Back Row:* Leona Hart, Annie Mae Beavers Hart, John V. Hart, Beulah Hart, Arthur Hart, Joanna Hart, Hattie Hart.

Mary Antionette "Nettie" Hart

without a mother:
1) Mary Beulah Hart Camp (b. 1873, d. 1920);
2) John Virna Hart (b. 1875, d. 1960);
3) Charles Arthur Hart (b. 1879, d. 1970);
4) Martha Joanna Hart (b. 1880, d. 1899);
5) Robert Lee "Bobby" Hart (who died as an infant, 1882-1882);
6) Hariet Emily "Hattie" Hart (b. 1883, d. 1926);
7) Infant son (b. 1885, d. 1885);
8) Susan Leona "Lena" Hart (b. 1886, d. 1960);
9) Samuel Stillwell "Sammie" Hart (b. 1888, d. 1911);
10) Celia Ethel Hart Newbern (b. 1890, d. 1974);
11) James Rufus "Doc" Hart (b. 1891, d. 1958). Nettie died one month after James Rufus Hart's birth.

Charles Arthur Hart had a son, Charles Raymond Hart (b. 1902, d. 1964), who became a prominent resident and pharmacist at Temple for forty years. Temple is three miles west of Hart Town.

14) Ella Hart (b. August 2, 1852, Carroll County, d. October 13, 1911) married Rufus Walker (b. May 22, 1847, March 6, 1904)) on December 22, 1870 in Carroll County.

Rufus and Ella Hart Walker had eight children:
1) Mary Walker (b. 1871, d. 1879);
2) Charles R. Walker (1873-1943);

3) Mattie Lena Walker (1877-1969);
4) Samuel Hart Walker (1879-1923);
5) George William Walker (1883-1966);
6) Joseph Lane Walker (1886-1962);
7) Mary Annie Walker (1889-1961) a
8) James M. Walker who was born in 1893.

Rufus and Ella Walker were buried at the Westview Cemetery in Fulton County.

Samuel, Jr.'s Ten Brothers and Sisters

According to information from the Roster of Revolutionary Soldiers in Georgia Volume 1, published by the Daughters of American Revolution in 1941: Samuel Hart, Sr. and Susanna Borin Hart's children:

1. Sarah Hart (b. circa 1778, Caswell, North Carolina, d. between 1856-1860, Taliaferro County) married Thomas Chapman, son of John Chapman.

2. Elizabeth Hart (b. January 30, 1780, Caswell County, North Carolina, d. May 29, 1863, Taliaferro County) was buried at Crawfordville in the family cemetery. Bible records show she married Nathan Chapman on February 20, 1800;

3. John Hart (b. circa 1782, North Carolina, d. November 1, 1832 St. Clair County, Illinois) married Peggy McDaniel.

4. James Hart (b. circa 1786, Orange County, North Carolina d. 1832, St. Clair County, Illinois) married Mary Beall on February 8, 1816.

5. Martha Susan Hart (b. 1787, Wilkes County, d. July 3, 1863, Talbot County) married James Monroe Veazey in Hancock County;

6. William Hart (b. 1788, Hancock County, d. St. Clair County, Illinois) married Nancy Beall on January 16, 1819 in Hancock County.

Some historians believe William Hart who lived in Hart Town in 1830 and was a Justice of the Peace was the "Judge" Hart who built the Hart House and started Hart Town well before Samuel C. Hart, Jr came to Hart Town, in 1843. See the Leathers' excerpt below.

William and Nancy Beall Hart had one child, a daughter, Mary (b. May 25, 1831, Scott, Johnson County, d. August 12, 1897, Johnson County). On May 1853, Mary Hart married David Redding Beasley (b. August 10, 1823, d. June 11, 1901. They had several children including a daughter, Sophronia.

7. Susannah "Phoebe" Hart (b. June 13, 1792, Wilkes County, d. August 29, 1867, Bowden, Carroll County) married Benjamin Franklin Chapman on January 12,

1809. Phoebe was buried at the Bowden First United Methodist Church Cemetery.

8. Eli Hart (b. July 2, 1793, Wilkes County, d. July 9, 1831, Taliaferro County) never married.

9. Rebecca Hart (b. May 1796, Troupe County, d. August 9, 1875, Tyus, Carroll County) married John Monroe Veal on September 30, 1838 in Talbot County. John Veal (b. July 28, 1790, Virginia, d. October 19, 1885, Tyus). The Federal Census record for 1850 shows this family lived in *Division 11* of Carroll County. John's real estate value was $3,000. He was age 55; Rebecca was 50; John D. was 17, Mary S. was 20 and two farm laborers are shown.

In 1860, the Federal Census shows John as age 67, Rebecca 63 and a Mary age 6. Their real estate value was $4,000 and personal estate value was $2,000. In 1870, the Census shows that John was 78; Rebecca was 75 and Mary was age 16. John's real estate value was $2,000; his personal estate value was $1,000.

Rebecca Hart Veal
Courtesy Wanda Haines

John and Rebecca Hart Veal had five children:

1) Allen Jones Veal (b. 1812, d. 1897);
2) William W. Veal (b. 1813, d. 1892); '
3) Benjamin F. Veal (b. 1821. d. 1889);
4) Mary Susanna Veal (Steed) (b. 1830, d. 1854);
5) John LaFayette Veal (b. 1833, d. 1899).

Both John and Rebecca Hart Veal were buried in the Veal Family Cemetery on their farm near Bowden.

10). Mary Hart (b. 1800, Wilkes County, d. August 29, 1869, Carroll County) married Alexander Colclaugh on December 28, 1831 in Taliaferro County. Alexander's father was William Colclaugh (Coolbaugh, 2nd). For more on the William Coolbaugh, see Chapter 3. For more information on Mary Hart Colclough, see Chapter 10. She was buried at the Bowden First Methodist Church Cemetery in Carroll County.

Abraham "Abram" Harrison Leathers

Abraham Leathers
Courtesy Milton Leathers

In 1881, the Hart home and estate was sold to the Abraham and Mary Jane Leathers family.

Abram Leathers (b. August 4, 1824, d. August 9, 1900) was the son of Samuel Lederer Leathers (b. 1792, Pendleton, South Carolina). Abram's mother was Mary Jane Swafford Leathers from Greenville, South Carolina. His father, Samuel, a Revolutionary War veteran, drew land in Paulding County, Georgia, and by 1827 had settled on the Pumpkinvine section of Sweetwater Creek on some of the richest farm land in west Georgia.

To this land, in Paulding County, Samuel brought his children, some of whom were grown: Samuel, Jr. and Mary Leathers, Joel Daniel and Mary McElreath Leathers and James and Lydia Leathers Dickson, who all cleared the area and set up houses nearby one another.

The story was told in the Leathers' genealogy book and in the family of how, as a boy of sixteen (1840), Abram worked as a day laborer when improvements were being made to Judge Hart's house just a few miles away in the next county, Carroll. Perhaps this was the time when the double porch was being added to the front. At supper one night after a long day of hauling stones and hoisting timber, Abram declared to his mother: "I am going to own that fine house one day!"

Two years later, when Abram was eighteen, he married Mary Jane Scoggins on January 8, 1842 in Carroll County. He and Mary Jane (b. November 1, 1825, d. September 20, 1905), had ten children:

1) One child born in 1844, stillborn.
2) Mary Amanda Jane Leathers (b. October 28, 1846, d. March 7, 1912);
3) William Franklin Leathers (b. October 6, 1848; d. December 22, 1918);
4) Annie Catherine Leathers (b. February 25, 1850; d. July 6, 1935);
5) Abraham Harrison Leathers Jr., (b. March 22, 1852, d. September 26, 1916);
6) Frederick Mortimer Leathers (b. March 30, 1854, d. July 28, 19230;
7) Nancy Margaret Leathers (b. June 3, 1855, d. March 2, 1881);
8) Samuel Elsberry Leathers (b. 1858, died 1930);
9) Martha Lee Leathers (b. April 7, 1860, d. September 15, 1914).
10) Bartow Leathers, infant girl, died at birth, 1862.

In 1850, 1860 and 1870, this family lived at Pumpkin Vine District in Paulding County. In 1880 they lived in District 642, Carroll County; his occupation was that of farmer.

On December 29, 1881, a deed was made out to Abraham Harrison Leathers

Hart Town Environs

for the property and home of Samuel Hart, some two years after Mr. Hart had passed. All the Leathers children were grown by then. But the fine two story home finally belonged to the Leathers' family and it was often filled with children, grandchildren and great-grandchildren. Before this couple died, Abram at 76 and Mary at 80 years old, they had 43 grandchildren and many great-grandchildren. This extended family was very close. This family enjoyed the home for about 19 years.

In 1900, Abram and Mary lived with their son Fred and daughter-in-law Mary and family in Fulton County as shown on the Federal Census Record.

Both Abram and his wife Mary Jane were buried at Friendship Baptist Church in Paulding County, about seven miles from Villa Rica. Many of their children are also buried at Friendship Primitive Baptist Church Cemetery.

1906 Guests Visit the Hart House
Courtesy Long Photo Collection

The William Jacob Brooks Jr. Family

William Brooks (b. December 31, 1870, Carroll County, d. September 4, 1951, Carroll County) was the son of William Jacob Brooks (b. 1843, d. 1883, Carroll County) and Martha Jane Pennington (b. 1842, d. 1925, Carroll County).

On September 13, 1894, William Brooks, Jr. married Lilla Alice Hayes in Carroll County. Lilla (b. June 23, 1875 d. February 9, 1958, Carroll County) was the daughter of Jasper Pickens Hayes and Carolyn Smith Hayes.

Will and his aunt Jane Ellen Brooks Wynn, (b. March 1839, d. December 7, 1923, Carroll County) together bought the house and 100 acres, on the corner of

Janie Brooks at the Hart House
Courtesy Barbara Wynn Mitchell

North Van Wert Road and Bankhead Highway, in 1919.

Janie Ellen Brooks had married William Thomas Wynn in 1889. On the 1910 Federal Census Record, she was listed, living alone, as head of the household in Temple, Georgia District 649. On the 1920 Federal Census Record, she was listed as aunt, age 81, living with this family.

The Brooks family made renovations to both chimneys and the house while they lived there from 1919 to 1958, a total of 38 years. Their children:

1) Gaudie (August 28, 1896);
2) Evie (b. 1898);
3) Addie (b. 1901) married Guy Hixon;
4) John (b. 1903);
5 Ena, fraternal twin (b. August 18, 1909) married Herman Clark Wynn on January 21, 1933;
6 Ina Katherine, fraternal twin (b. August 18, 1909 married Wyatt Hixon;
7) James Harry (b. 1912).

Ena and Herman Wynn lived in the Hart House with her parents Will and Lilla. Herman worked the farm with Will for a number of years, but later, both he and Ena worked in Bremen. They had one child, Barbara, who was born in the front left bedroom of the Hart House.

Will Brooks and Granddaughter Barbara
Courtesy Barbara Wynn Mitchell

In a 2016 interview, Barbara recalled as a child of roaming over the farm. She remembered playing in Samuel Hart's old gold mine across the road from the Hart house and behind the Allen house and store on the corner. She and the Allen's daughter, Sarah, went there, when their parents, who did not approve of their going into the old mine, but did not know where they were. In this interview Barbara remembered Felix and Rhoda Evans who lived in a tenant house for workers there on the farm for twenty years.

Barbara told of the carriage house that was converted to a chicken house. It burned one night and there was only a single well located on the right of the front lawn to get water. They could not draw water fast enough to put out the fire, so the old carriage house/chicken house perished.

Over the previous generations, travelers had used this well to water their animals or draw water for the radiators of their T-Models and even later vehicles. At one time there was a blacksmith shop close to the well, with tools the traveler might need. All who knew the Harts, Leathers and Brooks families felt comfortable using these accommodations.

Hart Town Environs

When William Brooks died in 1951, his funeral was held at Pleasant Grove Baptist Church, but his interment was at Asbury Cemetery in Temple. Lilla continued to live in the house and Rhoda Evans, who lived in the tenant house, took care of her until she died in 1958.

The Guy Hixon Family

After Lila Brooks died, the estate was divided among the surviving children. The big house and some acreage went to their third child Addie, who had married Guy Hixon. Guy and Addie Hixon had two children who both died tragically. Their daughter died while in high school. Their son, Oscar Hixon, perished in the Villa Rica explosion in 1957.

After they moved to the old Hart house, they made a great amount of renovations. They redid the curved stairway, added green tint to the narrow windows to the left and right of the front door, opened up the regular sized doors in the left and right first floor rooms off the front entrance, and upgraded the kitchen. They renovated the upstairs bedrooms.

The John Johnston Family

After Guy and Addie Hixon died, the John Johnston Family bought the house and seventeen acres in 1985. John Johnston added the side porch with the louver windows and made other renovations. He sold the house and property in 2002.

Hart House original location: circa 1843–2016: 33°44'09.44"N 84°57'37.15"W
Present Location 2020: 33°44'16.39"N 84°57'40.47"W

Remove not the ancient landmark, which thy fathers have set.
Proverbs 22:28

The Hart House
Georgia's Last Frontier, page 157A

Appendix A

Photos of artifacts found on the Hart property in the summer of 2016.
Photos by John Bailey

1848 Vest Button
Found by Trisha Mullinax Pope

1848 Vest Button - Back
Found by Trisha Mullinax Pope

An 1848 vest button, flower design, was found. The underside showed gold plating and enough print to reveal it was made by the Robinson Button Company of Attleborough, Massachusetts.

More Relics Found

Toy Car Found by Hamilton Pitts

Mule Bridle Buckle

Small Railroad Spike and Plow Points

Crowbar and Prybar Found Near the Well

The location of the original blacksmith shop was revealed by artifacts found near the front of the house, close to the only well and close to the highway.

Square Headed Nail

Native American Hand Axe or Hand Hoe (found under the house foundation after it had been moved).

Appendix B

MUSTER ROLL OF COMPANY I, 19th REGIMENT GEORGIA VOLUNTEER INFANTRY, ARMY OF TENNESSEE C. S. A., CARROLL COUNTY, GEORGIA, "VILLA RICA GOLD DIGGERS" OR "GOLD DIGGERS."

NOTE: This company appears to have been organized as Co. I, 2d Regiment, 4th Brigade, Georgia State Troops, June 22, 1861.

OFFICERS: Chambers, John T. Captain June 22, 1861. Resigned, on account of failing health, October 3, 1862.

Abercrombie, Thomas J.- 1st Lieutenant June 22, 1861. Elected Captain October 28, 1862.

Wylds, Francis A.(or Wilds)-2d Lieutenant June 22, 1861. Killed at 2d Manassas, Virginia August 30,1862.

Chambers, James L. (or James T.)-Jr. 2d Lieutenant June 22, 1861. "Resigned and went home, November 1861. Remained until July 1862, when, being conscripted, he concealed himself in the woods for 6 months, as he did not wish again to join C. S. Army. Captured in Carroll County, Georgia and released May 12,1865."

Adams, Robert A.- 1st Sergeant June 22, 1861. Admitted to Richmond, Virginia hospital June 30,1862. Died in Farmville, Virginia hospital July 20,1862.

Abercrombie, Isaac M.-2d Sergeant June 22, 1861. Surrendered, Greensboro, N. C. April 26,1865.

Dobbs, Doctor F.- 3d Sergeant June 22, 1861. Wounded at Mechanicsville, Virginia June 26,1862. Died of wounds at Richmond, Virginia July 10,1862.

Reaves, J. W.- 4th Sergeant June 22, 1861. Paid at Richmond, Virginia June 10,1862. No later record.

Chambers, Benjamin D. 5th Sergeant June 22, 1861. Wounded, Mechanicsville, Virginia June 26, 1862. Died. With 4th Georgia in Hospital: Richmond, Virginia July 28,1862.

Haynes, John M.- 1st Corporal June 22, 1861. Wounded at Chancellorsville, Virginia May 3,1863. In General Hospital #2, at Richmond, Virginia May 23,1863. Discharged, disability, August 1864.

Haynes, Jonathan G.-2d Corporal June 22, 1861. Wounded in eye, resulting in loss of sight.

Bivins, T. J.- 3d Corporal June 22, 1861. Captured at Sharpsburg, Md. September 17, 1862. Exchanged at Aiken's Landing, Virginia October 19, 1862. Wounded and disabled at Chancellorsville, Virginia May 3, 1863. Paid at Atlanta, Georgia April 3, 1864. No later record.

Caldwell, James R.-4th Corporal June 22, 1861. Pension records show he surrendered, Greensboro, N. C. April 26, 1865.

PRIVATES: Abercrombie, James- Private June 22, 1861. Died of typhoid fever in Belmont & Grove Hospital at Lovingston, Virginia August 21, 1862.

Adams, Joseph- Private June 22, 1861. Captured at Fredericksburg, Virginia December 13, 1862. Exchanged December 17, 1862. Wounded in head near Petersburg, Virginia June 20, 1864. Died of wounds in Confederate States Hospital at Petersburg, Virginia June 23, 1864.

Adams, Peter- Private June 22, 1861. Died September 8, 1862.

Adams, W.- Private June 22, 1861.

Anderson, D. - Private June 22, 1861.

Ayres, A. J. (or Ayers)- Private June 22, 1861. Captured at Fredericksburg, Virginia December 13, 1862, and paroled there for exchange December 17, 1862. No later record. Bagwell, Wiley H.- Private June 22, 1861. Surrendered, Greensboro, N. C. April 26, 1865. (Born in Georgia in 1840.)

Ballard, C.- Private June 22, 1861. Discharged in 1863.

Ballard, Robert Wesley- Private June 22, 1861. Died October 15, 1861.

Barnes, Thomas W.- Private June 22, 1861. Sick at Culpeper, Virginia January -February 1862. Discharged, disability.

Barnes, W.- Private June 22, 1861.

Bates, James W.- Private June 22, 1861. Admitted to C. S. A. General Hospital at Charlottesville, Virginia, with pneumonia, November 11, 1861. Returned to duty February 11, 1862.

Bates, Nathan S. Private June 22, 1861. Captured at Petersburg, Virginia August 19, 1864. Died of secondary hemorrhage, at Elmira, New York September 9, 1864. Grave

#1194, Woodlawn National Cemetery.

Bates, Samuel F.- Private June 22, 1861. Wounded at Fort Harrison, Virginia September 30, 1864. Died in Receiving & Wayside Hospital (General Hospital #9), at Richmond, Virginia October 24, 1864.

Binder, W.- Private June 22, 1861. Died at Richmond, Virginia May 23, 1862. Buried there in Hollywood Cemetery.

Bivins, M. (or Bevins)- Private June 22, 1861.

Blackburn, William H.- Private June 22, 1861. Wounded at Mechanicsville, Virginia June 26, 1862. Died of wounds July 2, 1862.

Blair, G.- Private June 22, 1861. Died at Richmond, Virginia May 24, 1862. Buried there in Hollywood Cemetery.

Brock, David N.- Private June 22, 1861. Captured at Winchester, Virginia December 2, 1862, and paroled there December 4, 1862. Paid at James Island, S. C., for commutation of rations while on sick furlough from March 4 to April 3,1863, and from June 20 to July 19, 1863 on December 17,1863. No later record.

Buckner, D. S.- Private June 22, 1861. Wounded, necessitating amputation of arm below elbow and leg above knee, at Mechanicsville, Virginia June 26,1862.

Buckner, M. J.- Private June 22, 1861. Died at Richmond, Virginia June 8,1862. Buried there in Hollywood Cemetery.

Buckner, William E.- Private June 22, 1861. Surrendered, Greensboro, N. C. April 26, 1865.

Burke, John T.- Private June 22, 1861. Died at Richmond, Virginia July 6,1862.

Carnes, Richard- private June 22, 1861.

Carter, James (or Joseph) - Private.

Carter, Samuel- Private June 22, 1861. Died at Richmond, Virginia in 1862.

Chambers, A.- Private June 22, 1861. Wounded at Chancellorsville, Virginia May 3,1863. Died from wounds May 1863.

Chambers, Merrill C.- Private June 22, 1861. Died near Camp Winder, Richmond,

Hart Town Environs

Virginia May 31, 1862. Buried there in Hollywood Cemetery.

Chambers, William Posey- private June 22, 1861. Elected 2d Lieutenant February 23, 1863. Surrendered, Greensboro, N. C. April 26, 1865.

Chance, William H.- Private March 4, 1862. Admitted to Chimborazo Hospital #3, at Richmond, Virginia August 17, 1862. Returned to duty September 2, 1862. Wounded at Shepherdstown, West Virginia, September 19, 1862. Died of wounds September 28, 1862.

Cheeves, A.(or Cheaves)- Private.

Cheeves, William A.(or Cheaves)- Private June 22, 1861. Appointed Sergeant. Elected 2d Lieutenant August 31, 1862. Wounded and captured at Fredericksburg, Virginia December 13, 1862. Paroled December 14, 1862. Captured at Weldon Railroad, Virginia August 19, 1864. Forwarded to Washington, D. C., August 24, 1864. Received at Fort Delaware, Del. August 29, 1864, and released there June 17, 1865.

Childress, H. K.- Private. Wounded in arm, necessitating amputation, at Cold Harbor, Virginia June 27, 1862.

Cole, Martin- Private June 22, 1861. Captured at Fredericksburg, Virginia December 13, 1862, and exchanged December 17, 1862. No later record. Born in 1838.

Cole, Tillman B.- Private March 8, 1862. Discharged, disability, at Richmond, Virginia June 25, 1862.

Crook, W. S.- Private June 22, 1861.

Crow, David- Private March 3, 1862. Discharged, disability, at Richmond, Virginia July 21, 1862. Died in Richmond, Virginia hospital July 1862.

Davis, L. H.- Private June 22, 1861.

Dobbs, Henry H.- Private June 22, 1861. Appointed Sergeant. Wounded at Mechanicsville, Virginia June 26, 1862. Captured at Fort Harrison, Virginia September 30, 1864. Paroled at Point Lookout, Md. and transferred to Aiken's Landing, Virginia March 17, 1865. Received at Boulware & Cox's Wharves, James River, Virginia for exchange, March 19, 1865. No later record.

Ellis, Calvin S.- Private June 22, 1861. Wounded and disabled at Chancellorsville, Virginia May 3, 1863. No later record.

Ellsberry, John B.- Private June 22, 1861. Captured at Fredericksburg, Virginia December 13, 1862. Paroled for exchange December 17, 1862. Died at Charleston, South Carolina in 1863.

Fennell, Samuel B.- Private June 22, 1861. Died in 2d Georgia. Hospital at Richmond, Virginia January 5, 1863.

Fields, T.- Private June 22, 1861.

Fullbright, Aaron- Private June 22, 1861. Captured at Fredericksburg, Virginia December 13, 1862. Exchanged at City Point, Virginia May 13,1863.

Fullbright, L.- Private June 22, 1861.

Fullbright, William E.- Private June 22, 1861. Wounded and captured at Fort Harrison, Virginia September 30, 1864. Paroled at Point Lookout, Md. and transferred to Aiken's Landing, Virginia for exchange, March 17, 1865. Received at Boulware & Cox's Wharves James River, Virginia March 19, 1865. No later record. (Born in Georgia July 22, 1844.)

Gasdin, F.(or Gosden)- Private June 22, 1861. Died in 1864.

Gasdin, James (or Gosden)- Private June 22, 1861.

Gilley, Taylor- Private June 22, 1861. Died in 1862.

Gray, J. A.-See Private , Co. G.

Gray, Lewis Harvey-Private June 22, 1861. Furloughed for 30 days February 9, 1862. No later record.

Grubbs, John- Private June 22, 1861. Appointed Sergeant. Captured at Cold Harbor, Virginia June 1, 1864. Paroled at Elmira, New York October 11, 1864. Exchanged at Point Lookout, Md. October 29, 1864. Leg disabled while in prison.

Hagens, W. T.- Private June 22, 1861.

Hannah, Allen H.- Private June 22, 1861. Killed in North Carolina April 1865.

Harrison, Benjamin- Private 1861.

Hart, F E.- Private June 22, 1861. Died of typhoid fever,"at home of Mr. Houtchins," at

Farmville, Virginia May 23, 1862. Buried in Hollywood Cemetery at Richmond, Virginia.

Hart, William R.- Private June 22, 1861. Killed in Seven Days' Fight, near Richmond, Virginia June 1862.

Haynes, Asa- Private June 22, 1861. Died in Florida in 1864.

Haynes, J. L.- Private July 19, 1861. Wounded and captured at Sharpsburg, Md. September 18, 1862. Transferred from Fort McHenry, Md. to Fortress Monroe, Virginia for exchange October 18, 1862. No later record.

Haynes, William W.- Private June 22, 1861.

Hazell, Milledge B. (or Hazle)- Private June 22, 1861. Killed at Mechanicsville, Virginia June 26, 1862.

Hewett, Jackson- Private June 22, 1861. Died at Richmond, Virginia in 1862.

Hewitt, James Madison- Private June 22, 1861. Wounded and captured at Sharpsburg, Md. September 17, 1862. Paroled at Fort McHenry, Md. and sent to Fortress Monroe, Virginia for exchange, October 13, 1862. Exchanged at Aiken's Landing, Virginia November 10, 1862. No later record. Pension records show he was wounded in both legs below knees, at Ocean Pond, Fla. February 19 and 20, 1864. Unfit for further duty. (Born in Georgia in 1848.)

Hewitt, William- Private June 22, 1861.

Hicks, W. L.- Private June 22, 1861.

Hill, Jackson L.- Private August 1, 1862. Admitted to Institute Hospital at Richmond, Virginia December 16, 1862, and died there December 25 or 28, 1862. Buried there in Hollywood Cemetery.

Hudgins, William P.- Private June 22, 1861. Admitted to General Hospital #13, at Richmond, Virginia June 18, 1862, and transferred to Petersburg, Virginia, date not stated. Wounded near Petersburg, Virginia June 1864. Died of wounds in Virginia Hospital at Petersburg, Virginia June 22, 1864.

Hunton, John T.- Private July 6, 1861. Granted certificate by Captain of his company, showing he was entitled to discharge by reason of disability, October 31, 1861. Died in 1864.

Hunton, Walter M.- Private June 22, 1861. Captured at Fredericksburg, Virginia

December 13, 1862. Paroled for exchange at camp near Falmouth, Virginia December 14, 1862. Killed at Petersburg, Virginia in 1864.

Hurt, J.- Private June 22, 1861. Died at Richmond, Virginia May 13, 1862. Buried there in Hollywood Cemetery.

Lawler, Nicholas David- Private June 22, 1861. Elected 2d Lieutenant June 3,1862; 1st Lieutenant October 28, 1862. Wounded at Fredericksburg, Virginia December 13, 1862. Surrendered, Greensboro, N. C. April 26,1865.

Leathers, James C.- Private June 22, 1861.

Leathers, J.- Private June 22, 1861.

Leatherwood, Jesse F.- Private June 22, 1861. Appointed Corporal. Died at Staunton, Virginia November 22, 1862.

Leatherwood, William B.- Private June 22, 1861. Captured at Fredericksburg, Virginia December 13, 1862. Exchanged there December 17, 1862. Wounded at Fort Sumter, South Carolina October 27, 1863. Surrendered, Greensboro, N. C. April 26, 1865.

Lee, William J.- Private June 22, 1861. Died at Fort Sumpter, South Carolina December 11, 1863.

Lindsey, J.- Private June 22, 1861. Wounded at Chancellorsville, Virginia May 3, 1863. Admitted to Chimborazo Hospital #2 at Richmond, Virginia with wound in knee joint, May 12, 1863, and died of wounds July 24, 1863.

Luther, John H.- Private June 22, 1861. Died at Richmond, Virginia May 29, 1863. Buried there in Hollywood Cemetery. Mann, Thomas J.- Private July 6, 1861. Captured and paroled at Warrenton, Virginia September 29, 1862. No later record.

McBrayer, A. J.- Private June 22, 1861. Captured at Fredericksburg, Virginia December 13,1862 , and exchanged there December 17, 1862. Deserted in 1864. Received at Washington, D. C., a Confederate deserter, October 12, 1864, where he took oath of allegiance to U. S. Government. and remained in Washington.

McBrayer, James Madison- Private June 22, 1861. Captured at Fredericksburg, Virginia December 13, 1862. Exchanged in 1862. Surrendered, Greensboro, N. C. April 26, 1865. Died in Villa Rica, Georgia in 1914.

McBrayer, John C.- Private June 22, 1861. Died of chronic diarrhea, in General Hospital at Danville, Virginia, August 7, 1862.

McBrayer, Samuel M.- Private June 22, 1861. Wounded in left thigh and arm at Ocean Pond, Fla. February 20, 1864. Captured near Petersburg, Virginia June 18, 1864. Paroled at Point Lookout, Md. and transferred to Aiken's Landing, Virginia for exchange, March 15, 1865. Received at Boulware & Cox s Wharves, James River, Virginia March 18, 1865. No later record. (Born in Paulding County, Georgia February 24, 1842.)

McCain, J.- Private June 22, 1861.

McCarley, H.- Private.

McCarley, John- Private June 22, 1861. Died in Virginia.

McCurdy, J. H.- Private June 22, 1861. Wounded at Cold Harbor, Virginia June 27, 1862. Transferred from General Hospital #9, at Richmond, Virginia to Chimborazo Hospital #4, there, with chronic diarrhoea, May 5, 1863, and to Lynchburg, Virginia May 11, 1863. No later record.

McRae, William S. S.- Private June 22, 1861. Killed in Virginia in 1864.

McVicker, James A.- Private June 22, 1861. Wounded in knee at 2d Manassas, Virginia August 30, 1862. Died, result amputation of leg, at Warrenton, Virginia Hospital September 20 or 23,1862.

Miles, J. H.- Private June 22, 1861.

Mills, John A.- Private June 22, 1861. Discharged, disability, March 29,1862.

Morris, Isham- private June 22, 1861. Died in Virginia December 11, 1861.

Morris, Moses- private June 22, 1861. Surrendered, Greensboro, N. C. April 26, 1865.

Payne, William Jasper - Private June 22, 1861. Died of measles in Richmond, Virginia hospital May 27, 1862. Buried there in Hollywood Cemetery.

Powers, Michael joined in Carroll County. He surrendered in N. C. at the end of the war.

Reaves, James B. (or Reeves)- Private June 22, 1861. Killed at Sharpsburg, Maryland on September 17, 1862.

Reeves, W.- Private June 22, 1861.

Richards, D.- Private June 22, 1861. Killed at Fredericksburg, Virginia December 13, 1862.

Richards, James C.- Private March 4, 1862. Captured at Frederick, Md. September 12, 1862. Exchanged at Aiken's Landing, Virginia November 10, 1862. Killed at Fredericksburg, Virginia December 13, 1862.

Richards, John W.- Private June 22, 1861. Discharged, disability, at Camp Barton, Virginia March 29, 1862. Reported to Provost Marshal, at Bermuda Hundred, Virginia, a Confederate deserter, October 24, 1864. Released at Camp Hamilton, Virginia and went to Philadelphia, Pa. November 12, 1864.

Richards, M.- Private June 22, 1861. Captured. Released from prison in 1865. Not on W. R.

Robbins, C. (or Robins)- Private June 22, 1861.

Robbins, James M. (or Robins)- Private June 22, 1861.

Ruffin, Samuel F.- Private June 22, 1861. Died in 1862.

Sampson, John F.- Private June 22, 1861. Killed at Cedar Run, Virginia August 9, 1862.

Scales, Joseph C.- Private June 22, 1861. Surrendered, Greensboro, North Carolina on April 26, 1865.

Scales, W.- Private June 22, 1861. Died in 1863.

Scoggin, John Thomas- Private June 22, 1861. Paid at Richmond, Virginia September 25, 1862. No later record.

Scoggin, W. M.- Private June 22, 1861. Captured at Fredericksburg, Virginia December 13, 1862, and paroled there for exchange, December 17, 1862. No later record.

Shannon, Richard- Private June 22, 1861. Captured near Kinston, N. C. March 8, 1865. Released at Point Lookout, Md. June 19, 1865.

Shannon, S.- Private June 22, 1861. Furloughed for 30 days from Jackson Hospital at Richmond, Virginia August 28, 1864. Died in service.

Skinner, Benjamin S.- Private April 1863. Died at Athens, Tennessee July 1865.

Smith, J. M.- Private June 22, 1861. Died at Richmond, Virginia May 27, 1862. Buried there in Hollywood Cemetery.

Stark, Henry H.- Private June 22, 1861. Died of typhoid fever at Camp Johnson, Virginia January 30, 1862.

Stephens, John D.- Private June 22, 1861. Admitted to Chimborazo Hospital 34, at Richmond, Virginia with typhoid fever, June 6, 1862. Sent to Lynchburg, Virginia June 10, 1862. Admitted to C. S. A. General Hospital at Danville, Virginia on account of debility, [sic] July 2, 1862. Returned to duty July 11, 1862. Captured at Fort Harrison, Virginia September 30, 1864. Died at Point Lookout, Md. January 12, 1865.

Stephens, Reuben C.- Private March 8, 1862. Died at Camp Winder, near Richmond, Virginia May 20, 1862. Buried there in Hollywood Cemetery. Tice, Henry- Private June 22, 1861. Discharged, disability, July 9, 1861.

Tice, William Wesley- Private June 22, 1861. Captured at Fredericksburg, Virginia December 13, 1862 , and exchanged there December 17,1862. No later record.

Tidwell, John W.- Private June 22, 1861. Captured at Fredericksburg, Virginia December 13, 1862. Paroled for exchanged, near Falmouth, Virginia, December 14,1862. Killed at Petersburg, Virginia.

Turner, Benjamin T.- Private June 22, 1861. Admitted to Chimborazo Hospital #3, at Richmond, Virginia, with diarrhea, March 12, 1862, and furloughed for 60 days April 28, 1862. Captured at Fredericksburg,Virginia December 13, 1862, and paroled there for exchange December 17, 1862. Died December 1862.

Velvin, James H.- Private June 22, 1861. Appointed Regimental Musician. Captured near Columbus, Georgia April 18, 1865. Transferred to Military Prison at Macon, Georgia April 23, 1865.

Vines, James W.- Private June 22, 1861. Wounded at Fredericksburg, Virginia December 13, 1862. Detailed for hospital duty September 12, 1863. Present at Summerville, South Carolina hospital October 31, 1863. No later record.

Waldrup, Herman- Private June 22, 1861. In Confederate Hospital at Culpepper, Virginia, with pneumonia, September 26, 1862. Captured at Fredericksburg, Virginia December 13, 1862, and paroled there for exchange December 17, 1862. Pension records show he was at home on furlough for 30 days close of war.

Webster, John W.- Private March 12, 1862. Wounded in eye, resulting in loss of sight, at Yorktown, Virginia April 1862. Discharged, disability, at Richmond, Virginia August 12, 1862. (Born in Georgia March 24, 1845.)

Webster, R.- Private June 22, 1861.

Whisenhunt, Benjamin M. Private March 4, 1864. Died of measles at Richmond, Virginia.

Whisenhunt, James- Private. Died in Virginia.

White, Thomas M.- Private June 22, 1861. Killed while on picket duty in 1863.

Williams, John P.- Private February 1862. Pension records show he was wounded in right hip, near Richmond, Virginia May 1864. Contracted tuberculosis from exposure. Furloughed home, was unfit for further service, May 1864. Died of tuberculosis in Paulding County, Georgia February 1869.

Willoughby, John- private June 22, 1861. Wounded, date and place not given. Admitted to Chimborazo Hospital #4, at Richmond, Virginia, with chronic diarrhoea, case hopeless, August 4, 1862, and died there August 27, 1862.

Wilson, Augustus C.- Private. Wounded through left breast and hand, resulting in amputation of forefinger, at Chancellorsville, Virginia May 3, 1863. (Born in Georgia.)

Woods, Joseph- Private July 1863. Killed in 1865.

Woods, William- Private March 4, 1862. In Huguenot Springs, Virginia hospital August 31, 1862. Killed at Petersburg, Virginia.

Wright, William M.- Private. Wounded and captured in 1862. Admitted to Harewood U. S. A. General Hospital at Washington, D. C., wounded in head, December 23, 1862. Died March 1, 1863. Buried at Arlington, Virginia.

Wynn, Robert W.- Private June 22, 1861. Wounded, date and place not given. Deserted from Jackson Hospital at Richmond, Virginia June 20, 1864.

Wynn, William Thomas - private 1862. Wounded at Fredericksburg, Virginia December 13, 1862. Paid to February 29, 1864. Pension records show he was at home on wounded furlough close of war. (Born in Georgia in 1843 or 1844.)

Hart Town Environs
Appendix C

1864 Census for Re-Organizing the Georgia Militia
37th Senatorial District - 642nd Militia District

Bagwell, C. N., 17 yrs. 10 mos., Farmer, b GA
Bagwell, Willis, 50 yrs. 3 mos., Farmer, b SC
Ballard, Eli, 48 yrs. 9 mos., Farmer, b GA
Blackburn, E. P., 53 yrs., Golddigger, b. TN
Blain, G. W., 50 yrs, 4 mos., Farmer, b. GA
Candler, Samuel C., 54 yrs, 7 mos., Farmer, b. GA
Candler, W. B., 16 yrs, 10 mos., Farmer, B. GA
Carnes, J. P., 49 yrs, 4 mos., Farmer, B. GA
Carter, Jno. A., 46 yrs, 7 mos., Farmer, b TN
Chambers, J. M., 32 yrs. 3 mos., Farmer, b. NC
Chambers, Jesse N., 17 yrs, 2 mos., Farmer, b. GA
Chambers, Joseph W., 43 yrs., Golddigger, b. GA
Chieves, Alison, 50 yrs, 11 mos., Farmer, b. GA
Cole, Jacob, 55 yrs, 1 mo., Farmer, b. SC
Crook, Jno. W., 59 yrs., Farmer, b. NC
Driskill, Wm. M., 29 yrs, 3 mos., Physician, b. GA
Flannigan, Giles, 38 yrs., Farmer, b. GA
Grubbs, Talton, 57 yrs, 4 mos., Shoemaker, b. SC
Hambrill, Jas. R., 25 yrs. 10 mos., Merchant, B. GA
Hamilton, Thomas M., 45 yrs. 6 mos., b. SC; Exemption: Postmaster
Harper, Terrell, 49 yrs., Farmer, b. GA
Haynes, Gen J., 25 yrs., 10 mos., Farmer, b. GA
Hazell, H. C., 44 yrs., 8 mos., Farmer, b. SC, Exemption: Mail Contractor
Hazell, Lafayette, 16 yrs. 3 mos., Farmer, b. SC
Hill., Wm. P., 59 yrs., 2 mos., Farmer, b. GA
Hodson, V. M., 45 yrs., 8 mos., Physician, b. DE
Howard, Stephen, 59 yrs., 8 mos., Shoemaker, b SC

Howell, H. P. 45 yrs. 10 mo., Farmer, b. NC
Kennedy, William 48 yr., Farmer, b. GA
Leathers, Peter, 50 yrs., 1 mo., Farmer, b. AL
Leatherwood, Wm. F., 47 yrs., 6 mos., Farmer, b. SC
Luther, Isaac, 50 yrs., 8 mos., Farmer, b. NC
McCanley, A. J., 17 yrs., 5 mos., Farmer, b. GA
McCurdy, R. T., 45 yrs., 6 mos., Farmer, b. TN
Massey, J. J. 44 yrs., 6 mos., Farmer, b. NC
Mitchell., R. L., 30 yrs., 8 mos., Farmer, b. GA
Morgan, Eli S., 49 yrs., Farmer, b. GA

Morris, Jesse, 17 yrs., Farmer, b. GA
Muse, Jno. M., 45 yrs., 3 mos., Minister, b. GA
Nalley, Ambrose, 16 yrs., Farmer, b. GA
Nalley, J. B., 50 yrs., 6 mos., Farmer, b. SC
New, James, 40 yrs., Farmer, b. GA
Newman, D. C., 45 yrs., 6 mos., Farmer, b SC
Omstead, M. T., 17 yrs.., 2 mos., Tanner, b. CT
Palmer, D. B., 55 yrs., Physician, B CT
Palmer, Joshua, 55 yrs., Miller, b. SC
Pope, Henry, 54 yrs., Farmer, b. NC
Rabun, John, 46 yrs., Mechanic, b. NC
Roberts, David, 54, Golddigger, b. SC
Roberts, John, 26 yrs., Farmer, b. GA
Roberts, Alfred, 50 yrs., 10 mos., Farmer, b. SC
Rogers, A. G., 32 yrs., 11 mos., Farmer, b. TN
Sasser, H. J., 45 yrs., 6 mos., Farmer, b. GA
Smith, P. M., 45 yrs., 1 mo., Farmer, b. GA
Stanley, G. W., 55 yrs., Farmer, b. GA
Strickland, Roswell, 59 yrs., 10 mos., Farmer, GA
Talbott, Richard, 48., 6 mos., Farmer, b. NC
Trussell, Franklin A., 33 yrs., 3 mos., Mechanic, b. SC
Velvin, J. H., 59 yrs., 8 mos., Mechanic, b. NC
Velvin, S. S., 38 yrs., 8 mos., Blacksmith, b. GA
Watson, M. C., 16 yrs., Golddigger, b. GA
Webb, M. H., 45 yrs., 10 mos., Farmer, b. TN
White, Franklin, 46 yrs., 2 mos., Farmer, b. SC
Willoughby, Thomas, 50 yrs., 4 mos., Golddigger, b. England
Young, J. W. C., 33 yrs., Farmer, b. SC
   N. J. Meaddor, Enrolling Officer; Charles W. Heard Aide de Camp

37th Senatorial District - 649th Militia District
Adams, Absalom, age not given, Farmer, b. TN
Adams, W. B., 33 yrs., 3 mos., Farmer, b. GA
Allen E. M., 16 yrs., 10 mos., Farmer, b. GA
Allen, L. A., 46 yrs., 1 mo., Farmer b. NC
Allen, Wm. M., 16 yrs., 5 mos., Farmer, b. GA
Anderson, G. W., 18 yrs., Farmer, b. GA
Anderson, J. W., 18 yrs., Farmer, b. GA
Autrey, G. W., 34 yrs., 8 mos., Farmer, birthplace illegible
Ballard, Wm. W., 32 yrs., 8 mos., Farmer, b. GA
Barnes, J. H. 53 yrs., Farmer
Brown, Thomas T., 49 yrs., Farmer, b. NC?

Hart Town Environs

Buckner, Leroy, 47 yrs., 11 mos., Farmer, b. GA
Chambers, A. M., 17 yrs., 3 mos., Farmer, b. GA
Chance, George W., 51 yrs., Farmer
Chance, James W., 16 yrs., 5 mos., Farmer, b. GA
Chance, Warren, 53 yrs., 3 mos., Farmer, B. SC
Cochran, J. F., 50 yrs., Farmer
Collins, Silas M., 16 yrs., 3 mos., Farmer, b. GA
Dale, John M., 56 yrs., 2 mos., Farmer
Dobbs, Joseph L., 16 yr., 8 mos., Farmer
Dobson, John F., 55 yrs., 7 mos., Farmer, b. NC
Dobson, Wm. L., 16 yrs., 2 mos., Farmer, b. GA
Drew, John S., 54 yrs., Mechanic, b. GA
Easterwood, John W., 50 yrs. 10 mos., Farmer
Emory, A. O., 56 yrs., 7 mos., Farmer
Evans, Fields P., 50 yrs., Farmer, b. GA
Evans, Richard L., 16 yrs., Farmer, b. GA
Garrison, B. J., 46 yrs. 10 mos., Farmer, b. SC
Gray, Jesse, 52 yrs., 11 mos., Farmer, b. SC
Gray, Z. T., 17 yrs., 7 mos., Farmer
Green, David, 17 yrs., 4 mos., Farmer
Hanson, O. A., 51 yrs., Farmer, b. SC
Hanson, W. A., 16 yrs., 2 mos., Farmer, b. GA
Hart, James M., 17 yrs., Farmer
Henry, William, 50 yrs., 3 mos., Blacksmith, b. GA
Hesterly, P. H., 53 yrs., 11 mos., Farmer
Hicks, James, 46 yrs. 4 mos., Farmer, b. SC
Higgins, R. Y., 53 yrs., 8 mos., Farmer, b. NC
Higgins, T. Y., 16 yrs., 9 mos., Farmer, b. GA
Martin, Nathan, 55 yrs., 6 mos., Farmer, b. SC
Meader, Newton J., 28 yrs., 7 mos., Farmer
Merritt, William, 34 yrs., Farmer, birthplace illegible
Morgan, Wm. H., 47 yrs., Farmer
Morris, Robert, 17 yrs., 6 mos., Farmer
Morris, Wyatt 59 yrs., Farmer
Mould (smould), A. P. S., 45 yrs., 4 mos., Farmer
Muse, Jesse W. 30 yrs., 1 mo., Farmer, b. GA
Muse, Jno. W., 27 yrs., Farmer, b. GA
Patterson, Emory, 56 yrs., 6 mos., Blacksmith
Reese (Ruse), John H., age not given, Physician, b. SC
Riggs, Alexander S., 17 yrs., 4 mos., Farmer, b. GA
Ringer, B. F., 34 yrs., 8 mos., Farmer, b. SC
Roe, Richard L., 36 yrs., 10 mos., Physician, b. GA?

Scales, Lewis, 55 yrs., 9 mos., Farmer, B. GA?
Scoggin, James J., 59 yrs., 10 mos., Farmer, b. GA
Sims, John N., 16 yrs., Farmer
Sims, John R., 46 yrs., Farmer, b. GA
Sims, Sterling T., 45 yrs., 2 mos., Farmer, birthplace illegible
Smith, J. T., 26 yrs, 11 mos., Farmer, b. GA
Smith, John, 54 years., 9 mos., Farmer, b. GA
Stripling, Nathaniel, 17 yrs., Farmer, birthplace illegible
Tidwell, S. J., 53 yrs., 5 mos., Farmer, b. GA
Turner, Hiram, 53 yrs., 5 mos., Farmer, birthplace illegible
Vines, Peter E., 30 yrs., Farmer, b. GA
Walden, Isaac, 46 yrs., 2 mos., Farmer, b. GA
Walton, Joseph L., 45 yrs., 11 mos., Farmer, b. GA
Walton, Rufus W., 16 yrs., 8 mos., Farmer, b. GA
Webster, John W., 18 yrs., 10 mos., Farmer b. Georgia
Webster, Joseph, 51 yrs., 10 mos., Blacksmith, b. MD
Williams, G. M., 29 yrs., 2 mos., Farmer, b. GA
Wright, Arthur S., 48 yrs., 2 mos., Farmer, b. GA
Yates, J. P., 38 yrs., 8 mos., Farmer, birthplace illegible

N. J. Meador, Enrolling Officer; Charles M. Heard, Aide de Camp

Hart Town Environs
Appendix D
Early Land Owners
From Abstracts 1827 - 1854
Carroll County, Georgia

When looking through this book my friend
If for purpose true
I hope success may crown your work
And give you courage anew.
[Written at bottom of page 47, book F]

Many of these abstracts mention mining, mineral, metal or gold rights and/or digging rights.

SOUTH OF HART TOWN
Land Lot #96, 6th District, Carroll County
Book A, page 268, Washington County, June 13, 1830. Thomas Hart (original drawer) to William Fish. $50.00. Land lot #96, 6th district of Carroll County (now Heard county) Attest: V. W. Stuart, N. F. Hand, J.I.C., July 15, 1830.

Land Lot #102, 6th District, Carroll County
Book C, page 141, Carroll County, 15 Mar 1837. JESSE CHAMBERS to SLOMAN WYNN. $350. Land lot #102, 6th district Carroll County. 202 1/2 acres, 1/2 interest in gold. Attest: William H. Taylor, James Baskin J. P. 19 May 1837

Land Lot #105, 6th District, Carroll County
Book A, page 165 Carroll County, 1 Jan 1829. JAMES UPTON to WRIGHT MAJORS. $225.00. 202 1/2 acres lying on the Little Tallapoosa River, drawn by RILEY HAROLL, Jasper County. Attest: Robert Cooper, John Long, J. I. C.

Book G, page 299, Carroll County, 26 Sep 1851. GREEN HICKS, guardian of the person and property of WRIGHT W. MAJORS, a minor to ANDREW J. BUTRAM, highest bidder. $203.50. 83 acres land lot #105, 6th district Carroll County. Estate of WRIGHT MAJORS, deceased. Attest: Willis Smith, John W. Palmer, J. P.

Land Lot #121, 6th District, Carroll County
Book G, page 374, Carroll County, 6 Nov 1850. JACOB L. CARTWRIGHT to JAMES TAYLOR. $100.00 S. E. half land lot #121, 6th district Cartwright reserves gold rights. Attest: Wm. H. Taylor, Sloman Wynn, P. G. Garrison J. P. 5 Jan 1854.

Land Lot #131, 6th District, Carroll County

Book B, page 452, Carroll County, 8 Apr 1835. JOHN RICHARDS to ELIZABETH KENNON. $500.00 Land lot #131, 6th district Carroll County. Attest: John A. Jones, (sic) Emsly P. Hogan.

Book B, page 462 Carroll County, 13 Apr 1835. WILLIAM KENNON to ANDREW AGNEW, JEREMIAH HARRISON, FRANCIS WINN and JAMES BASKIN, Trustees of Lebanon Campground. Relinquish of rights because of past (land) deeds. 4 acres of land lot #131, 6th district Carroll County including Lebanon Meeting House and Campground for use of the Methodist E. Church. Attest: Pennell Quales, A. M. McWhorter, J. P., 17 Jan 1835.

Land Lot 138, 6th District, Carroll County
Book A, page 241, Carroll County, 31 Mar 1829. WILSON CARTWRIGHT to JAMES MAJORS. $300.00. 101 1/4 acres of Lot #138, 6th District, Carroll County, Drawn by THOMAS T. NAPIER on the Little Tallapoosa River. Attest: Thos. Chandler, E. P. Hogan, Hiram Mehaffey.

Book A, page 506, Carroll County, 7 Feb 1830. JAMES MAJORS to WILLIAM N. DAVIS. $350.00 101 1/4 acres, Little Tallapoosa River, part of land lot #138, Carroll County originally granted to THOMAS I. NAPIER. ATTEST: William Majors, A. M. McWhorter, J. I. C., 17 Feb 1831.

Land Lot #114, 6th District, Carroll County
Book B, page 295, Jasper County, 4 Apr 1833. JOHN HILL late of Jasper County now of Carroll and securities D. A. REESE, JAMES WHITFIELD and FLEMING JOURDAN to A. SLAUGHTER and C. SABAYAN. $5.00 Land lot #114, 6th District Carroll. Gold mine and residence of John Hill. To secure a note of $3500.00. Attest: Mrs. E. Stokes, Jesse Loyall J. P. 24 May 1833.

Land Lot #154, 6th District, Carroll County
Book F, page 613, Carroll County, 30 May 1850. HENRY HAYNES to JAMES C. ECHOLS, Taliaferrs [sic] County. $800.00. Land lot #154, 6th district Carroll County. 202 1/2 acres. Attest: W. H. Awtry, Jos C. Williams, J. P. 12 Nov 1851.

EAST OF HART TOWN
Land Lot 158
Book A, page 337, Bibb County, June 7, 1830. John Poe of Carroll County. Sum of $150.00 and the right to mine minerals and metals, east half of land lot #158, in the 6th district of Carroll County. Attest: Finley Holmes, R. Turner, Thos. J. Mcleskey J.P., August 7, 1830.

Book A, page 332, Bibb County, 14 Jun 1830. JOHN POE, Carroll County to JOHN B. WICK, Bibb County. $150.00. 15 acres of lot #158, 6th district Carroll (diagram

Hart Town Environs

included). Attest: Finley Holmes, R. Turner, Thomas J. McLeskey J. P., 6 Aug 1830.

Book B, page 282, Carroll County. On the first Tuesday of April 1833. Jiles S. Boggess the Sheriff to John Poe. Sum of $6.00 for land lot #158, in the 6th district of Carroll County. Land lot containing 202 ½ acres. Sold to satisfy a suit in the Justice of Court in Fayette County. Waites Veal vs William Morris. Attest: Appleton Mandeville, S. Kingsbery, J.I.C. April 16, 1833.

Book B, page 318, Carroll County, September 10, 1833. Jiles S. Boggess to Lewis Baileau. Sum of $14.00 for land lot #158, in the 6th district of Carroll County land containing 202 ½ acres. Sold to satisfy a suit in the Superior Court, Carroll County vs. Lewis Davis and John Poe. Attest: John Dean, Sanford Kingsbery, J.I.C. September 10, 1833.

Book E, page 307, August 2,1846. John A. Jones of Paulding County to John T. Chambers. Sum of $300.00 for south east of land lot #158, 6th district of Carroll County. Bounded on the north west by Carrollton Road. Gold Interest reserved. Attest: Denison B. Palmer, Solomon Wynn, John Long, J.I.C. September 2, 1843.

Book F, page 566, Carroll County, September 13, 1850. Larkin H. Davis to Madison Wallis of Campbell County. Sum of $400.00 for north west half of land lot #158, in the 6th district of Carroll County. Containing 100 acres. Attest: R. G. Embry, Samuel C. Candler, Jos. C. Williams, J.P., August 30,1851.

Land Lot #159, 6th District Carroll County
Book B, page 291, February 27, 1833. Fereby Beall, widow to Charles C. and Jeremiah Beall. Sum of $10.00 for land lot #159, in the 6th district of Carroll County. Land lot containing 202 ½ acres, secure a promissory note of $130.00. Attest: George W. Calter, Salin Beall, J.I.C., May 23,1833.

Book D, page 267, Carroll County, July 4, 1837. JOHN DEAN the Sheriff to JOHN T. CHAMBERS. Sum of $60.00 for Land lot #159, Carroll County. 202 ½ acres. Sold to Satisfy a suit, in Carroll County, C. and J. Beall vs. Ferley Beall. Attest: Lee Bird, Jas. H. Rogers, J.I.C. January 27, 1842.

Book F, page 130, Chatham County, 2 May 1843. MORDECIA MYRES, General in Bankruptcy declares JOHN ROWLAND THURSTON a bankrupt and sells to LEWIS F. HARRIS for $23.00 land lot #162, 6th district Carroll County also digging rights land lot #161, 6th district, property of JACOB AWTRY. Attest: Robt. Macellary, J. George, N. P. 21 Jul 1848.

Land Lot #162 & Land Lot #163, 6th District Carroll County
Book G, page 284, Carroll County, 23 Aug 1853. JOHN A. JONES, Paulding County to

JOHN JONES, Carroll County. $5000.00. His portion of the estate. Land lot #190, part of land lot #163 to the edge of the (Little) Tallapoosa swamp, part of Land lot #162 all in the 6th district Carroll County. Attest: S. S. Strickland, Davis Irwin J. P. 24 Aug 1853.

Land Lot 163, 6th District Carroll County
Book B, page 157, Georgia, 6 Sept 1831. THOMAS ABERCROMBIE to JOHN A. JONES. $40.00 for the N. E. corner of land lot #163, in the 6th district in Carroll County, containing 10 acres, gold excepted. Attest: J.D. Chapman, John Camp.

Book E, page 261, Carroll County, 3 Oct 1843. THOMAS A. CROMBIE to JOHN T. CHAMBERS. $600.00. Land lot #163, 6th district Carroll County. 190 acres, except that deeded to John A. Jones. Land south, southeast and west of JOHN A. JONES line 2/3 of gold interest. Attest: Clayton Williams, R. V. C. Ruffin, J. P. 21 Aug 1845.

NORTH OF HART TOWN
Book G, page 548, Carroll County, 14 Jan 1854. THOMAS RABUN to SILAS DOBBS. $2415.00. Land lot #186, 6th district Carroll County. Land lot #199, 6th district Carroll County. Gold excepted on lot #199. Attest: A. H. Harrison. J. Chambers, J. P. 12 Oct 1854.

Land Lot 187 6th District Carroll County
Book C, page 127, Georgia, 16 Apr 1836. GEORGE SWAIN, Paulding County to THOMAS RABURN. $600. Part of land lot #187, 6th district Carroll County. 145 acres, N. W. of the clear fork of the Tallapoosa River. Attest: James Calthorpe, Phillip Chambers.

Book D, page 28, Carroll County, 1 Aug 1837. JOHN A. JONES to JAMES MAJORS. $300. Land Lot #187, 6th district Carroll County, South of the (Little) Tallapoosa (River), 59 acres. Reserving trees and other things growing between the Tennysee Road and Jones fence. Attest: Clayton Williams, Andrew McMullan.

Book D, page 115, Carroll County, 4 Oct 1839. JAMES MAJORS to ELIJAH McPHERSON. $300. Part of Land Lot #187, 6th district Carroll County, south of the (Little) Tallapoosa (River). 59 Acres. Attest: P. H. Majors, R. V. C. Ruffin J. P.

Land Lot 188, 6th District Carroll County Georgia. Book E, page 285, Carroll County, 15 Sep 1841. JOHN A. JONES to LEONARD C. HUFF. $1,000.00. Land lot #188, 6th district Carroll County. 202 1/2 acres. Attest: Clayton William, Jesse H. Chambers, William Chambers, J. C. Williams, J. P. 11 Nov 1845.

Book F, Page 518, Carroll County, 18 Oct 1850. LEONARD C. HUFF, Cass County to SAMUEL HART. Sum of $400.00 for 1/2 land lot #188, 6th district Carroll County. Land lot containing 101 1/4 acres. Attest: A.M. Northcutt, M. C. Awtry, O. H. Hansen, J.P. April 25, 1851.

Book F, page 518, 18 Oct 1850. WILLIAM P. ANDERSON, Cobb County to SAMUEL HART. $400.00. 1/2 land lot #188. 101 1/4 acres. Attest: A. M. Northcut, M. C. Awtry, O. H. Hanson, J. P. 25 Apr 1851.

Land Lot #190, 6th District Carroll County
Book B, Page 19, Carroll County, July 14,1830. HODGE RABUN to ALFRED IVERSON of Jones County. Sum of $2,000.00 for undivided 1/5 of land lot #190, in the 6th district of Carroll County. Land lot containing 202 ½ acres. All mineral rights. Attest: Benjamin Murphy, J. G. Hamilton.

Book E, page 275, 24 July 1844. JACOB AUTREY to HIRAM McKINNEY sum of $75.00 for 50 acres for the south east corner. Autrey reserves mining rights. Land Lot #191, 6th district Carroll County. Attest: Hendon B. Palmer, R. V. C. Ruffin, J.P. October 8, 1845.

Book E, page 408, September 1846. Hiram McKinney to Mary Ann McKinney. $100.00 for 50 acres. Land lot #191, 6th district reserves working Rights. Attest: L. B. Wear, Martin Holcomb, J. P. October 12, 1846.

Land Lot #197, 6th District, Carroll County
Book E, page 265, Carroll County, 7 Mar 1840. JOHN A. JONES, Paulding County to LEONARD C. HUFF. $1,200.00 Land lot #197, 6th district Carroll County. 202 1/2 acres. Attest: A. H. Harrison, R. V. C. Ruffin, J. P. 28 Aug 1845.

Land Lot #198, 6th District, Carroll County
Book G, page 384, Carroll County, 4 Jan 1850. JONATHAN CHAMBERS to WILLIAM H. YATES. $500.00. Land lot #198, 6th district Carroll County. Attest: George M. Hiden, Henry S. Chance, 24 Jan 1854.

Land Lot #199, 6th District, Carroll County
Book B, page 45, Coweta County, May 23, 1831. SARAH JOHNSON to THOMAS RABUN of Carroll County. Sum of $350.00 for land lot #199, in the 6th district of Carroll County. With rights to all gold excepted. Will pay all damages Rabun "may sustain by digging and washing for gold." Attest: Jonathan Hogan, James Stroud, J.I.C., July 6, 1831.

Book E, page 188, Carroll County, 23 Dec 1844. JAMES UPTON to HENRY S. CHANCE. $200.00. East half of land lot #199, 6th district Carroll County. Attest: Thos Chandler, B. S. Merrell, J. P. 24 Dec 1844.

Book G, page 548, Carroll County, 14 Jan 1854. THOMAS RABUN to SILAS

DOBBS. $2,415.00. Land lot #186, 6th district Carroll County. Land lot #199, 6th district Carroll County. Gold excepted on lot #199. Attest: A. H. Harrison. J. Chambers, J. P. 12 Oct 1854.

Land Lot #222, 6th District, Carroll County
Book E, page 293, Carroll County, 13 Oct 1845. JOHN B. WICK TO ROBERT F. McCurdy. $400.00. Land lot #222, 6th district Carroll County. 202 1/2 acres. Lumber, gold and mineral rights. Attest: Thomas H. Roberds, R. V. C. Ruffin J. P. 13 Nov 1845.

Page 318, Book A, June 13, 1830. Fleming Jordan of Jasper County to James Whitfield, John Hill, Edward A. Broaddus and Thomas Jefferson Smith, of Jasper County. Sum of $2,000. Land lot #224, 6th district Carroll County. 202 1/2 acres. Attest: Robert T. Hargrove, Jesse Loyall, J.P., August 3, 1830.

Page 295, Book B, Jasper County, April 4, 1833. John Hill Late of Jasper County now of Carroll County and securities D. A. Reese, James Whitfield and Fleming Jourdan to A. Slaughter and C. Sabayan. Sum of $5.00 for land lot #224, in the 6th district of Carroll County. Gold mine and residence of John Hill. To secure a note of $3,500.00 Attest: Mrs. E. Stokes, Jesse Loyall, J.P., May 24, 1833.

Page 282, Book E, August 18, 1841. John Hill of Augusta City by attorney in fact for Fleming Jourdin and David Reese to Needham Jarnagin of Carroll County. Sum of $900.00. Land lot #224, 6th district Carroll County. Know as the Hill Lot or Gold mine. Attest: J. W. Barney, Cas. Jourdin, J.I.C. November 10, 1845.

Page 282 Book E. Jasper County, 18 August 1841. J. E. A. Broddas. Jasper County to NEEDHAM JORNAGIN. $125.00. 1/6 interest lot# 224, 6th district Carroll County, known as the Hill Goldmine, all his rights and only reserving right to any gold veins. Attest: William Goolsby, Chas. Jordan, J. I C. 10 Nov. 1845.

Page 589, Book F, Carroll County, 10 Jan 1851. MARGARET JARNIGAN to THOMAS H. ROBERDS. $100.00. Mining interest land lot #224, 6th district Carroll County, with exception of veins deeded to John H. Davis. Attest: Saml C. Candler, Joseph C. Williams, J.P., 22 Oct 1851.

Land Lot #250, 6th District, Carroll County
Book G, page 445, Carroll County, 15 Apr 1844. GEORGE M. GLADDEN to THOMAS TURNER, ASBURY C. ARNOLD, JAMES TURNER, JOSIAH TOLBERT and L. H. DAVIS, trustees of the METHODIST EPISCOPAL CHURCH [sic SOUTH] north in [of] the COUNTY OF CARROLL. $15.00 S. E. corner, north half land lot #250, 6th district Carroll County. Running due west along the old original road from Villa Rica to Vanwert, the line between GEORGE GLADDEN and Mrs.

SUSAN STANFORD. Attest: James F. Davis, Thomas Stokeley J. I. C. 20 Apr 1854.

WEST OF HART TOWN
Land Lot 167 6th District Carroll County
Book B, page 46, 7 May 1831. JAMES JOHNSON to JAMES MAJORS. $505.00 Land lot 167, 6th district Carroll. 202 1/2 acres on the Little Tallapoosa River. Original grant to ELIJAH M. CALAWAY. Attest Y. J. Long, James Dickson, J. P. 6 Jul 1831.

Book D, page 106, Carroll County, 11 May 1840. PHILLIP BURROUGH, ELIJAH MCPHERSON and THOMAS CHANDLER to JOHN HOWELL of Tennessee. $200.00. Land lot #167, 6th dist Carroll County. Attest: Wilson Cartwright, John Dean.

Book A, page 485, Habersham County, 25 Dec 1830. JOHN STARRETT to WILLIS RABUN, Carroll County. $700.00. Land lot #168, 6th dist Carroll County. 202 1/2 acres drawn in the lottery by James Walker. Attest: Thos. Rabun, S. M. Norris J. P. 24 Jan 1831.

Book B, Page 216, Carroll County, April 24, 1832. WILLIS RABUN to JAMES H. McELRATH. Sum of $950.00. Land lot 168, Carroll County. 202 1/2 acres. Drawn in the lottery by JAMES WALKER. Witness: Daniel McDowell, Joseph McClure, Thomas Rabun. J. P. October 3, 1832.

Book B, Page 479, Carroll County, February 4, 1835. JAMES McGRATH to JOHN McGRATH. Sum of $400.00. 1/3 of land lot #168, 6th dist, Carroll County, on the Little Tallapoosa (River). Attest: James Majors, William Majors.

Book G, page 87, Paulding County. 16 Oct 1850. BURTON WATSON to JOHN THOMAS. $130.00. 40 acres N. E. corner of Land lot #168, 6th district Carroll County. Attest: Daniel Dulin, William Meret, O. A. Hanson, J. P. 10 Nov 1852.

Bibliography:

Abstracts:

Pitts, Sarah, *Abstract of Deeds Carroll County Georgia, Abstracts of Deed Books A, B, C, D, E, F & G for District 6*, 2017-2018. Unpublished.

Word, Mary Florence Authur. *Abstract of Deeds Carroll County Georgia, Abstracts of Deed Book A & B*, 1827-1836, *Volume I*. Pages 1-128. Family History Library, Salt Lake, Utah.

Word, Mary Florence Authur. *Abstract of Deeds Carroll County Georgia, Abstracts of Deed Book C & D, 1836-1843, Volume II*. Pages 1-98. Family History Library, Salt Lake, Utah.

Word, Mary Florence Authur. *Abstract of Deeds Carroll County Georgia, Abstracts of Deed Book E, F & G, 1843-1855, Volume III*. CGRS. Pages 1-221. Family History Library, Salt Lake, Utah.

Internet:

Ancestry.com: Public Member Trees; Carroll County, Georgia Federal Census Records - 1830, 1840, 1850, 1860, 1870, 1880, 1900, 1910; Federal Slave Census 1850 & 1860 Carroll County, Georgia

Ancestry.com: U. S. Appointments of U. S. Postmasters 1832-1971. Page 305 Volume 10, 1832-44; Volume 17 1844-1857; Volume 26 1857-1876; Volume 42 1876-1889; Volume 68A 1889-1930.

Carroll County, Georgia Mortality Schedule:

Crilley, Virginia. *Carroll County, Georgia USGenWeb Archives by varcsix@hot.rr.com*. US-GenWeb Archives http://www.usgwarchives.net/ga/carroll.htm http://www.usgwarchives.net/ga/gafiles.htm

DeVorsey, Louis. *Archaeology & Early History of Indian Trails. Indian Roads, Trails, and Paths*. University of Georgia, January 22, 2003. http://www.georgiaencyclopedia.org/nge/Article.jsp?id=h-790.

Find-A-Grave: Carroll County, Georgia and Douglas County, Georgia.

Fold 3 Military Program.

Georgia Property Tax Digests: Carroll County, Georgia 1873.

Google Earth Pro. U. S. Department of State Geographer @2020 Google Geo-Basis - DE/BKG.

Lucas, Jr., S. Emmett, *Carroll County, Georgia USGenWeb Archives Biographies*

Mock, Cary J., Jan Mojzisek, Michele McWaters, Michael Chenoweth, David W. Stahle. *The Winter of 1827-1828 over Eastern North America: A Season of Extraordinary Climatic Anomalies, Societal Impacts, and False Spring*. Pages 87 - 115. November 16, 2005. https://cpb-us-e1.wpmucdn.com/wordpressua.uark.edu/dist/1/224/files/2017/09/2007_Mock_etal.pdf

Moore, Sue Burns. *1829-1867 Membership New Hope Primitive Baptist Church Villa Rica, Carroll and Douglas County, Georgia*. File contributed for use in USGENWEB Archives by Georgia State Archives.

Native American Trails and Roads in Georgia. https://en.wikipedia.org/wiki/Category:Historic_trails_and_roads_in_Georgia_(U.S._state)

Newspapers.com.

Manuscripts, Official and Unofficial:
Anthony, Rev. J. D. *Cherokee County, Alabama Reminiscences of its Early Settlement, Alabama Historic Quarterly vol. 8 no 3*. Pages 319-342. 1946.

Bailey, Elaine Bolden. *The Cobb-Kittle House*. Self-published, 1988.

Bickers, Rev. Harvie E. Bickers. *A History of Wesley Chapel United Methodist Church Organized 1854*. Miles Wesley Arnold & J. W. Warelaw, Villa Rica Georgia, 1854.

The Carroll County Genealogical Quarterly: Spring 1983; Fall 1983; Fall 2003.

Duggan, M. L. *Educational Survey of Carroll County Georgia*. Page 69. Georgia State Department of Education, The University of Georgia Library, 1918.

The Family of Henry Haynes and Phoebe Eaton, courtesy Carl Lewis' Historical Documents. 2019.

Georgia Trust, *Letter Mark C. McDonald*. April 4, 2016.

"Handwritten Notes by Hart Genealogists," June Hart Wester, in possession of the authors. May 18, 2020. Courtesy Phyllis Smith Hart.

Hixon, Horace A. *History of Pleasant Grove Baptist Church Carroll County Georgia.* Pages 1-7. 1943.

History of Concord Methodist Church Hickory Level, Carroll County Georgia 1828-1966. Pages 1-7. Neva Lomason Library, Carrollton, Georgia.

Holland, Attorney, Hubert G. *Carnes Families of Bartow, Carroll, Cobb and Paulding Counties, Georgia.* Hubert B. Holland, Marietta, Furnished by Paulding County Public County Library. 1956.

Humphries, Nathaniel Harbin. *Deposition of April 12, 1872*. Taken at the house of G. E. Eidson's Cobb County. Judge Honor John L. Hopkins of Superior Court Fulton County, State of Georgia.

Leathers, III L. Milton. *The Leathers Family, 1607-1987*. Leathers Family, Athens Georgia, 1987.

Long, Calvin Luther. *The Progeny of John Long.* Pages 31 & 35. http://reocities.com/Heartland/valley/4561/progeny.html. 1913.

Nomination for the National Register of Historical Places. November 14, 1979, for the Dorough Round Barn.

Ruff, Sandra Pruett. *The Noland Family Tree.*

Samuel Hart Family Genealogy. Pages 1-183. Phyllis Smith Hart.

Southern Business Directory, Georgia, Carroll County, Villa Rica. 1854.

Wiggins, Rev. Wallis. *History of the Villa Rica Methodist Church.* Compiled by Mrs. S. C. Connally, Mrs. C. L. Roberds and Mrs. H. R. Marchman. 1951. Courtesy of Rebekah Willoughby Morgan.

Books:
Anderson, Mary Talley. *The History of Villa Rica.* Pages 15, 80, 89, 168. Carroll County Historical Society, 1976, 2000 Reprint.

Arthur, Mary Florence. *The Heritage of Carroll County Georgia.* 1826-2001, 2002.

Bailey, John B. *The History of Dark Corner Campbell County, Georgia.* Page 11. Lillium Press, 2015.

Bonner, James C. *Georgia's Last Frontier: The Development of Carroll County.* Pages 20, 37, 51. University of Georgia Press, Athens, 1971.

Carroll County Historical Society. *At Home in Carrollton 1827-1994.* Pages 13-15. Wolfe Publishing Fernandina Beach, Florida 32035, 1995

Cobb, Private Joe. *Carroll County and Her People.* Reprint 1976, Sesquicentenial-Bicentennial Committee Carroll County Chamber of Commerce, 1906, 1976, Reprint.

Cummins, Bertie Beall. *The Georgia Bealls and their Kinfolks.* Published Beall, Sr., Thomas Julian, May 7, 1964.

Daughters of American Revolution. *Roster of Revolutionary Soldiers in Georgia Volume 1.* Page 85-86, 1941.

Graham, Elizabeth Candler and Roberts, Ralph. *The Real Ones, Four Generations of the First Family of Coca-Cola.* Pages 1-341. Barricade Books, Inc., 1992.

Griffith, Jr., Benjamin W. *McIntosh and Weatherford Creek Indian Leaders.* The University of Alabama Press, 1988.

Hart Town Environs

Hart, Dorothy E. *Descendants of James Madison Hart*. Pages 1-144. 1993.

Henderson, Lillian. *Roster of Confederate Soldiers of Georgia 1861-1865*. Book 2, page 755. Book 5, page 903. Longino & Porter, Inc. Hapeville, Georgia; Funds for the publication of Volumes 1 and 2 were made available by S. Marvin Griffin, Governor of Georgia, 1955-1958.

Henderson, Ray. *The History of the Pony Club*. Lillium Press Historical books, 2011.

Holder, Burell Williams & Holder, Ruth Roberts. *A History of Temple, Georgia a West Georgia Town of Carroll County*. Pages 11, 14, 15 & 61. Vabella Publishing Carrollton, Georgia, 1976, 1982, & 2013.

North American Family Histories. Daughters of American Revolution. Lineage Book 1500-2000. Volume K 19: 1919. Pages 236 & 237.

Roster of Revolutionary Soldiers in Georgia. Volume 1. Pages 130 & 131.

Smith, B. Roger. *Descendants of James Chambers of Virginia 1738-1795*. 642 pages. Smith Publishing, 2009.

Southerland, Jr., Henry DeLeon and Brown, Jerry Elijah. *The Federal Road through Georgia, the Creek Nation and Alabama 1806-1836*. Sponsored by the Historic Chattahoochee Commission, 1989.

Yeats, W. S., State Geologist. *Geological Survey of Georgia: A Preliminary Report on a Part of the Gold Deposits of Georgia*. Pages 242-245. Franklin Printing and Publishing Company, Atlanta, Georgia, 1896.

Wiggins, Dr. David N. *Postcard History Series Carroll and Haralson Counties in Vintage Postcards*. Arcadia Publishing, 2004.

Photos:
More than 25 photos are from ancestry.com Public Member Trees. Others are from Carroll County Find-A-Grave; Fold 3 Military Program; Georgia Info Galileo 1883 map https://georgiainfo.galileo.usg.edu/histcountymaps/carrollhistmaps.htm; *At Home in Carrollton*; *Georgia's Last Frontier; The Heritage of Carroll County;* and *Times Georgian*..
One photo courtesy of Monroe Lee Joiner from the Villa Rica Gold Mine Museum at the Pine Mountain Stockmart Park in Villa Rica. Other photos found: Long Photo Collection; Villa Rica Archives, Villa Rica Area Historical Society, Inc.; Villa Rica Masonic Lodge Members; Photos contributed by individuals Courtesy: John Bailey; Hart Cobb, Ray Dial, Frank Duke, Cathy Gibson, Wanda Haines; Jack Hart, Phyllis Hart; Joe Jordan; Buford Kittle; Milton Leathers, Don Levans; Greg & Donna Lisenby; Barbara Wynn Mitchell; Mary Elizabeth Phillips, Sarah Pitts, Patricia Mullinax Pope; Pauline Roberts; Don Sharp, Amy Streeter; and Roger Smith.
Photo editing: Elaine Bailey, Jake Smith, Kevin Smith, Free Photo Restoration and Photo Colorizing & Restoration.

Interviews:

    Hart Cobb - May 2020
    Margaret Cobb - May 2020
    Frank Duke - October 2019
    Wanda Haines - April 2020
    Jack Hart - May 2016
    Phyllis Smith Hart - May 2016 & May 18, 2020
    Ray Henderson - July 2019 & January 2020
    Ruth Holder - January 2020
    Milton Leathers - June 2016
    Don Levans - January 2020
    Carl Lewis - December 2019, February 2020; March 21, 2020
    Greg & Donna Lisenby - October 2018
    John McFalls - February 2020
    Barbara Wynn Mitchell - September 2016
    Sarah Pitts - February 21, 2020; March 20, 2020
    Pauline Roberts - February 21, 2020.
    Rodger Smith - June 2019
    Monroe Spake - October 2019
    Jerry Vogler - July 2019
    Catherine Yates West - April 2020

Newspapers:

"History of Wesley Chapel Methodist Church." *Carroll County Paper [sic]*. Williams, Pastor M. S. September 20, 1891."

"Indian Trails through Carroll County, Georgia: the First Interstate." *Historic Preservation Series, The Carroll Star News*. Douglas C. Mabry. Sunday March 7.

"More on the 'first interstate': Indian Trails in Carroll County, Georgia." *Historic Preservation Series, The Carroll Star News*. Douglas C. Mabry. Sunday March 14.

"A Boy in a Covered Wagon in 1860 Comes to Carroll." *Carroll County Times*. J. A. Roberson, October 13, 1927.

"The Coming of the Civil War." *Carroll County Times*. J. A. Roberson, October 13, 1927.

The Temple Enterprise. Pages 1, 3 & 4. September 24, 1883.

"Wicks's Tavern Travels to New Home." *The Temple Enterprise*. Pages 1 & 4, December 3, 1998.

"Preserving History Restoration of Wick's Tavern." *Times-Georgian*. Pages 1 & 4. July 18, 1999

"Wick's Tavern is Open for 'bidness.'" *Times-Georgian. Page 1B*. Sunday, August 25, 2002.

"History Lies in our Backyard." *The Villa Rica Voice*. Stan Hardegree. Page 19. June 27, 2002.

"Discover Downtown Villa Rica." *The Villa Rican*. Page 7. 2008.

"Villa Rica, Reprinted From Carroll County & Her People by Private Joe Cobb." *The Historic News Southern Historical News*, Inc. Page 5. August 2002.

Bibliography by Chapters

Chapter 1: Native Americans, Early Pioneers & Early Roads
Ancestry.com: Carroll County Rangers, Carroll County, Georgia.

Anderson, Mary Talley. *The History of Villa Rica*. Pages 79. Reprinted by Carroll County Genealogical Society, 2000.

DeVorsey, Louis. *Archaeology & Early History of Indian Trails. Indian Roads, Trails, and Paths*. University of Georgia, January 22, 2003. http://www.georgiaencyclopedia.org/nge/Article.jsp?id=h-790.

Holland, Attorney Hubert G. *Carnes Families of Bartow, Carroll, Cobb & Paulding Georgia*. Marietta, Paulding Co Public County Library.

"Indian Trails through Carroll County, Georgia: the First Interstate." *Historic Preservation Series, The Carroll Star News*. Douglas C. Mabry. Sunday March 7, 2000.

Inferior Court Records, Early Roads in Carroll County, Georgia, 1831–1842. Carroll County Courthouse, Carrollton, Georgia.

Long, Calvin Luther. *The Progeny of John Long*. Pages 31 & 35. http://reocities.com/Heartland/valley/4561/progeny.html. 1913.

"More on the 'first interstate': Indian Trails in Carroll County, Georgia". *Historic Preservation Series, The Carroll Star News*. Douglas C. Mabry. Sunday March 14, 2000.

"Backtracking 100 Years" *The Temple Enterprise*. Pages 1 & 4, September 24, 1983.

"History Lies in our Backyard." *The Villa Rica Voice*. Page 19. Stan Hardegree, June 27, 2002.

Chapter 2: Waystation, Stores, Churches, Schools, Post Offices, Masons
Abstracts: Pitts, Sarah, *Abstract of Deeds Carroll County Georgia, Abstracts of Deed Books A, B, C, D, E, F & G for District 6*, 2017-2018. Unpublished.
Abstracts: Word, Mary Florence Authur. *Abstract of Deeds Carroll County Georgia, Abstracts of Deed Book A & B, 1827-1836, Volume I*. Pages 1-128. Family History Library, Salt Lake, Utah.
Abstracts: Word, Mary Florence Authur. *Abstract of Deeds Carroll County Georgia, Abstracts of Deed Book E, F & G, 1843-1855, Volume III*. CGRS. Pages 1-221. Family History

Library, Salt Lake, Utah.

Ancestry.com: U. S. Appointments of U. S. Postmasters 1832-1971. Page 305 Volume 10, 1832-44; Volume 17 1844-1857; Volume 26 1857-1876; Volume 42 1876-1889; Volume 68A 1889-1930.

Anderson, Mary Talley. *The History of Villa Rica* Carroll. p. 92. County Genealogical Society. 1976 & 2000.

Bickers, Rev. Harvie E. *A History of Wesley Chapel United Methodist Church.* Organized 1854 by Miles Wesley Arnold & J. W. Warelaw, Villa Rica Georgia, 1854.

"Buckhorn Tavern, Other Early Communities," *The Temple Enterprise 1883–Centennial Edition 1983.* Page 7. September 24, 1983.

Cobb, Private Joe. *Carroll County and Her People.* Page 19. Reprint 1976, Sesquicentenial-Bicentennial Committee Carroll County Chamber of Commerce, 1906

Carroll County Historical Society. *At Home in Carrollton 1827-1994 A History Illustrated.* Page 76. Photo Courtesy: Karl Steiner. Wolfe Publishing Fernandina Beach, Florida 32035, 1995.

Duggan, M. L. *Educational Survey of Carroll County Georgia.* Georgia State Department of Education. Page 69. The University of Georgia Library, 1918.

History of Concord Methodist Church Hickory Level, Carroll County Georgia 1828-1966. Pages 1-7. Neva Lomason Library, Carrollton, Georgia.

Google Earth Pro. U. S. Department of State Geographer @2020 Google Geo-Basis - DE/BKG.

"History Lies in our Backyard." *The Villa Rica Voice.* Page 19. Stan Hardegree, June 27, 2002.

Hixon, Horace A. Pamphlet: *History of Pleasant Grove Baptist Church Carroll County Georgia.* Pages 1-7. 1943.

Holder, Burell Williams & Holder, Ruth Roberts. *A History of Temple, Georgia A West Georgia Town of Carroll County.* Pages 13, 14, 15 & 61. Vabella Publishing Carrollton, Georgia, 1976, 1982, & 2013.

Holland, Attorney Hubert G. *Carnes Families of Bartow, Carroll, Cobb & Paulding Georgia.* Marietta, Paulding County Public Library.

Moore, Sue. 1829-1867 *Membership New Hope Primitive Baptist Church Villa Rica, Carroll and Douglas Counties, Georgia. Pages 1-24.* USGenWeb Archives.

Spears, Hilda and Chatt-Flint Staff. *Historic Preservation Study.* Article and photo prepared by Chattahoochee-Flint Area Planning and Development Commission, 1976.

Southerland, Jr., Henry DeLeon and Brown, Jerry Elijah. *The Federal Road through Georgia, the Creek Nation and Alabama 1806-1836.* Page 59. Sponsored by the Historic Chattahoochee Commission, 1989.

"Villa Rica Male and Female Institute," *Carroll County Free Press*, March 11, 1851.

Vintage Postcards, Arcadia Publishing, 2004

Wiggins, Rev. David N. *Postcard History Series Carroll and Haralson Counties.* http://www.eturner.com/GED/grpf00968.html. Coltharp Family Reunion, 2010.

Wiggins, Rev. Wallis. *History of the Villa Rica Methodist Church.* Compiled by Mrs. S. C. Connally, Mrs. C. L. Roberds and Mrs. H. R. Marchman. 1951. Courtesy of Rebekah Willoughby Morgan.

Villa Rica Board of Education. *A Manual for the Use of the Board of Education and Teachers of the Villa Rica High School in the City of Villa Rica, Georgia.* Pages 6, 12 and 20. Issued by the Board of Education, 1909-1910.

Chapter 3: Gold Deposits in Villa Rica & Climatic Anomalies
Abstracts: Pitts, Sarah, *Abstract of Deeds Carroll County Georgia, Abstracts of Deed Books A, B, C, D, E, F & G for District 6*, 2017-2018. Unpublished.
Abstracts: Word, Mary Florence Authur. *Abstract of Deeds Carroll County Georgia, Abstracts of Deed Book A & B*, 1827-1836, *Volume I.* Pages 1-128. Family History Library, Salt Lake Utah.
Abstracts: Word, Mary Florence Authur. *Abstract of Deeds Carroll County Georgia, Abstracts of Deed Book C & D, 1836-1843, Volume II.* Pages 1-98. Family History Library, Salt Lake Utah.
Abstracts: Word, Mary Florence Authur. *Abstract of Deeds Carroll County Georgia, Abstracts of Deed Book E, F & G, 1843-1855, Volume III.* CGRS. Pages 1-221. Family History Library, Salt Lake Utah.

Bonner, James C. *Georgia's Last Frontier: The Development of Carroll County.* Pages 50-51. University of Georgia Press, Athens, 1971.

Google Earth Pro. U. S. Department of State Geographer @2020 Google Geo-Basis - DE/BKG.

Mock, Cary J., Jan Mojzisek, Michele McWaters, Michael Chenoweth, David W. Stahle. *The Winter of 1827-1828 over Eastern North America: a Season of Extraordinary Climatic Anomalies, Societal Impacts, and False Spring.* Pages 87–115. November 16, 2005. https://cpb-us-e1.wpmucdn.com/wordpressua.uark.edu/dist/1/224/files/2017/09/2007_Mock_etal.pdf

Smith, B. Roger. *Descendants of James Chambers of Virginia 1738-1795.* 642 pages. Smith

Publishing, 2009.

"Villa Rica, Reprinted From *Carroll County & Her People* by Private Joe Cobb." *The Historic News Southern Historical News*, Inc. Page 5. August 2002.

Yeats, W. S., State Geologist. *Geological Survey of Georgia: A Preliminary Report on a Part of the Gold Deposits of Georgia*. Pages 242-245. Franklin Printing and Publishing Company, Atlanta, Georgia, 1896.

Chapter 4: Intruders, Pony Boys and Slicks
Ancestry.com: Public Member Tree. "Violence in Carrollton: The Pony Club." George C. Sharp. *Carroll Free Press*. Article and Cartoon.

Anthony, Rev. J. D. *Cherokee County, Alabama Reminiscences of its Early Settlement, Alabama Historic Quarterly Vol. 8, No 3*. Pages 319-342. 1946.

Henderson, Ray. *The History of the Pony Club*. Pages 196. 210, 217, 221-222, & 228-229. Lillium Press Historical books, 2011.

"Old Times in Carroll, Uncle George Sharp Continues his Reminiscences." *Carroll Free Press*. October 4, 1895, October 18, 1895, November 1, 1895.

Chapter 5: Early Settlers of Hart Town and Pleasant Grove
Abstracts: Pitts, Sarah, *Abstract of Deeds Carroll County Georgia, Abstracts of Deed Books A, B, C, D, E, F & G for District 6*, 2017-2018. Unpublished.
Abstracts: Word, Mary Florence Authur. *Abstract of Deeds Carroll County Georgia, Abstracts of Deed Book E, F & G, 1843-1855, Volume III*. CGRS. Pages 1-221. Family History Library, Salt Lake, Utah.

Ancestry.com: Public Member Trees; Federal Census Records; Carroll County Marriage Certificates; Carroll County Find-A-Grave, Temple and Villa Rica.

Anderson, Mary Talley. *The History of Villa Rica*. Pages 15 & 89. Carroll County Historical Society, 1976, 2000 Reprint

The Carroll County Genealogical Quarterly. The Yates Family. Fall 1983.

Cobb, Private Joe. *Carroll County and Her People*. p. 19, Reprint 1976, Sesquicentenial-Bicentennial Committee Carroll County Chamber of Commerce, 1906

Google Earth Pro. U. S. Department of State Geographer @2020 Google Geo-Basis - DE/BKG.

National Register of Historical Places Nomination Form, Dorough Round Barn and Farm. November 14, 1979.

Chapter 6: Early Settlers of Hickory Level
1873 Georgia Property Tax Digests.

Abstracts: Pitts, Sarah, *Abstract of Deeds Carroll County Georgia, Abstracts of Deed Books A, B, C, D, E, F & G for District 6*, 2017-2018. Unpublished.

Abstracts: Word, Mary Florence Authur. *Abstract of Deeds Carroll County Georgia, Abstracts of Deed Book A & B*, 1827-1836, *Volume I*. Pages 1-128. Family History Library, Salt Lake, Utah.

Abstracts: Word, Mary Florence Authur. *Abstract of Deeds Carroll County Georgia, Abstracts of Deed Book C & D, 1836-1843, Volume II*. Pages 1-98. Family History Library, Salt Lake, Utah.

Abstracts: Word, Mary Florence Authur. *Abstract of Deeds Carroll County Georgia, Abstracts of Deed Book E, F & G, 1843-1855, Volume III*. CGRS. Pages 1-221. Family History Library, Salt Lake, Utah.

Ancestry.com: Public Member Trees; Federal Census Records; Carroll County, Georgia Marriage Certificates.

Anderson, Mary Talley. *The History of Villa Rica*. Pages 15 & 16. Carroll County Historical Society, 1976, 2000 Reprint.

Carroll County Find-A-Grave, Temple and Villa Rica.

Henderson, Lillian. *Roster of Confederate Soldiers of Georgia 1861-1865, Book 2.* Page 755. Longino & Porter, Inc. Hapeville, Georgia; Funds for the publication of Volumes 1 and 2 were made available by S. Marvin Griffin, Governor of Georgia, 1955-1958. Book 2 pages 752-753.

Holder, Burell Williams & Holder, Ruth Roberts. *A History of Temple, Georgia a West Georgia Town of Carroll County.* Pages 11 & 61. Vabella Publishing Carrollton, Georgia, 1976, 1982, & 2013.

Chapter 7: The Civil War Affects Families: Candlers, Chambers, Haynes
Ancestry.com: Public Member Trees; The 1830, 1840, 1850, 1860, 1870, 1880 and 1900 Federal Census Record; Carroll County Marriage Records.

"A Boy in a Covered Wagon in 1860 Comes to Carroll." *Carroll County Times*. J. A. Roberson, October 13, 1927.

Carroll County Find-A-Grave for Temple and Villa Rica.

"The Coming of the Civil War." *Carroll County Times*. J. A. Roberson, October 13, 1927.

Google Earth Pro. U. S. Department of State Geographer @2020 Google Geo-Basis - DE/ BKG.

Graham, Elizabeth Candler and Roberts, Ralph. *The Real Ones, Four Generations of the First*

Family of Coca-Cola. Pages 1-341. Barricade Books, Inc., 1992.

Haynes, William Edgar. *The Family History William Haynes 1762–1843.* Shared by Leroy Haynes before 2002.

Henderson, Lillian. *Roster of Confederate Soldiers of Georgia 1861-1865, Book 2,* page 752–755. Longino & Porter, Inc. Hapeville, Georgia; Funds for the publication of Volumes 1 and 2 were made available by S. Marvin Griffin, Governor of Georgia, 1955-1958.

Smith, B. Roger. *Descendants of James Chambers of Virginia 1738-1795, 642 pages.* Smith Publishing, 2009.

Chapter 8: Early Settlers of Old Town—Hixtown & Chevestown
Abstracts: Pitts, Sarah, *Abstract of Deeds Carroll County Georgia, Abstracts of Deed Books A, B, C, D, E, F & G for District 6,* 2017-2018. Unpublished.
Abstracts: Word, Mary Florence Authur. *Abstract of Deeds Carroll County Georgia, Abstracts of Deed Book A & B, 1827-1836, Volume I.* Pages 1-128. Family History Library, Salt Lake, Utah.
Abstracts: Word, Mary Florence Authur. *Abstract of Deeds Carroll County Georgia, Abstracts of Deed Book C & D, 1836-1843, Volume II.* Pages 1-98. Family History Library, Salt Lake, Utah.
Abstracts: Word, Mary Florence Authur. *Abstract of Deeds Carroll County Georgia, Abstracts of Deed Book E, F & G, 1843-1855, Volume III.* CGRS. Pages 1-221. Family History Library, Salt Lake, Utah.

Ancestry.com: Public Member Tree; Federal Census Records; Carroll County Marriage Records.

Anderson, Mary Talley. *The History of Villa Rica.* Page 4. Carroll County Historical Society, 1976, 2000 Reprint.

The Carroll County Genealogical Quarterly, Spring 1983. Slaughter Family. Submitted Lee B. Nichols.

"Discover Downtown Villa Rica." *The Villa Rican.* 2008. Page 7.

Google Earth Pro. U. S. Department of State Geographer @2020 Google Geo-Basis - DE/BKG.

Henderson, Lillian. *Roster of Confederate Soldiers of Georgia 1861-1865, Book 2.* Page 755. Longino & Porter, Inc. Hapeville, Georgia; Funds for the publication of Volumes 1 and 2 were made available by S. Marvin Griffin, Governor of Georgia, 1955-1958. Book 2 pages 752-753.

"Interview with Appleton Mandeville," *The Atlanta Constitution.* Friday, September 28, 1887.

Lucas, Jr., S. Emmett. *Carroll County, Georgia USGenWeb Archives Biographies: Tolbert.*

Ruff, Sandra Pruett. *The Noland Family Tree.*

Southern Business Directory, Georgia. Carroll County, Villa Rica. 1854.

Chapter 9: Early Settlers of the Wesley Chapel Community
Abstracts: Pitts, Sarah, *Abstract of Deeds Carroll County Georgia, Abstracts of Deed Books A, B, C, D, E, F & G for District 6*, 2017-2018. Unpublished.
Abstracts: Word, Mary Florence Authur. *Abstract of Deeds Carroll County Georgia, Abstracts of Deed Book A & B*, 1827-1836, *Volume I.* Pages 1-128. Family History Library, Salt Lake, Utah.
Abstracts: Word, Mary Florence Authur. *Abstract of Deeds Carroll County Georgia, Abstracts of Deed Book C & D, 1836-1843, Volume II.* Pages 1-98. Family History Library, Salt Lake, Utah.
Abstracts: Word, Mary Florence Authur. *Abstract of Deeds Carroll County Georgia, Abstracts of Deed Book E, F & G, 1843-1855, Volume III.* CGRS. Pages 1-221. Family History Library, Salt Lake, Utah.

Ancestry.com: Public Member Trees; Federal Census Records; Carroll County Marriage Records. Carroll County Find-A-Grave.

"Clopton Gold Mining." *Carroll Free Press.* August 12, 1881.

"Clopton Mines at Villa Rica." *Carroll Free Press.* August 19, 1881.

Humphries, Nathaniel Harbin. "Deposition of April 12, 1872" taken at the house of G. E. Eidson, Cobb County by Judge Honor John L. Hopkins of Superior Court Fulton County, State of Georgia.

Chapter 10: Early Settlers of Hill's Crossing & Simsville
Pitts, Sarah, *Abstract of Deeds Carroll County Georgia, Abstracts of Deed Books A, B, C, D, E, F & G for District 6*, 2017-2018. Unpublished.
Word, Mary Florence Authur. *Abstract of Deeds Carroll County Georgia, Abstracts of Deed Book A & B*, 1827-1836, *Volume I.* Pages 1-128. Family History Library, Salt Lake, Utah.
Word, Mary Florence Authur. *Abstract of Deeds Carroll County Georgia, Abstracts of Deed Book C & D, 1836-1843, Volume II.* Pages 1-98. Family History Library, Salt Lake, Utah.
Word, Mary Florence Authur. *Abstract of Deeds Carroll County Georgia, Abstracts of Deed Book E, F & G, 1843-1855, Volume III.* CGRS. Pages 1-221. Family History Library, Salt Lake, Utah.

Ancestry.com: Public Member Tree; Federal Census Records; Carroll County Marriage Records.

Carroll County Find-A-Grave, Temple and Villa Rica.

The Carroll County Genealogical Quarterly. Elijah Daniel McPherson. Fall 2003.

Cobb, Private Joe. *Carroll County and Her People*. Pages 12 & 13. Reprint 1976, Sesquicentenial-Bicentennial Committee Carroll County Chamber of Commerce, 1906, 1976, Reprint.

Fold 3 Military Program: Jackson Lafayette Hill.

Google Earth Pro. U. S. Department of State Geographer @2020 Google Geo-Basis - DE/BKG.

Henderson, Lillian. *Roster of Confederate Soldiers of Georgia 1861-1865, Book 2*. Page 755. Longino & Porter, Inc. Hapeville, Georgia; Funds for the publication of Volumes 1 and 2 were made available by S. Marvin Griffin, Governor of Georgia, 1955-1958.

Holder, Burell Williams & Holder, Ruth Roberts. *A History of Temple, Georgia a West Georgia Town of Carroll County.* Pages 14, 15 & 18. Vabella Publishing Carrollton, Georgia, 1976, 1982, & 2013.

"Obituary of Cynthia Coleman." *Carroll County Times*. February 9, 1877.

Shole's Georgia State Gazette. 1879-80. Carroll County, Simsville.

Chapter 11: Families of the Hart Plantation

Ancestry.com: Public Member Tree by Marsha Gail Veazey; Federal Census Records; Carroll County Marriage Records.

Anderson, Mary Talley. *The History of Villa Rica*. Pages 15, 80 & 133. Carroll County Historical Society, 1976, 2000 Reprint.

The Carroll County Heritage Book Committee and County Heritage, Inc. *The Heritage of Carroll County, Georgia 1826–2001*. Pages 261-262. 2002.

Carroll County Historical Society. *At Home in Carrollton 1827-1994*. Pages 13-15 & 21. Wolfe Publishing Fernandina Beach, Florida 32035, 1995.

"Creek Lands Acquired by the State in 1825." *The Villa Rica Merchandiser*. Wednesday, 26 May 1965. Radford Herrick, author.

Cobb, Private Joe. *Carroll County and Her People*. Page 9. Reprint 1976, Sesquicentenial-Bicentennial Committee Carroll County Chamber of Commerce, 1906

Cummins, Bertie Beall. *The Georgia Bealls and their Kinfolks*. Published Beall, Sr., Thomas Julian, May 7, 1964.

Hart, Dorothy E. *Descendants of James Madison Hart*. Pages 1-144. 1993.

Fold 3 Military Program.

Georgia Trust for Historic Preservation. "The Georgia Trust's Board of Trustees, Letter, Mark

C. McDonald," April 4, 2016.

Google Earth Pro. U. S. Department of State Geographer @2020 Google Geo-Basis - DE/BKG.

"Hand written notes by Hart genealogists," June Hart Wester, in possession of the authors. May 18, 2020. Courtesy Phyllis Smith Hart.

Henderson, Lillian. *Roster of Confederate Soldiers of Georgia 1861-1865, Book 2,* Pages 752, 754 & 755. Book 5 page 903. Longino & Porter, Inc. Hapeville, Georgia; Funds for the publication of Volumes 1 and 2 were made available by S. Marvin Griffin, Governor of Georgia, 1941, 1955-1958. Book 2 pages 752-753.

Leathers, III L. Milton. *The Leathers Family, 1607-1987.* Leathers Family, Athens Georgia, 1987.

Long, Calvin Luther. *The Progeny of John Long.* Pages 31 & 35. http://reocities.com/Heartland/valley/4561/progeny.html. 1913.

Newspapers.com:

North American Family Histories. Daughters of American Revolution. Lineage Book 1500-2000. Volume K 19: 1919. Pages 236 & 237.

"Private Collection, Samuel Hart." 1822-1928 and 1760-1965, number GRG 9-434, Drawer 227, Box 64, The Georgia Archives. June Hart Wester. C. G. of Canton, Georgia.

Roster of Revolutionary Soldiers in Georgia. Volume 1. Pages 130 & 131.
Samuel Hart Family Genealogy. Pages 1-183. Courtesy: Phyllis Smith Hart.

"Samuel Hart Family Group Sheets." Lilma Hart Godsey, Pittsburg, Texas 75686.

Appendix A: Photos of Artifacts
By John B. Bailey and Elaine B. Bailey

Appendix B: Muster Roll of Villa Rica "Gold Diggers"
Carroll County Georgia Company I–19th Regiment. Crilley, Virginia. *Carroll County, Georgia USGenWeb Archives by varcsix@hot.rr.com.* USGenWeb Archives http://www.usgwarchives.net/ga/carroll.htm
http://www.usgwarchives.net/ga/gafiles.htm

Appendix C: 1864 Census for Reorganizing Georgia Militia
Ancestry.com. Carroll County, Georgia Company I–19th Regiment. Crilley, Virginia. *Carroll County, Georgia USGenWeb Archives by varcsix@hot.rr.com.*
USGenWeb Archives http://www.usgwarchives.net/ga/carroll.htm
http://www.usgwarchives.net/ga/gafiles.htm

Appendix D: Abstracts Carroll County, Georgia 1827–1854

Many of these abstracts mention mining, mineral, metal or gold rights and/or digging rights.

Abstract: Pitts, Sarah. *Abstract of Deeds Carroll County Georgia, Abstracts of Deed Books A, B, C, D, E, F & G for District 6*. 2017-2018, unpublished.

Abstract: Word, Mary Florence Authur. *Abstract of Deeds Carroll County Georgia, Abstracts of Deed Book A & B, 1827-1836, Volume I*. Pages 1-128. Family History Library, Salt Lake, Utah.

Abstract: Word, Mary Florence Authur. *Abstract of Deeds Carroll County Georgia, Abstracts of Deed Book C & D, 1836-1843, Volume II*. Pages 1-98. Family History Library, Salt Lake, Utah..

Abstract: Word, Mary Florence Authur. *Abstract of Deeds Carroll County Georgia, Abstracts of Deed Book E, F & G, 1843-1855, Volume III*. CGRS. Pages 1-221. Family History Library, Salt Lake, Utah.

About the Authors

Elaine Bolden Bailey has lived in Douglas County since 1970. She earned a Bachelor of Science degree in Education from the University of West Georgia and retired from West Georgia Technical College as the department head of Adult Education. Elaine and her husband, John, have two children, a son-in-law, and two grandchildren.

Elaine's interests are playing the piano, writing, history, and genealogy. She has written two poetry books, *Pompadour and Pearls: A Patchwork of Poetry* in 1991, *Buttermilk Clouds* in 1995; *Explosion in Villa Rica*, a non-fictional history in 2010; *Tracks*, a historical novel in 2011; and has collaborated with her husband in 2014 for his book, *History of Dark Corner Campbell County, Georgia*. In 2015, she and co-author, Patricia Lamar Mullinax wrote *Draketown Tragedy*, a story inspired by true events.

John B. Bailey was born in Charleston, South Carolina and moved to Georgia when he was twelve. He graduated from Villa Rica High School and attended West Georgia College. He is married to Elaine, has two children, a son-in-law and two grandchildren.

John has been published in *The Civil War Times, The Virginia Country Magazine and Military Images*. He was the Historical Editor of *Looking Good Douglas County* magazine. John has spoken to groups on the Civil War and Native American History for over thirty years.

He volunteered at the Villa Rica Gold Mine Museum for ten years, giving tours and demonstrating gold panning. He demonstrates flint napping at festivals and events. His hobbies are making arrowheads, metal detecting, blacksmithing, gardening and reading Civil War history. He was the president of the Villa Rica Area Historical Society for two years.

Index

(Index entries in all capital letters denote possible abstracts to deeds.)

A

If a name appears on a single page more than once, the indexing does NOT reflect this. So read the entire page for your search.

Adams
    Absalom Drury 156, 157
Adair
    James L. 19, 20, 40, 143
    James Lee 135
    John Bluett 135
    Judith 135
    Lucy 135
    Mitchell S. "Michael" 135
    Permelia 135
    Sarah Ann Harrington 135
    Sarah Ann Scott 135
    Sarah Sally 135
    William 135
    William Andrew 135
    William Bozeman 135
ADAIR
    BOZEMAN 136
Adams
    Absalom 157, 158
    Absalom Drury 156
    Absolom 14, 16, 17, 153, 154, 157
    Alley 156
    Edmund Hunt 156
    Elizabeth 158
    Gilbert Marion 156
    Gilles J. 17
    Jobe 17
    Jonah 156
    Lydia 156
    Mahala Jane 153
    Mahaley 156
    Margaret D. H. 156
    Mary Elizabeth Reid 153, 156
    Mollie E. 60
    Nathaniel 21, 22
    Phoebe Elizabeth 156
    Sarah 26, 157, 158
    Sarah Ann 156
    Sarah Blankenship 156
    William 26, 156
    William B. 157, 164
    William F. 156
    Zachariah Taylor 156
Aderhold
    Andrew J. 39
Aderholt
    Michael 16
AGNEW
    ANDREW 39, 202
Aimes
    John 18
Alexander Porter Green 28, 67, 79, 161
Allen
    Adeline Martha Jane 83
    Alcimus 14
    Alcimus Harris 83, 84
    Alysmus 32
    Cynthia Elvira 83
    James H. 154, 156
    James Harris 83
    Jane Moore McCain 83
    John A. 83
    Joseph H. 40
    Larkin 31, 32, 83
    Leanora R. 40
    Robert H. 83
    William Marcus 83
    Zachary J. 39
    Zachary T. 40
Allen, Sr.
    Adeline Martha Jane Steele 83
    Alcimus Harris 83
    Cynthia Kilgore Marcus Threadgill 83
ALLMAN
    NELSON 46
Allmon
    Nelson 104
Allum
    Nelson 154
Almon
    Mr. 58
    Nelson 147
Amis
    F. J. 29
Anderson
    George 75
    M. G. 18
Arney
    Henry 83
Arnold
    Asbury Coke 37
    Miles W. 32
    Miles Wesley 37, 38, 209, 214
    M. W. 32
    WIlliam 37

Index

ASBURY
   JOHN 43
Astins 28
Autrey
   Absalom James 120
   George W. 40
   Jacob 121
AUTREY
   JACOB 122, 205
Autry
   George W. 155
   M. C. 143
AUTRY
   M. C. 45
Awrey
   J. 40
Awtery
   Jacob 17
Awtrey
   Adeline M. 121
   Elizabeth Albina 121
   Emily Jerusha 121
   George W. 121
   Isaac 121
   Jacob 83, 120
   Lucy Naomi 121
   Merrell C. 110, 121
   Sarah 121
   Susannah "Susan" Fitzalin 121
   William Hill 121
AWTREY
   JACOB 121
Awtry
   Albinia 26
   Elizabeth A. 26
   George 154
   Jacob 21, 117, 121
   Merrel C. 26
   Nancy 26
AWTRY
   M. C. 45

B

Babb
   Clara Mae 176
Baggett
   Alfred 35
Bagwell
   Willis 14, 28, 76, 138
BAILEAU
   AUSTIN 45
   LEWIS 44, 45
Bailey
   Ezekiel 174
   Mary Steed 174
   Robert S. 18, 21
Ballard 31, 187, 197, 198
Bante
   John 16
Barber
   Elisha 16, 18
Bark
   Caswell 18
Barnapp
   Dunn and 139
Barnes
   James 159
   Judge 58
   L. P. 162
   Sarah McKenzie 159
Baskin
   Clark W. 84
   C. M. 148
   C. W. 156
   Henrietta Williams
   Harrison 84
   J. 40
   James 14, 18, 22, 31, 32, 39, 83, 84, 85, 86, 89, 92, 201
   James L. 39, 40
   James Lawrence 84
   Jas. 92
   Lawrence 148
   Margaret J. 84
   Martha 84
   Mary Ann Elizabeth 84
   Rhoda Chandler 85
   Sarah E. 84
   Thomas W. 84, 89
   Virginia J. 84
   Walter Colquit 84
   W. C. 40
   William Jasper 84
BASKIN
   JAMES 39, 202
Baxter 31, 32
Bayley
   John 17
Belk
   S. R. 38
Beal
   Auther 16
Beall 25, 28, 35, 45, 66, 68, 100, 101, 103, 121, 129, 172, 178, 203, 210, 221
   Hester P. 25
   Justiana Dickinson Hooper 100
   Justin 25
   Martha Bernetta Beall 100
   Mary 178
   Nancy 178
   Noble Peyton 100
Beall.
   Augustus Chandler 66
Beasley
   David Redding 69
   Sophronia 69, 178
Becker
   Josaah 17

Index

Belk
   S. R. 36, 38, 39
Bell
   Arthur 17
Bird
   Lee 16, 203
Bishop
   Eliza L. 75
   George 32
   Mollie 75
Black
   Peterson 19, 21
Blackwell
   Jessee 25
Bledsoe 89
Boggess
   Jiles 59, 117, 168
   J. S. 92
BOGGESS
   JILES 48, 116
Boggs
   Anderson 21
   Mary Ella 176
Bohanon
   Levi 17
Bolton
   Thomas 16
Bomar
   John 111
   Mary Louisa "Mary Lou" 111
   Sarah Tittle 111
Bone
   Sarah Sally Adair 135
Bonner
   J. A. 29
   Thomas 106
Boon
   Benjamin 46
   Jesse 21
BOON
   JESSE 46
Boone
   Daniel 171
   Rebecca Bryant 171
   Sarah Morgan 171
   Squire 171
Borin
   Joseph 170
   Susanna 170
Boring
   Thomas 32, 38
BOSWELL
   JOHN J. 49, 139
Bowen
   Christopher 21
   O. B. 40
   T. L. 40
Boyce
   Ann 143
Brady
   Jackson W. 32
   John W. 38
   J. W. 38
Brand
   W. H. 75
Brantley
   James 18
Braswell
   G. P. 35
   S. H. 32, 39
Broaddus
   Clopton and 117
   Edward A. 48, 117, 118, 206
BROADDUS
   DAVID 145
   EDWARD A. 36, 48
Brock
   Aaron Madison 86
   Charles Albert 86
   David 14, 83, 86
   David N. 86
   Eli Walker 86
   George William 86
   James Waddy 86
   John Cannon 86
   Marion Jackson 86
   Martha 86
   Mary Elizabeth Davis 86
   Robert Lee 86
   Rufus Wilburn 86
   Sarah Easterwood 86
   Sarah Jane 86
   Thomas Franklin 86
   Waddy 86
Brookes
   John 25
Brooks
   Elisha 33, 154
   Elizabeth 25
   James F. 155
   Janie Ellen 182
   John 25, 43, 46, 104, 154
   Lilla 167
   William 147, 156, 167, 181, 183
BROOKS
   ELISHA 33, 165
   JOHN 43, 161
Brooks III
   Catherine 147
   Catherine Matilda Clontz 147
   James Fletcher 147
   Janie E. 147
   John Wesley 147
   Lugeri Frances 147
   Mary Isabelle 147
   Mary "Polly" Burleson 147
   Sarah 147
   Thomas Sanford 147
   William Jacob 147
   William James 147
   William James Brooks II 147
Brooks Jr.
   Addie 181
   Ena 181

Index

Evie 181
Gaudie 181
Ina Katherine 181
James Harry 181
John 181
Lilla Alice 181
Martha Jane Pennington 181
William 181
William Jacob 181
Brown
  Jasper Aaron 176
  Jesse 17
  J. R. T. 29, 36, 37
Brown;
  James 16
Bryant
  Alice 171
  E. L. 48
  Elijah 47
  Helen B. 133
  Hillon H. 133
  J. M. 40, 116
  Joseph 171
BRYANT
  E. L. 48
  ELIJAH 47
Bryce
  Eleanor "Nellie" Ray Sharp 87
  Emily Margaret 87, 107
  Felix Sloman Chalmbers 87
  George Robert 87
  Henrietta Mahala 87
  Ira Bascomb 87
  J. 40, 92
  James 14, 31, 32, 87, 88, 92
  James Fulton 87
  James Young 87
  J. M. 83
  John Fulton 87
  John T. 39
  Joseph 87
  Mary Eleanor 87
  Mary Ellen Orr 87
  Nancy Ann Elisa 87
  Parthenia Ann Elizabeth 87
  Sarah Jane 87
  Thomas 16
  W. 92
  William 87
  William Hiram 87
Buckelew
  James 113
Burke
  Calloway 58, 59
  Thornton 35, 140
BURKE
  THORNTON 43
BURNAPP
  LYMAN 49, 139
Burnes
  William 21
  William R. 163
Burnett
  Valentine 16, 17
Burns
  William 19, 27
Burt
  Thornton 29
Burton
  T. W. 47
BURTON
  THOMAS W. 29, 47
Burtons 28
BUTRAM
  ANDREW J. 92

C

Cagle
  Susan M. "Susie" 71
Calhoun
  Col. 106
Camon
  Y. C. 16
Camp
  B. S. 21
  Mary Lucy "Mollie"
  Naomi 120
Campbell
  John A. 48, 116, 117
CANCELLER
  PHILLIP 45
Candler
  Elizabeth 129
  Elizabeth "Lizzie" Frances 101
  Elizabeth Slaughter 34, 129
  E. S. 21, 47, 141
  Eugenia 129
  Ezekiel S. 40
  Florence 129
  Martha 91
  Noble Daniel 101
  Samuel 100, 101, 102, 103, 117
  Samuel C. 20, 21, 35, 102, 103, 143, 203
  S. C. 40
  Warren 35
  Warren A. 31
  W. B. 33, 34, 42, 102, 103
  William Beall 129
  William Beall Candler, Jr. 129
CANDLER
  S. 91
Candler, Sr.
  Asa Griggs 100
  Ezekiel "Zekie"
  Samuel 100
  Florence "Fanny"
  Julie 100
  John Slaughter 100
  Milton Anthony 100
  Samuel Charles 100

Index

Samuel "Charlie" Charles 100
Sarah "Jessie" Justina 100
Warren Akin "King Shorty" 100
William "Willie" Beall 100
Cannes
   David 18
Cannon
   Watson and 118
CANSELLER
   PHILLIP 44, 45
Cardwell
   James 17
Carnes
   John 25
   Mary 25
   Polly 25
   Richard 94
Carroll
   Hannah McPherson 163
   James M. 163
Carson
   Atlanta H. Parker 174
CARTER
   JOHN 47
Cartright
   W. 40
   Wilson 21
Cartwright
   Thomas 164
   Wilson 45, 154, 157, 207
Cash 31
Chamber
   Sarah 143
Chambers 109
   Benjamin D. 105, 109
   Catherine 109, 110
   Doctor Porter 75

Doctor Porter "Doc" 105
Doctor Porter "Doc" 108
Elizabeth 103
Emily J. 71
Fannie 148
Francis Marion 105, 109
H. 26
Hannah 110
Hannah Minerva 105, 109
J. 39, 44, 47, 71, 76, 108, 204, 205
James 36, 211, 216, 218
James L. 105
Jesse 51
Jesse H. 109, 110
Jesse Harrison 107
John 15, 26
John T. 21, 28, 40, 51, 99, 100, 105, 106, 107, 118, 203
John Thaddus 103, 105
Joseph 32, 48, 50, 51, 103, 104, 105, 110, 117, 118
Joseph W. 25, 103
Joseph Washington 103, 105
Katherine 26, 182
Lucindy 26
Martha 103
Mary C. 103
Mary Elizabeth 110
Merrill Columbus 105, 108
Milton R. 75
Milton Rice 105, 108
Minerva Adeline 110

Nancy A. 103
Nelson Josephus 105, 107, 109
Nicholas F. 103
Nicholas Franklin 105
Phillip 20, 43, 204
Robert W. 105
Sarah 110, 143
Sarah Ann Elizabeth 105
Sarah Elizabeth Moody 103
Sarah L. 103
Washington 26, 103, 107
William K. 103
William Posey 105
CHAMBERS
   JESSE H. 36, 48, 51, 145
   JOSEPH 36, 48, 51, 145
Chance
   Henry J. 19, 21
   Henry S. 21, 32, 33, 39, 67, 91, 119, 157, 158, 163, 165
   Henry T. 17
   H. S. 40
   James 154, 155
Chandler
   Dorothy 88
   Harriet E. 88
   Harriet "Hattie 88
   Joseph 88, 148
   Marion 88
   Martha 88
   Mary Ann 88
   Mary Bell Jackson 89
   Newton J. 88
   Rhoda 88
   Sarah Farmer 88
   Sarah Framer 148

Index

Thomas 14, 88
Thomas H. 88
CHANDLER
  EZEKIEL S. 36, 48
Chapman
  Benjamin 19, 48, 117, 118
  Benjamin Franklin 178
  J. D. 92
  John 178
  Nathan 178
  Thomas 178
CHAPMAN
  BENJAMIN 36, 46, 48, 145
Chastain
  Dewren 134
  Frances 134
Cheaves
  Elizabeth Alford 119
  James L. 119
Cheeves
  Sarah Elizabeth 119
Cheney
  Sharp and 155
Cheves
  Addie Eugenia 119
  Allison 28, 71, 119, 120, 121, 125, 126
  Daniel Scott Mead 119
  Dora E. 119
  Earnest Jacob 119
  Jesse 119
  John A. 119
  Lucy Hitchcock 119
  Lula E. 119
  Mahala Ann Shinn 119
  Mary Ella 119
  Sarah Elizabeth 119, 125, 126
  William 119

  William Allison 119
Clark
  O. 51
  Oliver 51
  S. A. 38
  Samuel 32
Clarke
  Oliver 50
CLARKE
  OLIVER 51
Cleghorn
  William 56
Cline
  John 18
Clopton
  Alford 49, 139
  David 48, 117, 118, 136, 138, 140, 141
  David C. 136
  Martha 136
  Martha Jenkins 136
  Mary Ann Vanderwall 136
CLOPTON
  ALFORD 49, 139
  DAVID 36, 43, 48, 139, 141, 145
Clower
  Peter 47
CLOWERS
  PETER 47
Cobb
  Augusta Grow 149
  E. H. "Bud" 30
  Eldorado H. "Bud" 150
  Elizabeth Mitchell 148
  Esther Almeda Connell 151
  Francis Carter Chandler 148
  George H. 148
  Henry Hart 151
  Hugh B. 149

  Isaac 14, 23, 39, 147, 148, 149, 152
  Isaac E. 23, 24, 33, 148, 149, 154
  Isaac Eugene 148
  Isaac Osceola 151
  Isaac Osceola "Ossie" 150
  James H. 148
  Jane 28, 151
  Jane Hart 30, 148, 149
  J. L. 150
  J. M. 128
  John 30
  John M. 154, 156
  John Marion 148
  John T. 150
  Joseph 149
  Joseph Lafayette 148, 149
  Lewis Connell 151
  Lucy 151
  Martha S. 148
  Mary Ann 148
  Mary Chandler 148
  Ossie 30
  Pvt. Joe 149, 155
  Thomas B. 148
  William 14, 39, 147, 149, 150, 173
  William Frank 151
  William W. 24, 173, 174
  William Washington 28, 148, 149, 173
  W. W. 28
COBB
  ISAAC E. 33, 165
Cobb, Sr
  Isaac Osceola 151
Colclaugh
  Alexander 179
  Mary Hart 179
  William 179

Colclough
    Alexander 151
    Eli H. 151
    Mary Hart 151
    Susan Rebecca 151
    William 151
    William A. 151
Cole
    Gilbert 29, 33, 47, 67, 77, 154
    Jeremiah 17
    John 21
COLE
    GILBERT 33, 165, 166
Coleman
    Clara Kolbe 160
    Cynthia F. Riggs 159
    Elizabeth Ann 158
    Eliza M. 158
    George 158
    Henry 14, 154, 158, 159
    Henry Allen 158
    James P. 158
    John 159, 160
    John Henry 158
    John W. 159, 160
    Martha L. 158
    Mary F. 158
    Mollie Bailey 160
    Nancy Bufford 158
    Nancy Catherine 158
    Rebecca Catherine 158
    Sarah Ann Barnes 158
    Sarah Jane 158
    Sarah Ann Barnes 158
    W. A. 160
    William 14, 159, 164
    William Allen 154, 158, 159, 160
    William Forrest 159, 160
Coltharp
    Abel Bruce 66
    Beety 66
    Charlotte Elizabeth 66
    Emily Caroline 66
    J. 92
    James 14, 20, 21, 22, 65, 66
    James W. 65
    Jas. 92
    Joanna Adeline Mc-Spadden 65
    John III 65
    Majors & 23, 60, 61, 65, 66, 72
    Mary Cavendar 66
    Melissa Isabella 66
    Sarah Catherine "Kitty" 66
    Sophronia Adaline 66
    Susannah Horner 65
    William Henry 65
COLTHARP
    JAMES 45
Cone
    Reuben 50, 51
CONE
    REUBEN 51
Connell
    H. H. 29, 37
Conner
    John 14, 76, 79
Conners 25, 28
Cook
    D. A. 162
    Nancy W. Collier 162
    Tallulah Victoria 162
Coolbaugh
    William 69, 70, 152, 179
Cooper
    Charles Grady 176
Craven
    Myrtie 40
Creis
    Alexander M. 26
Crockett
    Susan Florida 164
Curry
    Benjamin 56
Curtiss
    J. L. 39

D

Daniel Boone 170, 171
Daughtery
    Mason 21
Davidson
    A. T. 103
Davis 28, 33, 35, 37, 40, 45, 80, 91, 92, 119, 141, 147, 154, 167, 189, 203, 206
    Lewis 20
    Margaret J. 71
    Mary Elizabeth 86, 165
DAVIS
    JONATHAN W. 145
    LARKIN H. 48, 49
    WILLIAM. N. 67, 165
    WILLIAM NEELEY 33
DEAN
    JOHN 45, 46, 141
DENNARD
    J. E. 44
Dickens
    Mary Elizabeth 165
Dickson
    James 25, 26, 50,

Index

52, 122, 207
Lydia Leathers 180
DICKSON
    JAMES 46
Dixon
    William 104
Dobbs 28, 173, 174, 186, 189, 199
    Fannie E. 174
    Lindsey 174
    Martha 174
    Mary "Mollie" 174
    Susan Hart 174
    Willard 174
Dobsons 28
Dorman
    Alford 32
    Alfred 32
Dorough
    Carrie Lee 89
    Carrie Louella "Lula" 89
    Charles Grady 89
    Edmond Herschel 89
    Edmond "Walter" 89
    Florence 89
    Florence Eufala Taylor 89
    Florence Taylor 89
    George Herschel 89
    George Preston 89
    John Wesley 89
    Lucinda Caroline Baughman 89
    Maggie Lee 89
    Robert Merle 89
    Walter 83, 89
Driscoll
    Will 14, 65
Dudley
    Elizabeth 26
Duke
    John 16, 17

Duncan
    Peter E. 158
Dunlap
    W. C. 32, 38
DUNN
    JAMES M. 49, 139
Dupree
    Benjamin 33
Dyer
    Amos 16
    Edward 16, 142
DYER
    JOEL H. 43, 139, 141

E

Easterwood
    John 17
ECHOLS
    JAMES 47
    JAMES C. 29, 47, 202
Edwards
    D. M. 36, 39
Ellington
    Martha Jenkins 136
Elliott
    T. M. 35, 36
Embry
    Abel 14, 76
    Adaline 148
Emery
    Able 154
Evans
    Felix 182
    Rhoda 182
EZZARD
    WILLIAM 51

F

Fain
    John 68
Fambrough
    Allen 56

FAMBROUGH
    ALLEN G. 116
Fannie Chambers 148
Farmer
    John 163
Felton
    Ezekiah 18
Few
    Ignatius W. 100
Fielder
    Florence 129
    F. M. 28
    Francis Marion 28
    Marion 28, 76
Fielders
    Frances 14
Florence 28
    Lucy Blaylock 164
    Thomas 164
Floyd
    B. F. 35
    W. A. 35, 131, 132
Ford
    Mary Ann Emily Schofield 140
    Olivia Eliza 140
FORT
    BENJAMIN 49, 139
Fowler
    Benoni 40
    Thomas 32
Freeman
    Bailey 35
    S. 35
Fullbright
    Leonard 16, 17, 29
FULLBRIGHT
    LEONARD 47, 76

G

Gan
    Nathan 17
GARNER
    THOMAS W. 141

Garrison
  James F. 20, 21
Gilley
  J. 92
  William B. 20
Gilmer
  Governor 56
Goggen
  Alexander 18
Goldin
  Franklin G. 153
Goldmine
  Hill 144, 206
Goodlin
  John 58
GOODSON
  MICHAEL 48
Gordon
  N. H. 40
Grace
  Nathaniel J. 154, 156
Granberry
  Ella B. 66
Gray 83
Green
  Alex 14, 67, 68, 154, 160, 161
  Alexander 15, 65, 68, 154
  Alexander Porter 28, 67, 79, 160
  Ambrose 160
  Anderson 16, 25, 33, 160, 161, 165
  Antoinette J. 67
  Eliza Ann Chappell 67
  James Walter 67, 68
  Jesse Mercer 67
  John Young 160
  Kizziah Stroud 122
  Martha 160
  Martha Lula Talloolar 67
  Martin Lafayette 160
  Mary Carrie Gorder 67
  Mary Elizabeth 160
  Mercer 14, 67, 68, 154, 160, 161
  Nancy 79, 160
  Nancy Porter 67, 160
  Nora Elizador 67, 161
  Rebecca 160
  Robert 160
  Sarah 122
  Thomas 160
  Tommie Lorena 67
  Virginia Caroline "Jennie" 67
  William 27, 122, 123, 160
  William Henderson 67
  William Mercer 67, 154, 160, 161
GREEN
  ANDERSON 161
  WILLIAM 67, 161
GREENE
  ROBERT A. 33, 67
Gresham
  M. 32
  Ned 32, 83
Grey
  David 154
  Samuel 154
Griffin
  J. P. 154, 155
Griffis
  Reverend 37
Griggs
  Asa 30, 91, 101, 118
  Lois McCants 91
  Louise C. 91
  Rebecca Elizabeth Davenport 91
  William 91
GRIGGS
  ASA W. 91
Groover
  Peter 38
Groves
  Phillips 32
Guierer
  Thomas W. 16

H

Hagood
  J. J. 29
Hall
  Ezekel 17
Hambleton
  John L. 16
Hambric
  Whitten 28
Hamilton
  J. T. 34
  Thomas M. 40
  T. M. 33
HAMILTON
  THOMAS 47
Hampton
  W. 99
Hamrick
  Nancy Rebecca 60
Hannah
  Carole Hannah Rodgers 141
  Celia Elizabeth 141
  Fannice J. "Fannie" 141
  Isaac 141
  Lucinda Jane "Lucy" 141
  Pritchard 141
  Reuben 141
  Richard Clark 141
  Richard Clark "Bud" 141

Index

Richard Hannah 141
Robert 141
Sarah Jane 141
HANVEY
   JOHN 47
Harass
   George 25
Harcrow
   James 17
Hardgrove
   Bright W. 136
   Fannie 136
Hardin
   William 56
Hargrave
   Bright Williamson 140
   Fannie Franklin 140
   Flora 140
   Frederick 140
   Frederick Clopton 140
   Hance Stephens 140
   Hannah H. 140
   Nellie Overtaker 140
   Ramath Rice 140
   Savannah 140
   Thornton Burke 140
   William Monroe 140
HARGRAVE
   BRIGHT W. 141
Hargraves
   Harris and 116
HARGRAVES
   BRIGHT W. 141
HARGROVE
   BRIGHT W. 141
   B. W. 141
Harlin
   Daniel 16
Harris
   Elizabeth 26
Harrison
   Abel 14, 142
   Abel H. 16, 20, 21, 118, 142, 143
   Abel Hill 110, 142, 143
   Hannah Chambers 142
   Joseph 142
   Margaret Hill 142
HARRISON
   ABEL 44
   ABEL H. 45
   JEREMIAH 39, 202
Hart 176
   Benjamin 170
   Bertha 176
   Bessie 176
   Catherine Elizabeth Parker 173
   Celia 176
   Celia Ethel 176
   Charles 176
   Charles A. 174
   Charles Arthur 176
   Charles Raymond 177
   Charles Stillwell 176
   Cicero Oscar "Cain" 174
   Cynthia S. 173
   Effie Teressia 175, 176
   Eldorado Hart "Bud" Cobb 173
   Elizabeth 176
   Ella 176, 177
   Enoch Tyre 176
   Eudorah T. 173
   Francis Eugene 175
   Francis Eugenius 172
   Francis Maxion 173
   George Barnes 173
   George Olin 174
   Hariet Emily "Hattie" 176
   Harriet Ann 173
   Isaac osceola "Ossie" Cobb 173
   James "Arthur" 176
   James Madison 176
   James Madison "Doll" 175
   James Rufus "Doc" 176
   John G. Cobb 173
   John Thomas 172, 174
   John Virna 176
   Joseph J. 173
   Joseph L. 24, 30, 39, 47, 149
   Joseph Lemuel 173
   "Judge" 69, 178
   Louisiana Hazeltine 176
   Lundah Bailey 174
   Martha 167, 175
   Martha Ann 175
   Martha Joanna 176
   Martha Velma 176
   Mary 69, 151, 152, 178, 179
   Mary Antionette "Nettie" Chambers 176
   Mary Beulah 176
   Mary Elizabeth 174
   Nancy 69, 170, 171, 173
   Nancy Ann Morgan 170
   Robert Lee "Bobby" 176
   Samuel 14, 28, 65, 68, 69, 148, 149, 151, 167, 168, 169, 170, 171, 172, 173,

Index

175, 178, 181, 182
Samuel "Lemuel" 170
Samuel "Ossie" 176
Samuel Stillwell "Sammie" 176
Samuel "Ossie" 175
Sarah 178
Sarah "Jane" 149
Sarah Jane 173
Susan 174, 178
Susan Leona "Lena" 176
Susanna Borin 170
Susannah Boring 171
Susannah Rice 170
Thomas 170
William 65, 68, 69, 152, 172, 178
William A. "Billy" 176
William M. 68, 69
William R. 174, 175
William S. 173
William W. 69, 70
William Washington Cobb 173
HART
   SAMUEL 45, 47, 76, 204
   SAMUEL C. 45
Hart, Jr
   Francis Eugene 171
   Harriet Ann 171
   Martha Susan Veazey 171
   Samuel Hart III 171
   Samuel S. 171
Hart, Jr.
   Samuel S. 171
Hartsfield
   Mary 143
Hart, Sr
   Eli 178
   Elizabeth 178
   James 178
   John 178
   Martha Susan 178
   Mary 178
   Rebecca 178
   Samuel 178
   Sarah 178
   Susannah "Phoebe" 178
   William 178
HARVEY
   JOHN 47
HATCHER
   JOSIAH 44
Hawkins
   Benjamin 14, 105
   Lucinda Malvina 105
   Sarah Hannah Chambers 105
Hay
   David R. 168
Hayes
   Carolyn Smith Hayes 181
   Jasper Pickens 181
   Lilla Alice 181
Haygood
   Appleton 32
Haynes 34, 40
   Alexander 19, 21
   Amelia 113, 114
   Arminda 78
   Cynthia 78, 110
   Edward 26, 76, 77
   Elizabeth 78
   Elizabeth Goodson 77
   Ephraim 76
   Estoria 111
   Hallie 112
   Henry 14, 15, 16, 26, 28, 35, 76, 77, 78
   James 76
   John 76. 110, 111
   John Bomar 111
   John Monroe 78, 110, 111, 112, 113
   Johnson 19, 21
   Johnston 76, 77
   Jonathan 14, 15, 16, 26, 76, 77, 78, 209
   Jonathon Ephraim 112
   Josephine 113
   Lafayette 78
   Leif 78
   Leonidas P. 111
   Lucinda 78
   Mary 76
   Mary Lou 111, 112
   Mary Louisa 111, 112
   Nancy 76
   Nancy Amelia "Mele" Norton 112
   Nancy R. 60
   Phoebe Eaton 76
   Riley 78
   Ruby 112
   S. T. 99
   Sam 113
   Samuel T. 112
   Samuel Tilden "Sambo" 112
   Samuel Tilton 111, 112, 115
   Sara 76
   Sara Hill 77, 78
   Sarah 76, 78, 79
   Sarah "Sallie" Jane 111
   William 14, 26, 76, 77
   William Henry 78
   William Randolph 112
Helton
   Amos 16

Index

Hembee
    William 94
Hembree 89
Hendon
    David 17
    Mr. 155
Henry
    Willie Elsie 89
Henry Allen Coleman 158, 159
HENTON
    CHARLES B. 36, 48
Herrin
    James 16
Hesterly
    Sarah C. 93
    Sterling Montgomery 93
Hewit
    Jackson 16
Hibbler
    Eldred M. 17
Hiccombeffon
    Ephriam B. 18
Hicks
    Eliza Jane Richards 15, 122, 123
    Ernest 122
    Helen 122
    Isaac Crayton 93, 122
    Isaac Crayton "Crate" 122
    John 122
    John C. 123, 124
    John Columbus 15, 122, 123
    Johnie 122
    Lennie 122
    Lillie 122
    Lizzie L. Doyal 122
    Mary 122
    Mary Winnie Lula Leatherwood 122
    Matthew 122
    Robert 122
    Sarah "Sally" Green 122
    Wallace 122
    William 48, 116, 117
    William A. 48, 115
HICKS
    GREEN 92
    WILLIAM 48, 116
Hiden
    D. 92
    David 16, 17, 23, 25, 147, 154
    George 16, 17, 154
    G. M. 33, 165
HIDEN
    DAVID 46, 161
Hilderbrand
    John 19, 21, 36, 49, 118
Hill
    Benjamin Newton 152
    Ellen Pemelia 152
    Isaac Abner 152
    Isaac Sion 152
    Isabella Baskin 152
    Isabella Virginia 152
    Isabelle Cox 152
    Jackson Lafayette 147, 152, 153, 220
    James Alexander 152
    J. L. 40
    John 144
    Margaret Jane 152
    Nancy 120, 121
    William H. 152
    W. P. 33
Hix
    Jesse L. 21
    William 41, 116, 132
Hixon
    Addie 167, 182, 183
    Billy 28, 65, 70
    Elijah Franklin 71, 80
    Elizabeth 72
    Emily Elizabeth Echols 70
    Emily J. Chambers 71
    Eva 71
    Guy 167, 182, 183
    Horace 71
    Howard M. 71
    James C. 28
    James Crawford 71
    John 71
    John Thomas 28, 65, 70
    Margaret Davis 80
    Margaret J. Davis 71
    Mary Elizabeth Witcher 71
    Olin Hugh 71
    Oscar 183
    Oscar W. 71
    Sarah Elizabeth 70
    William 14, 28
    Wyatt 182
Hodge
    Leona 176
Hodgen
    Mary 33
Hodgson
    Elizabeth Rice 130
    Elizabeth W. 130
    Valentine M. 40
    Valentine Mc 130
    V. M. 40
Hogan
    A. 92, 147
    Alexander 92

E. P. 92
HOGAN
   ALEXANDER 161
Hogue
   H. J. 47
HOGUE
   HENRY J. 47
   H. J. 47, 76
Hogues 28
Holcomb
   George 154, 156
Holland
   Edmund 117
   Edmund W. 36, 48, 116, 117, 118
   Edward W. 21, 118
   James H. 20
   J. W. 29
   Little & 116
HOLLAND
   CALVIN 141
   EDMUND W. 36, 48, 145
Holsenbeck
   Ray 113
Hope
   James 142
   John 142
HOPE
   JAMES 44, 45
   JOHN 44, 45
Howard
   Absolm 17
Howell
   Jas M. 143
Huckabee
   B. 18
Huff 143, 145
   Leonard 117, 118
   Leonard C. 22
HUFF
   LEONARD C. 36, 48, 76, 204, 205
Hughey

Thomas 21
Hulsey
   Charles 20, 43, 48, 50, 51, 52, 117, 141
   Henry 19
   William H. 113
Humphries
   Edna Emaline Holley 143
   James William 143
   John Wiley 143
   Nathaniel 143, 144
   Nathaniel Harbin 143
   Sarah Alice 143
   Sarah Harbin 143
   William Saddler 143
Hunt
   J. G. 29
HURT
   WILLIAM K. 76
Hutcheson
   Mahale Avarilla 165
Hyden
   David 27
   Geo. 155
   Mary 25

I

IVERSON
   ALFRED 47, 48, 139, 205

J

Jacobs
   James 40
Jarnagin
   N. 118
   Needham 21, 144, 206
JARNAGIN
   NEEDHAM 145
Jarnigan

   Margaret 117, 119
   Needham 117
JARNIGAN
   MRS. 91
   NEEDHAM 145
Jenkins
   J. B. 37
Johnson
   J. F. 19, 21
   Larkin 118
   Robert R. 32
   R. R. 36, 38
   Thomas 17
Johnston
   Anna 167
   John 167, 183
Jones
   Aaron 18, 60
   Colonel "Bat" 124
   James 32
   John A. 26, 45, 51, 117, 121, 124, 201, 203, 204
   John A. "Jack" 37
   John "Jack" Anselm 124
   S. P. 43
JONES
   JOHN 46, 203
   JOHN A. 46, 48, 116, 203, 204, 205
   SEABORN 46
Jordan
   Mariah 107
JORNAGAN
   N. 145
JORNAGIN
   NEEDHAM 144, 206
Jornigan
   Margaret Nuney 144
   Mary Ann Russell 144
   Needham 144
   Noah 144

Index

Sarah Niven 144
JORNIGAN
  N. 136
Jourdin
  Fleming 144

K

Keeton
  William 28
KENNON
  WILLIAM 39, 202
KERR
  ANDREW 44, 45
  JOHN 44, 45
Key
  John M. 29
King
  R. L. 34
Kinney 40
  Isaac 40
  Lucinda 79
  Zachariah T. 164
Kirkland
  Henrietta 66
Knight
  Guss F. 75
  Mathew 16
  Samuel 17
  Willoby 21

L

Lambert
  L. P. 29
Land
  W. A. 36
LAND
  JESSE 51
Landrum
  Samuel B. 17
Lane
  W. A. 29
Lasseter
  James 21

Lassetter 28, 52, 65
  Addie Mae Green 72
  Erie 72
  George Washington Lassetter, Jr. 72
  James Green 72
  John George Washington 72
  Marion Annette 72
  Mary E. Barnett 72
  Mary Parthenia L. Brown 72
  William Casper 72
  William Cheadle 72
Lassiter
  J. G. W. 14
Lassiters, 28
LAWHORN
  ALLEN 139
Leak
  Sanford 39
Leake
  Sandford 36
  Sanford 36
Leathers 19, 28, 29, 69, 167, 178, 181
  Abraham Harrison 180
  Abraham Harrison Leathers, Jr. 180
  Abram 180
  Annie Catherine 180
  Arminda 26
  Bartow 180
  Frederick Mortimer 180
  James 26
  James C. 93
  Joel 56
  (Maria) 26
  Martha Lee 180
  Mary 26, 167, 180
  Mary Amanda Jane 180
  Mary Jane Scoggins 180
  Mary Jane Swafford 180
  Mary Swafford 180
  Nancy Margaret 180
  Samuel 19
  Samuel Elsberry 180
  Samuel Lederer 180
  William Franklin 180
Leek
  Sanford 32
Leeke
  Sanford 32
Liles
  David 16
  James 16
Little
  F. M. 40, 76, 145
Long
  Benjamin 14
  Benjamin McFarland 15, 168, 169
  Calvin 169
  Caroline Eliza Grantland 169
  Charity Taylor 169
  Isabella 15
  Isabella Jane 168
  Isabelle Leeper 15
  Isabell Leeper 15
  James Young 15, 167
  Jane 15, 168
  Jane Walker 167
  Jane Young 167
  John 14, 15, 17, 25, 46, 65, 167, 168, 169
  John Orville 168
  Looney James 168
  Louisa Susan 168
  Louise S. 15

Nancy D. 169
Nancy Davis 15, 167
Robert 15, 167
William Leeper 15, 168, 169
Long III
   John 15
Lott
   Rebekah 26
Lovell
   Floyd 90
Lowery
   Warren Spencer 75
Lucas
   B. E. 32
Lucy
   William E. 32
Lupo
   James 32
   J. L. 38
LUTHER
   F. 47, 76
   FREDRICK 47
Lyle
   Hoke 71
   Johnnie Lou Hixon 71

M

Mabel
   John 34
Mabry
   H. P. 21
Majors
   Alexander W. 73
   Amanda 72
   Augustus A. 73
   Brother 25, 27
   Calvin 92
   Caroline 92
   Elbert Lee 73
   Emaline 72
   Isaac Barton 72
   James 18, 46, 72, 92
   James B. 72
   James M. 92
   James W. 72, 73
   Jane Upton 72
   Mablean 72
   Marshal Lee 72
   Martha 73
   Martha Jane 72
   Mary Ann 72
   Mary Brightwell 73
   Mary Wright 72, 73
   Nicey 73
   Peter 72, 73
   Peter Lafayette 72
   Pleasant Henry 72
   Sarah McColphin 73
   Susannah Scaggs 73
   Susan Upton 92
   Widow 92
   William 16, 26, 27, 65, 73, 74
   William B. 73
   William J. 73
   William W. 92
   Wright 14, 18, 31, 72, 73, 83, 92
MAJORS
   J. 46
   JAMES 46, 202, 204, 207
   W. 46
   WILLIAM 46, 139, 141
   WRIGHT W. 92
Malone
   G. B. 35
   W. H. 35
Maltbie
   J. T. 37
Mandeville
   Appleton 21, 116, 203, 219
Martin
   Jim 140
Mason
   Adell Alfred 175
   Henry H. 175
   Homer 175
   Lucian 175
   Martha Ann 175
   Martha Ann Hart 175
   Robert Ridley 175
   Robert Wood 175
MASON
   WILEY W. 49, 139
Mastenn
   H. M. 154, 156
Mathas
   Hiram Miles 89
Matthis
   Mr. 98
Maxwell
   W. A. 35
Mayfield
   Jesse 17
McCain
   Benjamin 156, 162
   Benjamin J. 154, 161
   Benjamin Jasper 161
   Billy 32, 83
   B. J. 40, 155
   Hugh 161
   Ida Tallulah "Lou" 161
   Isabella Baskin 152, 153
   Margaret Nisbet 161
   Mary Jane 164
   Samuel E. 161
   Tallulah 161
   William Baskin 161
   William Benjamin 161
McCarley

Index

James "Jim" Knox Polk 109
Lydia Yates 107
Moses 107
Tabitha Sarah Jane 107
McCLAIN
  CHARLES 44
McClung
  John Benjamin 176
McClure
  Mr. 137
McClutcheon
  T. E. 37
McCorcle
  John 21
McCurdy
  R. T. 40
McDaniel
  Peggy 178
McDowell
  Daniel 19, 207
  James B. 17
  James S. 16
McDOWELL
  DANIEL 44
McElrath
  James 147
McElreath
  John 20
McGahee
  George 162
  John 162
McGee
  William 154
McHand
  W. B. 32
McIntosh
  William 13, 55
McKee
  Richard W. 39
McKenzie
  Joe 60
McKinney
  Benjamin 147

McKINNEY
  HIRAM 122, 205
McKleroy 19, 20, 21
McLains 19
McLarty
  A. N. 40
  G. W. 40
  Sarah Temperance "Sallie" 129
  S. W. 40
McMichael
  Annie 71
  Walter 71
McMullan
  Andrew 16, 204
McPherson
  Amanda 162
  Charles Lafayette 162
  Charles Lewis 162, 163
  Daniel 162
  Delphia 162
  E. 92
  Elijah 154, 162, 163
  Elijah Daniel 162
  Elijah Houston 162, 163
  Emily 162
  H. 155
  Henry Livingston 162
  John "Jack" Howell 162
  Louisa 162
  Mary Ann 162
  Sarah Ann 163
  Susannah Kincheloe 162
  William Barton 162
  William Nelson 162
McRea 92
  M. 92
McSpadden
  Green C. 66

McSPADDEN
  GREEN 45
  GREEN C. 45
McWalker
  Riley 17
McWhorter
  Abbott M. 40
  A. M. 17, 18, 20, 39, 40, 202
  E. B. 40
  Leroy 28
  Lovick Eugene 89
McWhorter.
  A. M. 18
Mehaffey
  H. 92
  James 92
Mehaffy
  Hiram 17
Meigs
  Return [sic] 57
Merrell
  Benjamin 92
  B. S. 154, 205
  William W. 106, 154
  W. W. 147
Merridith
  John 18
Michael
  James 16, 18
Miller
  Eli 17
Mirkinson
  Rora 17
Mitchell
  John 40
  Underwood & 116
Monk 92
Moody
  George S. 50, 52
  John 104
  Reuben 104
Moon
  Octavia 75

Index

Moony
  Mr. 92
Moore
  Jas. P. 138
  J. M. 35
  Mr. 138
Morgan
  A. J. 29, 36
  John 49, 139
  John D. 59
  Nancy Ann 170
  Rebecca Alexander 170
  Reverend 37
  Sarah 170
  Thomas 170
  William 154
MORGAN
  JOHN E. 49, 139
Morris
  Moses 16
Moseley
  Edwin 125
  Sarah Gathright 125
  Sarah "Sallie" Mozley (Moseley) 125
Moss
  William B. 32, 40
Mosteller 83
Mote
  Mary 108
Mullins
  Nell 176
Mulwee
  S. 92
Murkinson
  Keneth 17
Murphy
  John 32, 38
Muse 28, 29, 40, 60, 198, 199
  J. M. 28
Myers
  J. N. 32, 36, 38

N

Newborn 28
Newman
  William Jasper 165
Newton
  Thomas 17
Noland
  Annie Pathon 124
  Battavia Jane 126
  Buddy Aubrey 126
  Cleveland Dorman 126
  Edward Moseley "Edwin" 124
  Edward Peyton "Edwin" 126
  Elsy Jane 124
  E. M. 125
  Francis "Fannie" Evelyn 126
  George Avery 124
  George Franklin 127
  George R. 124
  Georgia Ann 126
  Henry Terrell 124
  James Edwin 127
  Lesbia "Lisby" Kate 126
  Marthy "Mattie" 126
  Mary Elizabeth "Lizzie" Burnes 127
  Nathan 126
  Ora Emily 126
  Ora J. 127
  Peyton 124
  Samuel 124
  Samuel Burns 127
  Samuel Clemen 126
  Sarah 125
  Sarah A. 127
  Sarah "Sallie" L. 126
  Sarah "Sallie" Mozley 126
  Seaborn Jackson 126
  Seaborn W. 40, 125, 126, 127
  William Allison 126
  William Aubrey 119, 125, 126
  William P. 127
Norton
  Amelia 113
  John Marion 113
  M. D. 36

O

Oxford
  J. I. 37

P

Palmer
  Denison B. 50, 52, 203
  Dennison B. 40
PALMER
  DENISON B. 36, 48
Parish
  Reverend 37
Parker
  Atlanta H. 174
  Enoch 18
  George Washington 172, 174
  George William "Willie" 174
  S. C. 16
Parker, Jr.
  George William "Willie" 174
Parr
  Daniel N. 17
  William L. 18, 19, 106
Parsons
  Cora Belle 176

Index

PATRICK
  WILLIAM A. R. 36, 48
PATTON
  M. L. 141
Pentecost
  Fredrice 136
  Mr. 137
Perddy
  Lemuel 18
Perkerson
  Tom 35
Peteet
  Emma Josephine 88
Philips
  William 18
Phillips
  Harkin 17
  Joseph 16
Pierce
  Newton 83
Poe
  James 92
  John 133
Poes 19
Polk
  C. 40
Pollard
  Irwin 92
Powell
  B. C. 35
  George W. 32
  Thomas G. 31, 32
  Thomas T. 83
Pritchett
  Frank A. 34

Q

Qualls 19

R

Rabun
  Brother 27
  T. 47
  Thomas 27, 43, 46, 207
RABUN
  HODGE 139, 205
  THOMAS 29, 47, 204, 205
Raburn
  Thomas 20, 22, 141
  Willis 147
Rainwater
  James 29
Read
  George 16
  Henry T. 16
  Mathew 16
  Reubin 18
Reaves
  James 21
Redus
  James Adams 174
  Lundah 174
Reed
  Reuben 60
Reese
  David 144
  Mary Virginia 165
Reeves
  James 14, 28, 29, 35, 76
Reid
  Henry L. 17
  Mathew 17
  Robert A. 39
REID
  MATTHEW 45, 48
Reynold
  F. F. 39
Reynolds
  F. F. 32, 36, 39
Rhodes
  R. C. 29
Rice
  Parker 14, 76
  Parker M. 28, 118
Richards
  Andrew Jackson Richards 92
  Angelina Mahala Hale 92
  Arminda Amanda 92
  Elizabeth A. 92
  Elizabeth Fowler 92
  Eliza Jane 92
  Emily Mahala 92
  Frances 19
  Francis Marion 92
  Francis Marion Richards Jr. 92
  James C. 92
  John 92
  John W. 92
  Joseph Denman 92
  King Henry 92
  Susan Idelia 92
  William Milburn 92
RICHARDS
  FRANCIS 95
  FRANCIS M. 95
Riggs
  Alice Florence 165
  Alice W. 164
  Anna V. Crockett 164
  Cynthia Florence 164
  Emma B. 164
  James Madison 164
  Jane Florence 164
  John 14, 155, 159, 164
  John Q. 164
  Josephine B. 164
  Lizzie D. 164
  Sarah M. 164
  Stephen 155, 156
  Stephen Alexander Hamilton 164
Roberds
  Thomas 118

Index

Roberts
   James H. 93
   Leonidas 119
ROBERTS
   JAMES 145
   THOMAS H. 48
Robinson
   John 92
Roddy
   Hogan T. 92
Rodgers
   S. W. 32
RODGERS
   WINIFRED 47
ROGERS
   JOHN 145
Rooks
   William 20
Roop
   W. W. 29
Rowe
   Allen 140
   Richard L. 155
   Richard L. (S.) 40
   R. L. 155, 156
Ruben
   Thomas 104
Ruffin
   R. V. C. 21, 22, 47, 118, 141, 145
Russell
   Harrison & 116
   R. N. 40, 45

S

Sanders 135
   Britton 32, 39
   Jonathan 21, 48
SANDERS
   JONATHAN 47
Sawtell
   I. Y. 162
Scales
   Franklin Seaborn 32
Scarcsey
   David 136
Scoggins
   Gilliam Andrew 176
Sewell
   J. M. 39
   W. M. 32
Shackleford
   Richard 17
Sharp
   George 60, 216
   George S. 16, 17, 59, 60, 61, 62, 63, 87
   George Spencer 59
   G. S. 128
   Hiram 18, 60
   Hiram Jackson 59
   John Wilkes Booth 60
   Martha A. 59
   Mary Ellen 60
   Nancy Rebecca 60
   Nancy R. Haynes 59
   Phebe Jane 59
   Sarah Ann Owens 59, 60
   Victoria 59
   William Franklin 59
Shaw
   Elsie 112
   Frank 111, 112, 114
Sheats
   Charles 120
Sheets
   Charles 21, 27, 120
Shepard
   John 51
Sheppard
   John 50, 104
Sherdon
   Abner 17
Shields
   Carrie Long 15
Shinn 28, 71, 120
SHORTER
   ELI S. 49, 139
Simmons
   A. J. 35
   O. C. 36, 39
Simons
   O. C. 32
SIMPSON
   JAMES 141
Sims
   Emily Bradberry 164
   Hiram Thomas 164
   James Newton 164
   John Hiram Newton 164
   John Sterling 164
   Lorinda "Lavada" 164
   Mary 164
   Mary Luncinda Abercrombie 164
   Millard Fillmore 164
   Robert Toombs 164
   Sterling Tucker 156, 164, 165
   Sterling Tucker "Uncle Tuck" 155, 164
   Uncle "Tuck" 155
   William J. 164
   William Jasper 164
Sims, Junior
   Mahale Avarilla Hutcheson 165
   Sophronia Elizabeth Turner 165
   Sterling Tucker 165
Skinner
   Luke 14, 76
Slaughter
   Angelina Castleberry 127
   John 35, 101, 127, 128, 129

Index

John B. 40
John Thomas 127
John Thomas, Jr. 127
J. T. 40, 128
Martha Elizabeth 127
Melvina Eugenia Freeman 127
Nathaniel Garrett 127
N. G. 35
Richard W. 130
Small
   Sarah Ann 163
Smiley
   Robert B. 141
Smith
   David 17, 21
   F. R. 39
   Honest 83
   J. Blakley 32
   John 32
   Sidney M. 32
   William 147, 153, 154
Smythe
   Gus 162
Sneelgroves 28
Snellgrove
   Hallie 68
SPARKS
   THOMAS H. 46
Spencer
   Joseph N. 16
Spinks
   J. M. 37
Springer
   William 78
Stacy
   James 33
Stallings
   Charles Eugene 79
   Eliza Ann 79
   Festus Harrison 79

J. M. B. 29
John Wesley 79
Nathan Vincent 79
Robert E. 79
Sarah Ann 79
Steadham
   Era Hixon 71
   W. L. 71
Steel
   John M. 155
Stegall
   William 32
Stephens
   Bob 83
   Francis 88
   Martha Kansas "Mattie" 108
   Simeon L. 32
   William D. 17
Stokely
   T. 40
Stone
   James D. 155, 156
   J. O. 14, 76
   W. P. 35
Street
   J. M. 155
Stripling
   D. 40
   Dave 31
   David 32, 38, 83
   James 16, 32
Summerlin
   Nancy Odessa "Susie" 94
Summerline
   Alice 93
Susanna Borin 170
Suttles
   J. M. 37
   W. M. 29
Swain
   George 44, 46
SWAIN
   GEORGE 46, 204

Sykes
   Annie Belle 79
   Darling 79
   Darling Franklin 79
   Frank 14, 28, 68, 79, 80
   Hariet 79
   Lois 79
   Mary 79
   Mary Rosanna "Rosie" 109
   Sarah 79
   Sarah Ann Cochran 79
   Sarah Ann Frances 79
   Sarah Margaret 68
   Stephen Alexander 79
   T. F. 14, 76
   Thomas "Frank" 79, 80
   Thomas Frank 14, 68, 80
   Thomas Franklin 79
   Virginia Caroline "Jennie" Green 79
   Walter C. 79

T

Taylor
   Billy 31, 32, 83
   Eliza H. McKinney 89
   Florence Eufala 89
   John W. 40
   John Walker Glenn 89
   Theodosia Carolyn McEachen 89
   William H. 32, 201
   William Harvey 89
   William Harvy 89
TAYLOR
   WILLIAM H. 91

Index

Teal
    Lunas Martin 176
    Susie 176
Thomas
    N. G. 46, 143
    Nicholas G. 142
    Thomas W. 32
THOMAS
    N. G. 45
    NICHOLAS G. 45
Thompson
    Joseph 17
Thornton
    Fabius Maxwell 74
THORNTON
    WILLIAM 43
Threadgill
    Alcimus 84
    Cynthia Kilgore
    Marcus 83
    Eliza Ann 84
    Eugenia 84
    Harriett 84
    Harriett Virginia 84
    Henry Ledbetter 84
    Martha 84
    Mary Francis 84
    Mary Francis Allen 84
    Thomas 84
Thrower
    Joseph William 89
Tidwell
    Mansell 16
Tolbert
    Abby Estelle 130
    Albert 104
    Allen 50, 51
    Clark C. 129
    Elba 130
    Elizabeth 130
    Elizabeth Hodson 131
    Elizabeth W. 129
    Elizzie 130
    Josiah 37
    Josiah Thomas 129, 130, 131
    J. T. 131, 132, 134
    J. Thomas 130
    Lucy Emmaline 129
    Lucy Minerva 129
    Minnie 130
    Montra May 130
    Permelia Adair 135
    Roland 130
    Roland Andrew 129
    Roland Harrison 129
    Thomas Sanford 129
    Thomas Wilburn 130
    William H. 129
Toombs
    Robert 88
Trusell 38
Trussell
    Claiborn 35, 37, 38
    Cleyburn 32
    F. A. 35
Turner 16, 31, 37, 40, 85, 165
    Alice 148
    L. L. 16
    Rev. T. 40
    Sophronia Elizabeth 165
Turners
    Tom 28
Tuttle
    Delia Johnson 133
    Temperance 133
    William 133

U

Underwood
    J. H. 40
Upson
    James 31
Upton
    James 58, 83, 92

V

Veal
    Allen Jones 179
    Benjamin F. 179
    John LaFayette 179
    John Monroe 179
    Mary Susanna 179
    Rebecca 179
    William W. 179
Veazey
    James Monroe 178
    Martha Susan 171
Veazey, Sr
    John 171
    Sarah Jane Raburn 171
Velvin 28, 68, 134, 195, 198
    Antoinette "Annette" Jane Green 132
    Delilah Moore 131
    Elizabeth 131
    Frances Kilgore 131
    James Henry 131
    Jesse Deila 132
    John 132
    John Henry 131
    John Jethro 131
    Louella 132
    Mary Frances "Frannie" 131
    Rilla 132
    Robert 140
    Robert Jones 131
    Robert Michael 131
    Sydney Smith 131
    Thomas B. "Tom" 131
Verdell
    C. M. 36, 39

W

Index

Waddell
  A. L. 155
  Alford 147, 155
  Alfred 156
  Nancy 155
  Simon 147, 155
  'Sims' 155
WADDELL
  ALFRED 33, 166
Wagner
  William O. 17
Wagnon
  Wm. O. 16
Wagnow
  Colonel 55
Waldrop
  Glenn 29
Walker 92
  B. 40, 94
  Charles R. 177
  Ella 177
  George William 177
  James M. 177
  Jane 15, 167
  John 68, 89
  Jonathan 18, 19, 25
  Joseph Lane 177
  Larkin 31
  Lizzie 148
  Lula 80
  Mary 177
  Mary Annie 177
  Mattie Lena 177
  Rufus 177
  Samuel Hart 177
  William 60, 178
Wallis
  C. Ermon 113
Walls
  Jeremiah 16
Walton
  F. 36
  Fletcher 39
Wapner
  Wallas 18

Ward
  George W. 16
  John 18, 19
Wardlaw
  W. J. 32, 37, 38
Ware
  Alexander 55
  George W. 17
Warran
  John 49, 139
WARRAN
  JOHN 49, 139
Warren
  Peter 21
Warwick
  Loy 36
Wasson
  Eliza 140
Watson
  Robert 48, 117, 118
  Sarah 86
  Tyre 16, 142
Webster
  W. W. 138
Weems
  D. J. 36
  J. D. 32
Weims
  D. J. 39
West
  Allen Absalom 153
  Antha Willie 153
  Elizabeth W. 153
  Gilbert Taylor 153
  Martha Ella 153
  Robert William 153
  Talulah Jane 153
  T. H. 76
  Thomas Smith 153
  William 14, 23, 40, 147, 153, 154
  William Smith 153
  William Wester 153
  Winnefred Tankersley 153

Whisenhunt
  John 92
White
  David W. 16
  William 17
Whitley
  Thomas H. 32
Wick
  Daniel Wick 132
  Hannah Jane 132
  Hannah Jane Butler 132
  John 117, 129, 133
  John B. 36, 40, 49, 118, 132, 133
  John Butler 132
  Mary C. 132
WICK
  JOHN B. 48, 49, 202, 206
WICKS
  Mr. 91
William
  Clayton 118, 204
Williams
  Arling 89
  Barnes 59
  Brother 28
  Clayton 20, 48, 117, 118, 142, 154, 158, 204
  James F. 154
  Judith Adair 135
  Lucinda Parks 124
  Margaret Mary 93
  Mary Ann 157
  M. S. 35, 36, 38, 39
  Peter Jones 124
  Susan C. 124
WILLIAMS
  CLAYTON 36, 45, 48, 145
WILLIAMSON
  WILLIAM 139

Index

Willingham
    Carrie 75
Willis
    Thomas 93
Wilson
    Ethel Hixon 71
    J. N. 34
WINN
    FRANCIS 39, 202
Witcher
    B. M. 40
    D. H. 40
    Mary Elizabeth 71
    Roberts & 117
WITCHER
    D. H. 122
Witcher's 91
Wood
    E. H. 32, 36
    James Madison 75
    John N. 75
    Puckett 18
    Robertson 147, 149
    William 106
    W. J. 32
Woods 109
WOOTEN
    JESSEE 144
Worley
    J. G. 32
Worsham
    William 18
Wright
    J. Gilbert 89
    John 45, 155
    Martha Velma "Vella" 176
Wylds
    F. A. 40
Wynn
    Barbara 182
    Ena 182
    Herman 182
    Herman Clark 182
    Jane Ellen Brooks 181
    Janie Ellen Brooks 182
    Mollie 31
    Sloman 19, 21, 59, 201
    Slomman 31, 32, 83
    Slomon 16
    William Thomas 148, 182

Y

Yarbrough
    J. W. 32
Yates
    Ada O. Hixon 71, 80
    Elijah Matthew 80
    Elizabeth 74
    Eller Lenora 74
    Georgia Ann Caroline 74, 108
    Hannah Catherine 74
    Harrison P. 74
    James 74
    James F. 74
    James M. 74
    Joel L. 74
    Joel Pickney 74
    Joseph E. Brown 74
    Lydia Elizabeth 74
    Margaret Alene 81
    Martha Jane Stewart 74
    Martha Matilda Steed 80
    Martha "Mattie" Slaughter 74
    Mary 74
    Minnie Kate 81
    Myrtie Mae 81
    Robert Atticus 71, 76, 80
    Rufus M. 74
    Sallie Adella 74
    Sarah Jane Josehene 74
    Sarah Josephine "Josie" 108
    Synthia Lenore 74
    Tabitha 74
    Tabitha Yates 74
    William E. 74
    William Raymond 81
    Willis Alvin 74
YATES
    JAMES 76
    J. F. 47, 76
    JOEL P. 76
    JOHN F. 76
    TABITHA 76
    W. H. 76
    WILLIAM F. 76
Young
    J. J. 92

Z

ZUBER
    CHARLES B. 76

www.ingramcontent.com/pod-product-compliance
Lightning Source LLC
Chambersburg PA
CBHW080536170426
43195CB00016B/2580